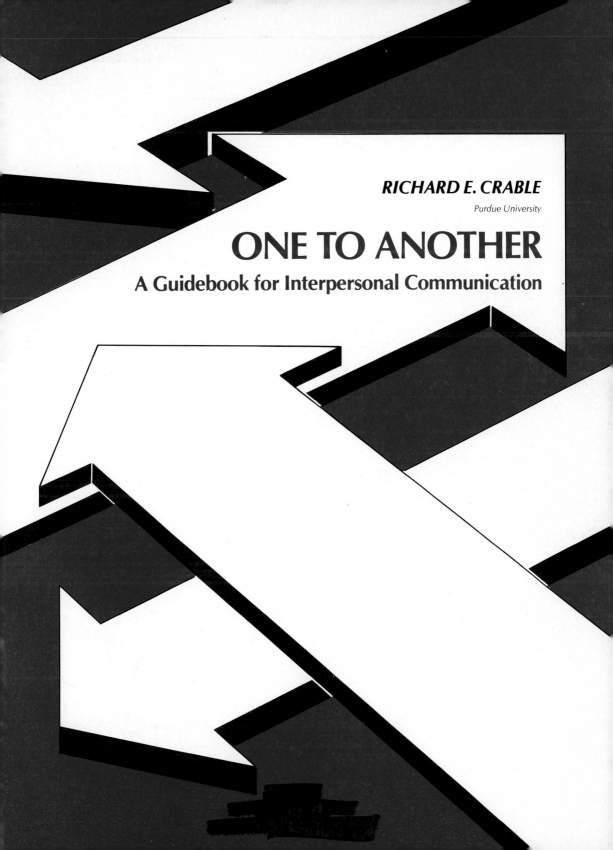

RICHARD E. CRABLE

Purdue University

ONE TO ANOTHER

A Guidebook for Interpersonal Communication

Sponsoring editor: Alan M. Spiegel
Project editor: Claudia Kohner
Text and cover designer: Gayle Jaeger
Production manager: Jeanie Berke
Photo researcher: Myra Schachne
Compositor: Ruttle, Shaw & Wetherill, Inc.
Printer and binder: Halliday Lithograph Corporation
Art studio: E. H. Technical Services, Inc.

Extract material from p. 246, "Mankind Owes the Child the Best It Has to Give," excerpted from the U. N. Declaration of the Rights of the Child.

ONE TO ANOTHER: *A GUIDEBOOK FOR INTERPERSONAL COMMUNICATION*

Library of Congress Cataloging in Publication Data

Crable, Richard E.
  One to another.

  Includes index.
  1. Interpersonal communication.   I. Title.
BF637.C45C7   153.6   80-21887
ISBN 0-06-041395-6

BRIEF CONTENTS

v

DETAILED
CONTENTS

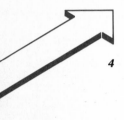

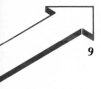

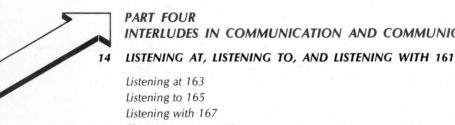

PREFACE

The 1970s have been called the "me" decade: The social activism so characteristic of the 1960s gave way to an American concern for "self." Physical fitness, personalized religions, the individual drive for jobs with executive washrooms, and the magazine *Self* all testify to the quest for personal satisfaction.

And yet, there is no overwhelming evidence that the "me" decade brought personal happiness. It may be that the drive to develop the "me" may need to be balanced by the development of "us." It may be that improved interpersonal relationships may be the key to a happier "us," "you" – and "me."

One to Another is based on the belief that the human relationship is one of humankind's great and largely unknown frontiers. I have written this book as a "guidebook" through the crucial, complex, and often confusing problems you and I encounter as we interact with people who are important to us.

Basic assumptions
Several assumptions have guided my writing of this book, and I would like to share them with you.

First, I assume that *human communication is a process in which we must emphasize "human."* Though later in the book I discuss the nature of communication in detail, we should never forget that we are dealing with the humans who *use* that process. The book's focus, then, is on how the process of communication can help in attaining important human goals. Communication is, of course, interesting for its own sake. In this book, however, effective communication is viewed as a tool to help improve human relationships. In that way, I intend the focus to be always upon the humans engaging in human communication.

Second, I assume that *no human relationship ever remains exactly the same for long.* Only in fairy tales do people – parents/children, friends, lovers, spouses – ever truly live "happily *ever* after." A relationship that survives is one in which at least one person works hard to sustain the relationship. The best that anyone can hope to achieve in most relationships is "stability." Yet, stability does not mean a changeless, flawless relationship; instead, stability refers to a relationship in which rebalancing and readjustment are fairly constant activities. Since I believe that no relationship remains stationary for long, human communication becomes a vital element in maintaining the desired quality of human relationships.

Finally, I assume that *almost any human relationship can be improved by effective interpersonal communication.* Some relationships are casual, and we are content to have them stay that way. More important are those relationships that we want to deepen. Indeed, relationships can become so deep and so strong that the two people involved sense a genuine "oneness" with one another. This absolute ultimate in human relationships is rare, difficult to achieve—but possible. It is what I shall call "interpersonal communion" in this book; and it is what I assume to be the goal in certain special relationships enjoyed by you and me. The "communing relationship" is the ultimate human situation. Though much of the rest of this book develops this concept of communion, let me simply state here that effective interpersonal communication can improve your chances of experiencing such a relationship with another person.

These, then, are the major assumptions of *One to Another.* They are not only the biases of this book, but my biases—biases that I cheerfully defend.

Major goals My three specific goals in writing a book that emphasizes human relationships are the following:

First, *to help you gain insight into interpersonal communication.* I combine traditionally discussed ideas and beliefs with some very untraditional, but important, concerns in interpersonal communication. The result is, I hope, a happy mixture of the old and the new, the tested and the hypothesized, the safe and the risky. It is just that combination that makes interpersonal communication such a challenging and important area of study.

Second, *to help you gain an appreciation of interpersonal communion.* Appreciation is an imprecise term that may mean either "understanding" or "awareness of worth." I use this term because both of those ideas are relevant: I want you not only to understand the nature of human communion but also to realize its value in your personal life.

Third, *to help you learn to use interpersonal communication to better achieve interpersonal communion.* This, of course, is the most important of the three goals. The first two are cognitive or mental in orientation; this one emphasizes your ability to use communication in your efforts to commune with others. Although the success of this third goal depends heavily on the success of the first two, it is the major thrust of this book. These three are academically justifiable goals, but that is not my main concern. These goals are also important aspects of what it is to be human and what it is to need to be close to another human being.

Structure of the book This book is in four parts for very good reasons.

Part One introduces major terms, ideas, and directions for the upcoming discussions. Three brief chapters create a framework that will help you understand the rest of the book.

Part Two is a study of the basic elements and concerns of interpersonal communication/communion. In some respects this is the most traditional part of the book. In another sense, its traditional flavor is balanced by the application of basic communication concepts to our concern for communion. Chapters 4 through 8 include discussions of communicators, meaning, goals in communication, and levels of communication.

Part Three describes the communion process in detail by focusing on the central concern for "sharing" in communication and communion. Chapter 9 introduces the next three chapters. Together, these four chapters verbally and visually describe the sharing, communal relationship. Chapter 13 concludes this part by discussing an "ethic" of human relationships.

Part Four deals with what I enthusiastically call "interludes" in communication and communion. These chapters are not structured around available research or traditional approaches to the study of communication. Instead, they are structured around the kinds of human problems faced in day-to-day life. Consequently, the chapters involve concerns such as "feeling," "being," and "knowing." Yet these topics are dealt with, I believe, by walking a narrow line between the highly esoteric and abstract, on the one hand, and the grossly concrete and specific, on the other. The topics, in fact, have *not* been approached as if they were *topics* to be explored; they have been approached as if they were *human problems* to be understood on the level (and in the language) of human beings.

Intended characteristics of the book In writing this book I had very specific intentions in mind regarding *how* the book should be created and perceived. I would like to share these with you.

First, I have intended for this book to be *clear and readable.* I have tried to use lucid and accurate descriptions of the discussion topics. Yet I have attempted to avoid jargon and technical expressions as much as possible. I want you as the reader to easily understand my main points as well as the more subtle ideas. Where there are research and other discussions that might appeal to your desire to "find out more," I have included references and related ideas (even some digressions) as footnoted material. The book is meant to be a self-contained and clear treatment of some very common human problems and needs.

Second, I have intended for this book to be *well illustrated.* Whenever appropriate, I have included short examples as well as more detailed illustrations and accounts of situations. In addition, each chapter, except for those in Part One, contains at least one "case study" that provides a detailed example of the idea, concept, or problem discussed in the chapter. The pictures and sketches are intended to provide further illustrations of what I would like you to understand.

Third, I have intended for this book to be a *mixture of discussion levels.* By this I mean that I have tried to tread a path between two kinds of books: those that are so heavily laden with research findings and specific details that the generalities are lost, and those that are so esoteric and abstract that no specific insights emerge. In other words, the book is intended to fall somewhere between a textbook and a book for the popular press. I mean no disrespect to either kind of book. It simply seems to me that the strength of a textbook is its substance; the strength of popular books tends to be their humanness and readability. I have attempted to create a book that is both substantive and enjoyably human.

Finally, I have intended in several ways to make the book as *flexible* as possible. (1) I have tried to make the book relevant to the ordinary reader as well as to the student. Certainly, college students are not the only people who want to learn about people. (2) I have tried to make the chapters in Parts Two and Four readable in virtually any order. This is particularly true of Part Four; indeed, the "interludes" can be read when the reader is most interested in reading them. (3) I have tried to make the book both complete and compact so that it can be used in a wide variety of courses, classes, workshops, and less structured settings—as either the primary or supplementary text. Such flexibility is aimed toward making **One to Another** *your* book.

RICHARD E. CRABLE

PART **ONE**

COMMUNICATION: ONE TO ANOTHER

COMMUNICATION AND COMMUNION

Let me begin by using a comparison to tell you what this book is about.

For as long as I can remember, I have enjoyed building things of wood. As I watched my father work, I marveled at how bits and pieces of wood could be turned into something attractive and usable. I, too, wanted to learn to build such things. What I discovered was that no one simply learns to build. I had to learn how to use the tools of the carpenter—the hammer, the saw, the screwdriver, and the rest. My first real tool was a hammer. It and a package of nails were delivered by "Santa" on my fourth birthday. I learned to use this first tool by hammering dozens of nails into a single board—if there was space on the surface of the board, it needed another nail. Through the years, I mastered other tools. At last, I was able to build! In that process I had to begin by learning to use those tools that would help me build attractive and useful things from wood.

This book applies that same principle to more important aspects of life. I will attempt to explore with you the activity we call interpersonal communication—communication between two people. I will focus on the communication process as a tool for the improvement of your relationships with others. So the main focus in the book is not on communication itself, but on interpersonal relationships. Our attention will be on learning communication tools that can be used to "build"—and sustain—better human relationships.

This is a "people" book. Let me explain why that is important.

Homo sapiens:
why we miss
understanding
Everyone knows that people are classified, biologically, as *homo sapiens.* Not everyone knows that the Latin phrase means "primate-wise," or "a smart two-legged, upright-walking beast." There are other primates, of course, and some of them have been taught to do elaborate tricks and even to communicate—a little. I will not argue whether or not chimpanzees will some-day communicate as effectively as we humans are supposed to do. I *will*

4

argue my bias that only humans seem able to communicate about their communication. That is, while apes and other primates someday may be taught to communicate, I do not believe that they will ever sit around saying, "Gee, I really tried to explain what I mean – wonder why old Mary misunderstood me?" I simply think the more sophisticated kinds of self-analysis and doubt about communication are reserved for humans.

As the (only) "wise" primates, humans seek understanding between and among one another – in fact, we're even dismayed to find out that dogs don't fully comprehend the English language. We seek understanding through gestures, smiles, letters, songs, poems, paintings, bumper stickers, textbooks, blueprints, and so on. When we succeed in communicating, we know it. We are even so "wise" that we know that we know that we have succeeded. Our humanly superior abilities allow us to realize the immense pleasure of communicating and achieving understanding. On the other hand, when we fail, we also know that. It is not – as with apes – simply a matter of getting or not getting our banana. We know something far more important has occurred: We have not been understood. As humans, we tend to acutely *dislike misunderstanding* – and to severely *miss understanding*. Only humans seem to be capable of suffering the great pangs of distress over misunderstanding. Only humans have created a history of seeking whatever means are available to "get together."

Communication: the magical mystery cure

With the human need for understanding, it is no surprise that humans have traditionally placed a great emphasis on "communication." The study of communication has always been interesting. For the past 2300 years or so communication has been systematically studied. It was as important to Aristotle as it is to contemporary scholars.

The 1960s, however, seemed to be the turning point in the fortunes of "communication." Communication was advertised as a magical cure-all for just about everything. We needed (someone pointed out) better communication between politicians and voters, blacks and whites, young and old, employees and employers, Moscow and Washington, wives and husbands, and – in a way – between here and eternity. "Communication" has been marketed formally and informally as a magic elixir having the curative properties usually reserved for patented liquids sold from the back of a medicine-show wagon.

This new status of communication which I have only slightly exaggerated causes me some misgivings as both a person and a professor of communication. On one hand, as a professor I should be happy about the perceived importance of my field; as a person, I am paid to teach what I know about this allegedly magical process. On the other hand, as a professor, I am aware of the limitations of communication as a cure-all; as a person, I am uncomfortable at the thought that "communication" has been misrepresented to most of society. Now, I believe that improved communication

5

. . . I do not believe that communication is a magical answer to all the world's problems. [Prelutsky, Stock, Boston]

can be a positive and constructive force in human lives. But I do not believe that communication is a magical answer to all the world's problems. Communication, then, is high on my list of the good things in life; I simply feel some dismay at the way it has been marketed.

Communication: the beginning of the end

With all this as background, you may be asking why I have written yet another book "about communication." The best answer I can provide is that this book is an attempt at trying to shift the emphasis in human communication away from "communication" and toward "human."

My goal is to convince you that improved communication is not—or should not be—the goal of most interpersonal situations. I think the fundamental problem is that communication is basically a *tool*—which is all right. Yet it has been merchandised by people as an *end product.* Let me explain the difference. Tools are seldom important for their own sake. They are important for what they can *do.* Communication as a tool is important because it may be a way of helping you and others improve your relationship or mediate a problem. It seems to me, however, that there is a tremendous temptation to see communication as a goal or an end product: or, as I have heard it said, for example, "We want better communication in our relationship!" That strikes me as silly. I can understand someone wanting a better relationship, which may be possible by using communication as a tool; I cannot understand why anyone would wish to communicate solely for the purpose of being better able to communicate. So let's change the phrase to: "We want a deeper, better relationship—and hope communication can help us." To me, that makes much more sense.

But, then, what might a "better relationship" be? Ironically, I think a "better relationship" can be understood by noting that the English words "communicate" and "communion" come from the same root meanings. In each case the emphasis is on "making common" or "sharing in common." Well, these may be the denotations, but the connotations of the words have developed over the years and by way of human use of the terms. "Communion," for example, probably means a religious service to most people; a secondary meaning might relate to "mixing in with"—as in "communing with nature." "Communication" most prominently has come to stand for a process of using words or nonverbal message symbols. It might seem that the different commonsense meanings of the two words would serve to make each irrelevant to the other. That, however, is not necessarily the case.

"Communion," as I use the term in the book, is not a religious ceremony nor a completely abstract feeling of "mixing" with nature. Instead, *communion is the "oneness" experienced between two people.* A human relationship is based on the sharing of reactions, thoughts, feelings, needs, and desires. All of us experience this sense of sharing in different degrees—and with different people. Only rarely do two individuals find their sharing so deep and so consistent that something special happens: they seem almost perfectly "in tune" with one another. In the terms I shall use in the book, these two have experienced a "oneness"—a state of interpersonal "communion." Communion is the ultimate level of human relationship.

Types of relationships   To explain better the nature of the "communing" relationship, let me contrast it to some other types of relationships. This will not be a list of all the possible kinds of human relationships but will suggest some ways of describing the nature of a two-person interaction.

1. There are relationships based on "threat" or force. Parents or work

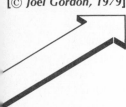

supervisors may pose some sort of threat – and this can become the essence of the relationship. The reason such a relationship can work is that one of the individuals experiences fear – fear of physical force, social stigma, emotional trauma, or something. The possible negative result of ending such a relationship is that what is feared will occur: beatings, emotional stress, or social stigmatization ("I will tell the neighbors that. . . .").

2. There are relationships based on "duty." Because of a formal agreement such as a marriage "contract" or because the person *is* after all a parent, formal or informal commitments are perceived. These commitments are what can hold the relationship together. The penalties possible for ending a relationship based on duty may include shame or failure for not having fulfilled those commitments.

3. There are relationships based on "debt." This may at first seem very similar to duty. Here, though, I mean specific feelings that a person has done something that makes you "owe" them: "Jack has been such a good friend – How can I . . .?" or "Gloria has given me the best years of her life – How can I divorce her?" In these situations the relationship works because of feelings of personal obligation. Stepping out of such a relationship can result in feelings of guilt or a sense of being unfair.

4. There are relationships based on "exchange." Each party gives the other something he or she needs. Such relationships work because of the

mutual advantage of the relationship. Correspondingly, ending such a relationship can mean the end of the mutually advantageous situation. The outdated stereotype that women "trade" sexual activity with a husband for security is a stumbling way of attempting to see the exchange relationship in interpersonal relationships.

5. There are relationships based on—for lack of a better term—"no choice." The people stay together as friends, lovers, spouses, or parents and children because they either have not explored or have not found alternatives to their relationship. The implications of ending such a relationship include complete uncertainty. With no alternatives, there is an absence of being able to project the future.

Let me make a few observations about each of these types of relationship. First, any one relationship may be characterized by two or more of these terms or types. In different circumstances the relationship might seem to be one of threat, exchange, or duty. Second, all these types of relationships emphasize the *differences* between people: for threat to work, there must be a difference in perceived power or force; for duty to be a factor, there must be a varying set of commitments; for debt to operate, there must be certain "things" owed to another person; for exchange to function, there must be different things to be exchanged; for relationships based on "no choice" to work, there must be a feeling that the people are doing the only thing they can—even if it means staying (perhaps unhappily) together. But a third observation is even more crucial: any relationship that is best characterized by one of these terms can be changed into a different kind of relationship—that is, if the people involved are interested in change. Relatedly, any of these relationships can change into what I call a "communing" relationship.

The communing relationship   The relationship between two people can be called "communing" or "communion" when what holds it together is a "feeling of oneness"—a feeling that "who you are" is bound up with "who I am." There is, then, a communion of "identities"—who each of us is. And the result of ending such a relationship is a loss of part of what "you" and "I" are. Communion, interpersonally, is not where two people actually become mere "halves" of a single relationship. Instead, each is more like he or she wants to be *because of the relationship.*

Communion probably does not occur accidentally. Those two people who feel so close to one another have spent some length of time exchanging thoughts, ideas, feelings, and dreams—they have been actively engaged in the process of communication. Communication—that process involving verbal and nonverbal symbols—seems to be an essential part of the development of communion. Better interpersonal communication can improve interpersonal relationships. These relationships may eventually become

9

"communing" relationships. And here, I think, is a key to truly understanding what some people refer to as "interpersonal communication." In the interpersonal process of communication the *tools needed* are words and nonverbal symbols; the *end product desired is communion.* Communication is the beginning of that end.

The concern in this book is with the nature of interpersonal communion. "Communication" is important; however, it is most important to the extent that it is instrumental in achieving the goal of interpersonal communion. In this way *our focus will be communication* and *communion.*

This perspective is much more comfortable for me, and I suspect it will be helpful to you as well. As a human being, you will come into contact with a large number of other individuals. In this process, you will want to establish very close relationships with some of these people — so close that "communion" seems to be the appropriate term. The book is written as a help with that sort of goal and those kinds of situations. At other times you may have no great desire to establish communion between yourself and another. What you will find, however, is that your understanding of communion will be a great asset in functioning more humanely in even casual relationships. Indeed, you may discover that communion may be possible and desirable for your relationships with a widening circle of people. This book is for those who need and desire to know something more about being people — singly and in pairs — for those needing to communicate one to another.

CHAPTER SUMMARY

The chapter attempted to make clear that One to Another *is a book about people and their relationships with one another. Communication is the focus, studied in terms of how it can be used as a process to help human relationships. In this sense, communication is a tool.*

Humans want and, indeed, need to understand and to be understood. In our efforts to achieve this, we might emphasize the magical quality of communication to solve all our problems. Communication, however, is not magic; it is a very special and complicated process that can help people attain or maintain satisfying relationships.

The chapter detailed several sorts of human relationships, building toward the most intimate of relationships—communion between two people. Some description of interpersonal communion was given, but this chapter is only the beginning. In the chapters to come, you will learn more and more about how to use communication in interpersonal relationships.

LEARNING
BY APPLYING

1   Try to recall a recent instance of when you and another person "failed" to understand each other. Explain. How did you feel? Angry? Hurt? Frustrated? Helpless? Confused? Try to explain your feelings.

2   Try to recall a time when you finally succeeded in getting another person to "see what you meant"—after some initial misunderstanding. Explain. How did you feel when you succeeded? Happy? Relieved? Smart? Powerful? Lucky? Try to explain your feelings. How do you think the other person felt when he or she began to understand you?

3   Keep a list, for several days, of times you observe people thinking "communication" is the answer to a problem. Use newspapers, television, magazines, and your own experiences. You will probably see that kind of thinking in relation to labor–management negotiations, accusations of improper political activity, marital "disagreements," classroom discussions, and so on. What other situations do you observe? Do you think people are being realistic about communication as an all-powerful cure?

4   Think about a person in your life with whom you feel "closest." How would you explain this "closeness"? You may find that the rest of the book will help you to better explain this feeling of "oneness."

LEARNING
BY DISCUSSING

1   Why do you think "understanding" is important? How do your ideas compare with the ideas in the chapter?

2   The chapter—and the book—focuses on improving communications so that relationships can be improved. Discuss important ways in which communication can be an effective tool for interpersonal relationships.

3   What were your ideas about "communion" before reading the chapter? Do you see that communion can be an important goal in various sorts of human relationships?

4   Without having read the rest of the book, what ideas do you have about communication helping to build toward a "communing" relationship?

COMMUNICATION: SO FAMILIAR AND YET...

STUDY OF THIS CHAPTER WILL ENABLE YOU TO

- *have a working definition of communication*
- *understand the basic characteristics implied in that definition*
- *understand the basic elements of the communication process*
- *use the basic elements of communication to describe communication situations*
- *understand the activities or subprocesses of communication*
- *use the activities or subprocesses of communication to explain a communication situation*

Communication. You and I spend a great deal of our lives engaged in communicating. As humans, we spend hours thinking about our communication. At one time or another we are pleased about it, we worry about it, we regret what we said, we regret what we did not say. . . . But what exactly is this thing called communication? How does it work?

On defining **Unfortunately, it isn't *exactly* anything. There are nearly as many definitions**
communication **of the term as there are people who write about it. I suspect that you would not gain much from a listing of numerous different definitions. It is, however, desirable that I explain what I mean when using the term communication in the course of this book: *Communication* can be viewed as the *recreation of similar meaning by symbolic transaction.*[1] That is not nearly so difficult to understand as it may seem at first. The definition states that *meanings* are *recreated* as *similar* meanings in someone else's mind by using *symbols* in a *transaction.* Let me explain the definition – and those five major terms – by using the following conversation.**

Hi!
Hello, Dan. . . . What's that silly smile for?
Oh, I was just struck by how beautiful you really are.
Oh, Dan. . . .
I don't mean to embarrass you. Sometimes I just need to tell you how I feel.
Well, . . . thank you. . . . I appreciate that.

The conversation was brief, but it was long enough for me to explain my conception of communication. Let me take each of the five major terms in the definition, using the conversation as an illustration.

[1] The essential parts of this definition first appeared in Richard E. Crable, "What Can You Believe About Rhetoric?" in *Exploration in Speech Communication,* ed. John J. Makay (Columbus, O.: Merrill, 1973), pp. 28–38.

First, communication involves *"meaning": the attachment of impor-*
tance or significance to something. The "meaning" of a class ring—to you
—may be accomplishment or pride. This might be the importance or significance you attach to the ring. The American flag, income tax forms, and
doves can all be important because of the meaning people give them. What
the woman "meant" to Dan was beauty and—though he did not use the
terms—perhaps admiration and love. These were the meanings that *he at-*
tached to this other person.

Second, communication implies a focus on the *"recreation" of mean-*
ing: the sharing of the meaning you have with another. In the example
Dan was not content to *have* meanings for the woman. He wanted to share
them with her. He wished to tell her about them. In a real sense he wanted
to recreate the meanings *in her mind* that he had *in his.* The problem is
that, as far as we know, no one can ever completely and flawlessly recreate
someone else's meaning. At best, the person recreates something that
approaches the other person's meaning. So, third, communication involves
the recreation of *"similar" meanings: approximations or something near*
to what the meaning actually is. The recreated meaning is never exact.
When I say, "Oh, I see what you mean," I am really saying, "Close enough!
Now I see *just about* what you mean." The worst communication is when
the created meaning and the recreated meaning have little or nothing in
common. The best communication is when the meanings are highly similar. That seems to be all we can expect, but that is quite a lot.

But, then, how are "similar meanings recreated"? Fourth, communication depends on *"symbols": words, actions, or things that can "stand for"*
or represent meanings. Almost anything can be used as a symbol.[2] Wedding
rings are used to represent a timeless bond between lovers. The bald eagle
is meant to stand for a proud and brave country. A herd of cattle is used to
represent an investment firm that is "bullish"—aggressive, confident—
about America. When the thing that represents a meaning or idea is a word
—either orally spoken or written—it is called a "verbal symbol." Anything
not a written or spoken word that still stands for a meaning or idea is typically termed a "nonverbal symbol."

In communication no one can *transfer* a meaning directly to another
person. So once I have a meaning, I try to translate that meaning into symbols—verbal and/or nonverbal. My goal is to have you translate the symbols
and recreate a meaning similar to what I have. The meanings, then, are not
communicated. Symbols are exchanged in the hope that a meaning can be
recreated in the other person's mind.

---

[2] The view that "one cannot not communicate" has been popularized by Paul
Watzlawick, Janet Beavin, and Don Jackson, *Pragmatics of Human Communi-*
cation (New York: Norton, 1967). Anything can be a symbol, but there are differences among what I shall call "intentional" communication, "accidental"
communication, and "mis-communication" in the following pages.

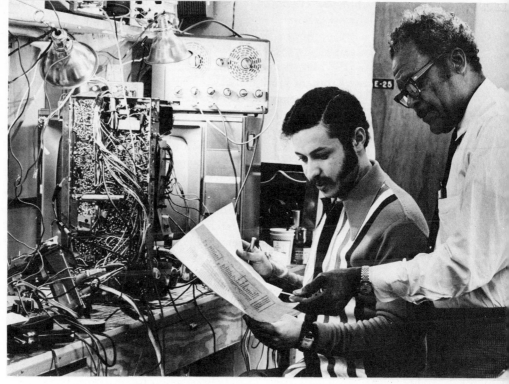

When symbols are exchanged, what occurs is a *"transaction": a process or ongoing activity that involves change*.[3] This fifth and final part of the definition means that all communication involves ongoing changes. When you engage in a bank transaction, you may exchange cash for a deposit slip—or exchange cash for an agreement to pay it back with interest (a loan). Both you and the bank have been affected by the process. If you were buying an automobile, you would exchange cash or a loan agreement for the car. Both you and the car dealer will have been affected. Similarly, when you engage in communication, changes will occur because of the process. You may know something that you did not before—even if it is just a fact about the other person. The other person may receive new information or new insights. You may even change your original meanings as you try to recreate them in someone else. There are all sorts of ways in which change occurs. The important point is that communication is a process of transaction: you, the other, the meanings, or something else will have

---

[3] "Transaction" is preferred to the more static-sounding "interaction" which had been popular in the field for years. Interaction seems to imply a movement among or between variables—without any particular change.

changed. The changes may be slight—hardly noticeable—or dramatic, but they will occur. Communication is a transaction.

Communication, then, involves meanings that are recreated as similar meanings in someone else's mind by using symbols in a transaction. These major terms can be used to restate the definition: Communication is the recreation of similar meaning by symbolic transaction. The problem with the conversation between Dan and the woman is that communication does not always occur so pleasantly or straightforwardly. You may be interested in the differences among what can be called "intentional" communication, "accidental" communication, and "miscommunication."

In Dan's case, for example, the woman recreated in her own mind something very similar to what Dan wanted. He attached complimentary meanings to her and wanted her to know that. Since he intended—or meant —to recreate such meanings, we can speak of this as "intentional" communication. But what if Dan had been too shy to tell her how he felt? He may have answered her question about the smile with, "Oh, no reason." Still he may have wanted to tell her how he felt, but used loving eyes and deep sighs to communicate. If she had understood those silent symbols and knew the reasons for them, he still would have intentionally communicated.

But there are other possibilities. He might not have *wanted* to communicate deep feelings for her at all. She might have seen his smile, not asked him anything, and said to herself, "He likes me . . . a lot." If Dan had not meant for that meaning to occur to her—even though he *did* like her, we can call that "accidental" communication: She would have recreated a meaning he had, although he had not intentionally tried to communicate it. On the other hand, let's assume that the woman did not ask the reason for the smile and that she still decided that he might like her. Let's also assume that Dan, in fact, did *not* like her. The situation would not involve a recreation of similar meanings: She would be creating a meaning by herself, instead of recreating a meaning Dan had. I call such situations "miscommunication."

The major point to be made in relation to intentional communication, accidental communication, and miscommunication is that they are all important to the study of interpersonal communication. All of them will occur from time to time in human relationships and will affect the relationships. The study of interpersonal communication, however, should help you reduce the number of miscommunications and unpleasant accidental communications. Such study should help you become more effective in recreating meanings that are similar to those you intend.

Earlier, I defined communication as the "recreation of similar meaning by symbolic transaction." The discussion of those various ideas may have made the definition less awesome and more practical. The discussion, however, should become more specific: What are the major elements of the communication process?

Since the stress in this book is on human communication, communicators, then, are the most important elements of the process. *"Communicators"* are the *people engaged in symbolic transaction.* Sometimes the communicators will be "sending" sets of symbols, and at other times they will be "receiving" those sets. More often, during the communication process communicators will be both sending and receiving sets of symbols. The term *"message"* – a second important element of communication – is *the set of verbal and nonverbal symbols used by communicators.* When two people are engaged in communication, we can say that they are sending and receiving messages. Sometimes the messages they send will be a response to an earlier message. This *response to the initial message is called "feedback,"* a third important element of the process.[4] The feedback to an initial message might be a sentence, a head nod, a frown – in short, any sort of verbal or nonverbal symbol or set of symbols.

In order for messages or feedback messages to be sent and received, they must "flow through" or be "carried by" something. *"Media"* – a fourth element of the communication processes – are *those means by which messages are exchanged.* A piece of paper, for example, is the medium for a letter – as would be the postal service that "sends" the letter. Sound waves are the medium of the spoken word. Light waves allow sight to occur; so they are the medium for most nonverbal messages and feedback messages. Media – also called "channels"[5] – are necessary for the sending and receiving of messages.

A fifth basic element of communication is what I call *"conceptual screens": the knowledge, values, beliefs, experiences, and so on of individual communicators.*[6] Water, for instance, flows through pipes (media or channels) in the same way for everyone. No variations in the people receiving the water affect what is sent or received. That is not the case with communication messages. One of the reasons that we can hope only for the re-creation of *similar* meanings in another person is the existence of these screens. The meaning of a message will depend a great deal on the kind and level of knowledge, the social beliefs, and so forth of the individuals involved. Your message – filtered through your screens and biases – will not

[4] Feedback was originally a term from electrical engineering. It referred to the feeding back of sound through a system that caused the familiar whine in public address systems. Some writers – and I am tempted myself – consider a message as feedback only when it influences (is actually "fed back" through) the original communicator.

[5] I avoid the word channel as much as possible since common channels such as pipes and riverbeds allow the "flow" in only one direction. Communication "channels" usually (but not always) serve both initial messages and feedback – in reverse directions.

[6] The idea of conceptual screens is similar to what are called "fields of experience" in Wilbur Schramm, "How Communication Works," in *The Process and Effects of Mass Communication*, ed. Wilbur Schramm (Urbana, Ill.: University of Illinois Press, 1954), pp. 3–10.

17

be the same message when it is filtered through the other person's screens and biases. These conceptual screens are a way of describing how individual meanings are created.

A final element of communication processes is perhaps the most general. *"Interference"* is what I shall call *anything that hinders or lessens the efficiency of communication.*[7] This is the most general of the elements since interference can exist in any of the other elements. Chattering or a loud stereo is interference in the medium for oral messages. Sloppy handwriting or an inefficient postal delivery is interference in written communication. Vague language or a foreign language can be interference in a message or feedback message. Fatigue or anger can be interference in one or both communicators. In addition, factors such as political bias or lack of knowledge can be interference in the conceptual screens. In short, there are a number of sources of handicaps in trying to communicate. The point is not that interference *may* occur but, rather, that it *will* occur. Thus the recreation of similar meanings is not so easy as it sounds. Interference *is* a constant factor in communication and will be discussed further in the next chapter.

With an awareness of the roles of communicators, messages, feedback, media, conceptual screens, and interference, you have a general knowledge of the elements of the communication process. Figure 2-1 illustrates how these elements can be visualized. Note that each of the communicators performs the roles of receiver and sender of messages or feedback —that is, each person receives messages from him- or herself and from others as well as sends messages to him- or herself and to others. So each "simple" communication process is really a whole complex *system* of incoming and outgoing messages.

Activities in the communication process

Still there is more to the process of communication. The messages "sent" to someone else are the product of several activities or subprocesses. Similarly, the reaction to a message—the feedback—is the result of the same sorts of activities. These activities include reception, interpretation, choice, symbolization, and transmission.[8] Let's briefly examine each.

"Reception" is simply *the process of sensing symbols and other stimuli.* The ears, eyes, nose, sense of touch, and even taste are the primary means of receiving or sensing stimuli. Without this reception, there could be no communication. Yet the reception of stimuli is only the first of several important activities. These stimuli must undergo *"interpretation": the at-*

---

[7] The term "noise" has been used by Claude Shannon and Warren Weaver, *The Mathematical Model of Communication* (Urbana, Ill.: University of Illinois Press, 1949), p. 5, to indicate problems that can occur in the channel or medium. I prefer the term interference since problems are not at all restricted to the channel.

[8] I first developed discussion about these particular ideas in Richard E. Crable, *Argumentation as Communication: Reasoning with Receivers* (Columbus, O.: Merrill, 1976), chap. 4.

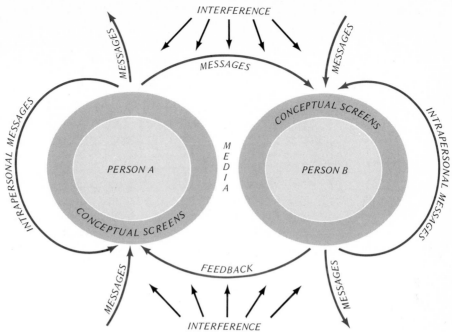

**Figure 2-1
The elements of
communication**

taching of meaning or significance to stimuli. It is possible, for example,
to receive messages without knowing what meaning to give them – without
being able to interpret them. More often, however, reception and interpretation of messages occur together or almost simultaneously. These two activities or subprocesses of communication are so generally linked that some
writers combine them into one activity: *perception*. Perception is the general term for the simultaneous reception and interpretation of messages.

Once messages have been received and interpreted (or perceived), the
next important activity becomes *"choice": the decision about how or if to
respond to the message as interpreted.* Any reaction – even the decision
not to react – is largely a matter of human choice. Will the choice be to ask a
question, shout back, write a letter, leave the room . . . or what? A decision
will be made.

When a choice is made, there will be some effort at *"symbolization":
the translating of a response back into a verbal or nonverbal (or both)
message.* Symbolization is the opposite process of interpretation. Interpretation involves the *decoding* of messages – What does this symbol mean?
Symbolization is similar to the *encoding* of messages – How can I use symbols to recreate what I mean?

But symbols or sets of symbols that are supposed to be a message or
feedback message must be "sent" to the other person. *"Transmission"* is

19

Figure 2-2
Activities in the
communication
process

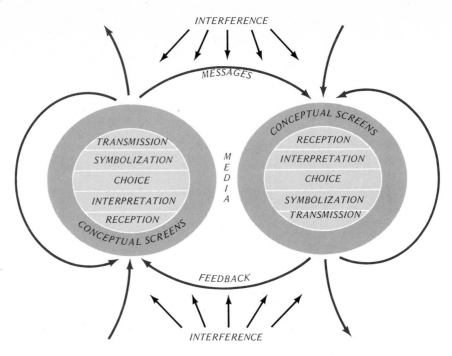

the activity or subprocess of sending messages to the other person. Transmission is the opposite process of reception. Instead of sensing stimuli—
including messages—the person who is transmitting presents stimuli for
the other person. Sheets of paper sent through the mail, the spoken word,
the hand movement are all ways of transmitting messages.

Figure 2-2 illustrates how the communication process can be visualized when the activities of communication are added. Notice that without
the elements of communication, the activities make no sense. Without the
activities or subprocesses of communication, the elements would be unimportant. Consider these ideas as you study Figure 2-2. You will see that
reception, interpretation, choice, symbolization, and transmission describe
the major activities or subprocesses of communication.

*Applying
the terms,
elements, and
subprocesses of
communication*

At this point, let me show how the material in this chapter can be used to
understand better the communication process. As an illustration, I will use
a very relevant situation: I have written this book, and you are reading it.
What can be said about the situation from a communication perspective?

First, I hope that I have been communicating with you and that I have
used symbols during the transaction so that you have recreated the meanings that I attach to "communication." More specifically, I have tried to
play the role of communicator. For years, I have received information, in-

sight, viewpoints, and additional messages from others as well as from my own study and research. I have attached different kinds and degrees of importance and meaning to these messages—partly because of all my conceptual screens made up of education at particular schools, my own set of biases, the social environment in which I grew up, and so forth. I have made choices about what to write and how to write—and, before those choices, had decided that I would in fact write. I have tried to symbolize what I wanted to write for you into words, diagrams, and case studies. These have been transmitted to you by way of my typewriter, my secretary, typing paper, copying machines, a postal service, Harper & Row, Publishers, a book called *One to Another*, an air or trucking company, and your bookstore.

At that point, you become the principal communicator as a receiver of my messages. You will react in a particular way depending on your own biases, preferences, background, and other conceptual screens. In part, you will react to what I have to say on the basis of any interference in any of the messages or media that have been used in the process. You will receive certain messages, interpret them, and decide how you will respond. You will symbolize your reaction and transmit it as feedback to your instructor, to

Yes, I have written the book and you are reading it. But there is so much involved in this very common communication process. [© *Joel Gordon, 1976*]

friends, to classmates, or maybe even to me directly. On the basis of that feedback the communication process can continue . . . on and on.

Yes, I have written the book and you are reading it. But there is so much involved in this very common communication process.

CHAPTER SUMMARY

In this chapter the discussion began with a definition of communication as the recreation of similar meaning by symbolic transaction. That definition was explored by analyzing each of those major terms. Next, we discussed the primary elements of communication, including cummunicators (as senders and receivers), messages, feedback messages, media, conceptual screens, and interference. The first five help explain how communication works. The last—interference—explains why it never works perfectly. Finally, we examined the subprocesses or activities of communication to understand more specifically how communication works. Reception, interpretation, choice, symbolization, and transmission are convenient ways of explaining the process.

In sum, the chapter has been an introduction to the process of communication—something so familiar, and yet so complex and difficult.

LEARNING BY APPLYING

1 *Consider the following situation:*

Mary	You know, there is something I meant to tell you the other day, and I forgot.
Harry	Oh?
Mary	I would like you to come over Monday night for a little get-together. Dinner and drinks.
Harry	I'd love to. How formal is it?
Mary	Oh, wear something comfortable, but nice. About 6:30, okay?
Harry	I'll be there.
	Harry arrives at the dinner in jeans, old sweat shirt, and sneakers.
Mary	Harry! What are you wearing that for?
Harry	You said something nice and comfortable!
Mary	I said something comfortable, *but* nice. . . . Oh, Harry. . . .

Communication can be viewed as the recreation of meaning by symbolic transaction. In the preceding example, use the terms, meanings, recreated meanings, symbols, similar, and transaction to explain the "misunderstanding."

2 *Consider the following situations:*

a. *Jack and Bill are discussing an upcoming class assignment. Bill has just called to* get directions from Jack who resents the fact that Bill missed class when the assignment was given.

b. Sarah and Kelly are tenderly embracing one another on a sofa. Kelly is trying to convince Sarah that an intimate relationship between them will not affect their working relationship in which she is his supervisor. Sarah does not believe it.

Answer the following questions in relation to each situation:

(1) Who were the communicators? In what way do you suspect they both sent and received messages?
(2) What do you think were the initial messages? the feedback?
(3) What were the main media for the communication?
(4) What can you say about the conceptual screens of each party?
(5) Where do you think interference might have been most serious?
(6) What can you relate about the activities or subprocesses of communication (including reception, interpretation, choice, symbolization, and transmission)? In which of these subprocesses did a possible problem seem to exist?

LEARNING BY DISCUSSING

1 Discuss what you feel are the main strengths and weaknesses of the definition of communication presented in the text. Are there ways in which you would change the definition? If so, what are they?

2 Discuss the basic characteristics of communication as explained in the text. Why are they all important? Would you add others?

3 Discuss the basic elements of the communication model as described. Do you think these are useful in explaining how communication "works"?

4 Discuss your understanding of the activities or "subprocesses" of communication. Do you see how all these apply to every communication transaction?

LEARNING BY READING FURTHER

Crable, Richard E., Using Communication. Boston: Allyn and Bacon, 1979.
Darnell, Donald, and Brockriede, Wayne, Persons Communicating. Englewood Cliffs, NJ: Prentice-Hall, 1976.
Larson, Carl E., and Dance, Frank, Perspectives on Communication. Milwaukee: Speech Communication Center, 1968.
Miller, Gerald R., and Nicholson, Henry E., Communication Inquiry A Perspective on a Process. Reading, MA: Addison-Wesley, 1976.
Mortenson, C. David, and Sereno, Kenneth K., Advances in Communication Research. New York: Harper & Row, 1973.
Wenburg, John R., and Wilmot, William W., The Personal Communication Process. New York: Wiley, 1973.

ME/US: WHY INTRAPERSONAL AND INTERPERSONAL COMMUNICATION CANNOT BE SEPARATED

STUDY OF THIS CHAPTER WILL ENABLE YOU TO UNDERSTAND

- *the meaning of "types of communication"*
- *the concept of "self-concept"*
- *the various "selves" of the self-concept*
- *the nature of perception*
- *the selectivity devices of perception*
- *how self-concept and perception both involve intra- and interpersonal communicatio*
- *why intrapersonal and interpersonal communication can never be completely divided*

Communication as a process was the focus of the last chapter. The basic ideas discussed can be related to virtually any "type" of human communication. Traditionally, writers and teachers in the field of communication differentiate types of communication on the basis of "settings" or "situations." So there is such a thing as "mass communication" where an audience of perhaps millions of people watch, listen to, or read one set of symbols. "Public address" or "public communication" usually refers to one person speaking to audiences of various sizes without the use of mass media. "Group communication" generally involves at least three people who recognize themselves as a unit, share a common goal, and more equally share the roles of senders and receivers. "Interpersonal communication" refers to two people and "intrapersonal communication" usually means one person "talking with" or "speaking to" him- or herself. The study of communication can be divided into these types.[1]

*Inter*personal communication – the focus of this text – can be understood more clearly by having some idea of how *intra*personal communication works. I am tempted to discuss intrapersonal communication first, followed by a more detailed discussion of interpersonal communication. The problem with this is that neither occurs without the other: Intrapersonal communication is continually affected by interpersonal transactions, and intrapersonal communication occurs at the same time interpersonal communication is occurring. Dividing interpersonal and intrapersonal

---

[1] It is important to note that there are various ways of identifying each of these types. This division – indeed, any division – of the study of communication is simply for the sake of convenience. When something is studied, it must be broken down into smaller segments to allow clear analysis. Many of the concerns in one "type" of communication, however, are of concern in other types as we shall see in this chapter.

communication—even for convenient discussion—seems to hurt the understanding of both.

In this chapter, then, I shall (1) discuss the nature of something called "self-concept"; (2) elaborate on what we have already called "perception"; and (3) show why these two concepts make it impossible to divide intrapersonal and interpersonal communication.

Self-concept

"Self-concept" involves your thinking and feelings about who you are and what you are. A conception is a mental impression or formulation. Self-concept, then, is the impressions you have about yourself as an individual. Psychologists, psychiatrists, and those in communication have long recognized that a positive self-concept is important. People who are bitter, depressed, hostile, aggressive, and so forth frequently do not like others and furthermore, usually do not like themselves. Seeing little good in themselves, they may also see little good in others. On the other hand, activities such as athletics, competitive speech activities, and drama are often said to help one's self-concept. Through it all, self-concept gets considerable attention among people in communication, sociology, psychology, and related fields.

One of the problems with self-concept is that it can seem so terribly abstract. "Who am I?" "What am I?" Such questions can appear so vague that the question-asking itself can be depressing. Why spend time asking something that seems impossible to answer? Fortunately, there are more specific ways of approaching the idea of self-concept, which have to do with the realization that a number of "selves" make up who you are.[2]

One of these selves can be labeled the *"actual self": a definition of who you are*—really. Popular books and other sources provide various means by which you can discover your "real," "true," or actual self. The major flaw with this conception of the actual self is that it is, in fact, a *conception* or an impression. It seems to me that no one has a true, real, or actual self that can be defined once and for all. But even if it really exists, I do not think that people with their conceptual screens would be able to recognize it. You may wish to launch a search for "who you are—your actual self," but I suspect a more practical approach is to concentrate on the *"perceived present self": a conception of who you* are, *which depends on your interpretation.* By the perceived present self I mean that you begin to understand or to discover your thoughts, feelings, and behavior. This perceived present self is probably as close as possible to the usual meaning of self-concept. When asked about your self-concept, you might well say, "Well, I see myself as

---

[2] Various other terms are used for these same concepts. What I call the actual self, for example, is sometimes referred to as the "real" self. I use the terms that I think are most easily understood—and the easiest to apply in studying the self.

being shy, fairly intelligent, gentle. . . ." This might be an accurate description of the picture *you* have of yourself. But it may not be how others who know you would describe you; what an objective observer would say; and/or how you will always see yourself. That does not matter. By expressing to yourself and to others at that time how you perceive yourself, you have explained part of your own self-concept.

Besides the actual self and the perceived present self, another important conception is the *"becoming self": an idea you have about who and what you are becoming.*[3] Change is a natural thing for individuals to experience. It can occur in your environment or in your thoughts, feelings, and behavior. Some of this change will go unnoticed by you, but part of it, however, will be quite noticeable and may even be dramatic. You may have the impression that you are "in transition": You were shy, but now you are becoming more outgoing; you were very jealous, but now you are more relaxed; or you were once loving, but now you see yourself as becoming more self-centered. Whether the change is consciously being made or is accidental, you may perceive it. Whether it is something you welcome or dislike, you may perceive it. Whatever the situation, you may find yourself changing — becoming different. You may create a conception of your "becoming self" that may be different from your perceived present self, which is a description of what you think you are; the becoming self is a description of what you think you are *becoming.*

Even when you do not sense any kind of change in yourself, other conceptions of self are also important. We can speak of a *"feared self"*: a conception of what you *do not want to be.* You may fear you will become too sensitive or too brash; you will become too unstable or too set in your own ways; or, more personally, you will become like Sue, Larry, Irving, Aunt Harriet, Cousin Pete — or anyone else. Regardless of the specific "you" that you do not wish to become, the feared self is important. It provides guidelines that can help you avoid what you do not wish to become. Relatedly but in contrast, we can recognize *"desired selves": conceptions about how you* would like to change *or qualities you would like to have.* The desired self is positive in direction by reversing the discussion of the feared self. You may wish that you were more sensitive or that you could be more calm during a discussion. Again, in personal terms, you may find yourself wanting to be more like Sue, Larry, Irving, Aunt Harriet, or Cousin Pete in specific ways — perhaps not exactly like them, but sharing some of their better characteristics.

Finally, the discussion of self-concept would not be complete without realizing that everyone has a number of *"metaperceptions"* or *"yourself as*

[3] The concept of the becoming self is also developed in Richard E. Crable, *Using Communication* (Boston: Allyn and Bacon, 1979), pp. 37–38.

you *think others see you": conceptions of what you think others think about you.*[4] You have various perceptions of who and what you are but often speculate about how others view you. Such "metaperceptions" include: "She thinks I'm exciting," "He figures that I'm too sensitive to take the criticism," and "They can't think any worse of me." You can have very different perceptions of how you think different people "see" you. These perceptions may not be accurate; but they are how you think others perceive you, or what we call "metaperceptions."

What, then, is the self-concept? It is really a collection of perceptions about who you think you are now, what you think you are becoming, what you would like to be, what you fear you might become, and what you think others think about you. As you and I seek relationships with others, we must know something about ourselves. These concepts can help that self-discovery process. Let me illustrate by sharing with you some elements of my own self-concept.

First, I should say that I spent years trying to discover the "real" Dick Crable. That was a search for my actual self. The problem was that as soon as I had "found myself," I discovered that I had changed. Getting older, meeting new people, and involving myself in new situations—all these and more seemed to change who I thought I was. Eventually, I began to concentrate on my perceived present self: Who I thought I was at any one point in time. At present, I see myself as (among other things) hardworking, reasonably intelligent, outgoing on the outside but still shy on the inside, successful, responsible, ambitious, moody, and prone to lose my temper. I have always feared being a failure or being too hard to love. But I have always wanted to be more relaxed in new situations, and more patient, gentle, and caring. I have a becoming self, too. Lately, I think that I have been able to care much more deeply for my family, students, and even casual friends and acquaintances. Metaperceptions are also relevant: I believe that I am seen (by different people) as too demanding, more loving than previously, hardworking, witty, goal-oriented—and, maybe, a bit overly enthusiastic and aggressive. All of these perceptions may not be accurate, but they are *my* perceptions.

The self-concept, then, is a whole collection of factors: your perception of your present self, your becoming self, your feared self, your desired self, and your metaperceptions of self. "Who are you?" then is a very broad question. "You" are a creation of different kinds of perceptions—perceptions that may contradict as easily as they may be consistent. The idea of self-concept is, like you, complex. Why it is complex relates to our next topic: perception.

[4] The prefix "meta-" means a second layer of something. So there are, for instance, "theoretical studies"—studies of or using theories. There are also "metatheoretical studies"—*the study of the study of* theories. Here, there is a perception of another person's perception.

Perception   Perception, as we mentioned earlier, is a term that combines the processes of reception and interpretation. When bombarded by stimuli, you receive some of them and attach certain significance or meaning to some of them. Perception cannot be perfectly accomplished, for the formulation of meanings generally—whether original or recreated—is hindered by interference and the conceptual screens of the individuals involved in the communication process. There are four different ways to describe more specifically how meaning creation and recreation are affected by this concept of perception.[5]

First, meaning creation and recreation can be affected by *"selective exposure": simply not allowing stimuli to be received.* To explain selective exposure let's consider, for example, the staunch Republican who will not listen to a Democratic candidate speak—or vice versa. By doing this, the partisan voter "screens out" any potential ideas of the other candidate and is being *selective* in terms of what sorts of stimuli can reach him or her. Intentionally reading only certain magazines or newspapers, visiting only with people we like, or knowing only about your own religion are all examples of selective exposure. Often, this selectivity occurs in more immediate ways: "Don't even talk to me about Mary," "I don't want to hear it," or "I never want to see you again." Selective exposure can also be accidental. There is no way, for instance, to read every magazine printed. For whatever reason, some meanings cannot occur because selective exposure is taking place.

Some opportunity for meaning creation and recreation is also lost because of *"selective attention": attending to or paying attention to only certain things.* A person, for example, may choose to expose him- or herself to a political meeting. This does not mean that he or she will receive every bit of stimuli present. People tend to pay attention to things that truly interest or affect them: a pleasant word, a life-threatening situation, an agreeable comment or one that infuriates them. Here, too, paying attention to only certain stimulation can be either accidental or purposeful. You may be tired and therefore accidentally inattentive. Or you may be angry and purposefully inattentive. Everyone seems to engage in selective attention, which can affect the creation and recreation of meanings.

Further, meaning creation and recreation may be affected by what can be called *"selective interpretation": the individual attaches significance and meaning to a stimulus.* As discussed in the last chapter, because of any number of factors, your interpretation and mine of some stimuli might differ. What you found artistic, I might find offensive; what I see as beautiful or good might seem ugly or dangerous to you; or what you considered important, I might think trivial. Since people are naturally different in so

---

[5] These concepts of selectivity have become commonly accepted terms. A similar treatment of them is in John R. Wenburg and William W. Wilmot, *The Personal Communication Process* (New York: Wiley, 1973), chap 7.

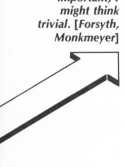

. . . what you considered important, I might think trivial. [Forsyth, Monkmeyer]

many ways, they tend to interpret things in different ways. From all the possible interpretations, you will probably decide on one way of interpretation. The result is that selective interpretation has again affected the whole perceptual process.

Finally, even after you selectively expose yourself to something, selectively pay attention, and selectively interpret, you selectively retain information. *"Selective retention,"* then, means that *only certain things will be remembered.* Whether called selective retention or selective forgetting, the point is the same. People generally forget certain things and remember others—either accidentally or on purpose. Clearly, some try to forget things that were unpleasant: mistakes, sins, crimes, and so forth. And yet these may be the very things that others remember and cannot forget. Although forgetting is a part of life, we are concerned here with perception and how it is affected by the details, thoughts, feelings, and incidents that you either remember or forget.

Earlier, perception was described as the joint process of receiving and interpreting stimuli. That same definition applies here. We have seen in this section that perception has various stages: From all available stimuli, we expose ourselves to only certain ones; of these, we pay attention to only some; of the various interpretations of these, we chose only certain interpretations; and these are often forgotten or "modified" in memory.[6] These four activities of selection form an analogy to four screens with consistently smaller openings. We expose ourselves to certain stimuli, attend to fewer, screen out most of the possible interpretations, and then remember only some of them. Figure 3-1 illustrates this process.[7] Given the visual impression of the diagram, perception is seen in a new way. The question is

[6] The idea that things are remembered in a particular way is an important part of selective retention. Often when we say, "I didn't remember that," we mean, "I didn't remember that . . . in that way."

[7] The diagram is modeled after the kind of illustration Korzybski uses to explain levels of abstraction. Korzybski's most important work, *Science and Sanity* is extremely difficult to understand. A more readable interpretation of the ideas is in William H. Youngren, *Semantics, Linguistics, and Criticism* (New York: Random House, 1972), chap. 1.

Figure 3-1
The continual
narrowing by
selection

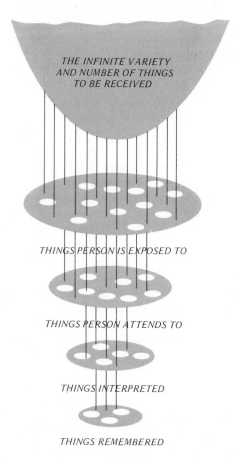

THE INFINITE VARIETY
AND NUMBER OF THINGS
TO BE RECEIVED

THINGS PERSON IS EXPOSED TO

THINGS PERSON ATTENDS TO

THINGS INTERPRETED

THINGS REMEMBERED

not, "Why was this perceived so poorly?" but, rather, "How was it ever perceived so clearly—considering what has to occur?"

Self-concept,
perception,
and intra/
interpersonal
communication

At this point, self-concept and perception can be linked to the relationship between intrapersonal and interpersonal communication. Traditionally, self-concept is discussed in intrapersonal terms: What you "say" to yourself or "discuss" with yourself may all revolve around who you think you are, want to be, fear being, and so on. Your conception about your behavior, thoughts, and feelings—your self-concept—is based on your own intrapersonal processing. And just as traditionally, perception—creating and recreating meaning based on how we perceive ourselves, others, and things and events around us—is considered the basis for all communication. Here, I will discuss, more specifically, how perception and self-concept make it impossible to divide intrapersonal from interpersonal communication. I will describe (1) how self-concept is based on interpersonal feedback and (2) how interpersonal perception and communication are based on the self-concept.

Self-concept and
interpersonal
feedback

Without doubt, I believe that self-concept is a product of *intra*personal communication. In order to understand "who we are," we have to take the time and make the effort to analyze ourselves. But that process seems dependent on others, and the feedback from them is, of course, *inter*personal. The self can be viewed as a conception we get by using other people as a "mirror," and seeing our reflection through them tells us much about who we are.[8] Let me give an illustration.

One of the necessary housekeeping chores at the start of the classes at my university is completion of "class cards" by students, which are retained in the department for future reference. Students are asked to provide on these cards a number of bits of information: name, student identification number, class rank (freshman, etc.), course name and number, and so forth. In addition, I request information on the back of the card pertaining to their reasons for taking the course and their occupation or occupational goals, which may help me to adjust the course to their needs.

All of this is routine, and generally students may have already completed several of these cards. Answers to the questions tend to be short and straightforward: "Course is required for a major" or "I thought I could benefit from the course"; "I want to be a public relations person" or "I am a registered nurse." This is helpful information but none of it is very creative —for obvious reasons, given the nature of the questions.

---

[8] The concepts of mirrors and reflections is developed clearly in Robert Monaghan, "Self-Concept: Through the Communication Looking Glass," in Richard E. Crable and Richard O. Forsythe (with Steven L. Vibbert), *Fundamentals of Communication*, 2d ed. (Columbus, O.: Collegiate, 1978), pp. 48–53.

And then there was Vicki. For "occupation" she wrote, "daughter, wife, mother, student, artist, and human being." My first thought was that she was being sarcastic. My second thought was that she probably had a better awareness of her "occupation" than anyone else in the class. Let me explain.

Vicki, seemed to realize that *"who" she was was very much determined by her relationship to others.* In relation to her mother and father, she was a daughter; in relation to me, she was a student, and so forth. These were not simply roles she played. Her relationship with various people helped define who *she* was. And, more specifically, in her relationship to me, she was a bright, enthusiastic student; in her relationship to her children, she may have been a caring, concerned mother. The relationship was not just one of structure—parent–child, for example; it was also one of characteristics. She may have been enthusiastic in certain relationships, but less so in others. She may have been assertive in one relationship, yet more shy in another. Part of her *intra*personal conceptions of herself was forever tied to her *inter*personal relationships.

Also, I have the feeling that Vicki realized that *feedback from others is indispensable to the development of the self-concept.* These same people

33

with whom we share relationships provide clues about ourselves.[9] Our self-concept is affected by what others verbally and nonverbally communicate to us. Their approval or disapproval, their admiration or hatred of what we do affects our self-concept. If there is no reaction that can be detected, we may feel uneasy and still be affected. Without feedback, there is little with which to develop a self-concept—that is, without interpersonal transactions, intrapersonal processing seems to occur "in the dark." With feedback, the self-concept can be developed by using others as a mirror, and then responding in some way. We may not always be affected by specific reflected feedback, but feedback generally is indispensable in the creation of the self-concept. In short, we see ourselves —in part—as we believe others see us.

Interpersonal perception and self-concept

Earlier, I stated the importance of a good self-concept. The positive development of your self-concept most likely has been more of a concern to your parents than you think. For years in small-group communication, there has been concern for the person who plays the *projector* role: someone who blames others for his or her own problems—or hates in another what is actually one of his or her hated personal characteristics.[10] This "projecting" activity seems to be consistent with, but opposite to, the situation involving a positive self-concept. The person with a positive self-concept generally feels better about others because he or she feels better about him- or herself: The good a person sees in others is very much related to the good he or she sees in him- or herself. Combining the projector and the person with a positive self-concept, we might say that much of our *inter*personal perception is due to our *intra*personal perception. In other words, "We see others as we see ourselves." Surely, the point can be taken too far. Interpersonal perception depends on a variety of factors that affect the selectivity in exposure, attention, interpretation, and retention. Political biases, religious beliefs, personal grudges—these and more—affect how people and things are perceived. And yet we cannot afford to ignore the factors of self-concept that may act as a more efficient screen than these other factors. In fact, all these factors themselves may be filtered through the screen of self-concept. In sum, self-concept as an intrapersonal concept may be a primary factor in interpersonal communication.

Two ideas should be highlighted here because of their importance. (1) You cannot separate yourself from others and still expect to grow as an individual. The development of "who you are" can take place best—and perhaps only—in relation to those people you come to know. The discussions in

[9] These clues are important whether the reflections from others "confirm," "disconfirm," or fail to react to our self-perceptions.

[10] The concept, usually used in group study, seems traceable originally to Kenneth D. Benne and Paul Sheats, "Functional Roles of Group Members," *Journal of Social Sciences* 4 (Spring 1948): 41–49.

this book are intended to help you develop those relationships with others. (2) You cannot develop relationships with others without concentrating to some extent on who you are and what you want to be as a person. This book should also help you to develop your self-concept as a way of helping with interpersonal relationships. Intrapersonal communication depends on interpersonal communication just as much as interpersonal communication depends on intrapersonal communication—it goes around in a circle. In fact, as the title of the chapter indicates, there is no good way to divide interpersonal and intrapersonal communication.

CHAPTER SUMMARY

Although interpersonal and intrapersonal communication can be seen as different types of communication, I am more concerned with how they affect one another. Indeed, I have argued that intra- and interpersonal communication cannot really be separated. Where one occurs, the other will have an effect.

The chapter began with a discussion of self-concept and the variety of selves that make up that conception. Then, attention was shifted to the process of perception and the various ways in which screening occurred in the perceptual process. Finally, the discussion turned to how interpersonal and intrapersonal communication are so intimately related. Self-concept—usually treated as an intrapersonal concern—develops in response to relationships and by reflected feedback. In the same way, interpersonal communication is based on interpersonal perception, which may be more affected by the self-concept than we usually recognize.

The text, of course, focuses on interpersonal communication. Yet you will read much that sounds like a discussion of intrapersonal communication—how you respond to yourself. The interweaving of interpersonal and intrapersonal communication seems to me to be the only realistic way of studying communication. Interpersonal and intrapersonal communication cannot—or at least should not—be considered as separate processes.

LEARNING BY APPLYING

1 *For the chapter to be of real benefit, you must have some ideas about your own self-concept. To discover those ideas, think or write or share a way or several ways of ending the following statements:*

a. *The perceived present self (use several phrases if necessary):*
Physically, I think I am _____
Emotionally, I think I am _____

Ethically, I think I am _____

Interpersonally, I think I am _____

Socially, I think I am _____

In general, I think I am _____

_____

b. *The becoming self (use several phrases if necessary):*
    I think I am becoming more _____

    I think I am becoming less _____

c. *The feared self (use several phrases if necessary):*
    Qualities I hate in people are _____

    _____

    I hope people never think I'm _____

    _____

    The person I would least like to be like is _____

    _____

d. *The desired self (use several phrases if necessary):*
    Qualities I most admire in people are _____

    _____

    I wish people thought I was _____

    _____

    The person I would most like to be like is _____

    _____

e. *Metaperceptions (use several phrases if necessary):*
    My closest friend of the other sex thinks I am _____

    _____

    My (circle one) mother, father, parents, guardian think(s) I am _____

    My closest friend of the same sex thinks I am _____

    _____

    My favorite (circle one) co-worker, classmate, instructor thinks I am ____

    In general, I think I am viewed by others as _____

    _____

2 *Try to recall the last time you and another person disagreed about something. Was one (or more) of the following perhaps involved? selectivity in exposure, attention, interpretation, or retention. Explain.*

3 *Examine your answers to exercise 1a through e. How has feedback from others affected those judgments? You may need time to think about this one.*

4 *Examine your answers about the "desired self" and the "feared self" in 1c and d—especially, the answers to whom you would most and least like to be like. How does the perception you have of these people affect how you perceive yourself? Again, this one may take some time.*

5 *Speculate about how your relationships with others can affect—in general*

—how you feel about yourself. Chapters 9 to 13 will demonstrate even more clearly how you and another become more like each of you wants to be. If this idea seems crucial to you now, you may wish to read those chapters at this time.

LEARNING BY DISCUSSING

1 Discuss what the book describes as "types" of communication. Do you find these helpful in explaining the communication in which you become involved?

2 Does the book's conception of self-concept help you understand the importance of "human" in the phrase "human communication"? How?

3 Does the discussion of various types or interpretations or "facets" of the self help you understand your thoughts about yourself? Explain.

4 Discuss how selectivity devices account for some of the differences in how people perceive.

5 Discuss how perception and self-concept involve both intrapersonal and interpersonal communication.

6 React to the book's position that intrapersonal and interpersonal communication can never be separated entirely.

LEARNING BY READING FURTHER

Condon, John C., Jr., *Interpersonal Communication*. New York: Macmillan, 1977.
Crable, Richard E., *Using Communication*. Boston: Allyn and Bacon, 1979.
Del Polito, Carolyn M., *Intrapersonal Communication*. Menlo Park, CA: Cummings, 1977.
Shuter, Robert, *Understanding Misunderstandings*. New York: Harper & Row, 1979.
Stewart, John, and D'Angelo, Gary, *Together*. Reading, MA: Addison-Wesley, 1975.
Wilmot, William W., *Dyadic Communication*. Reading, MA: Addison-Wesley, 1975.

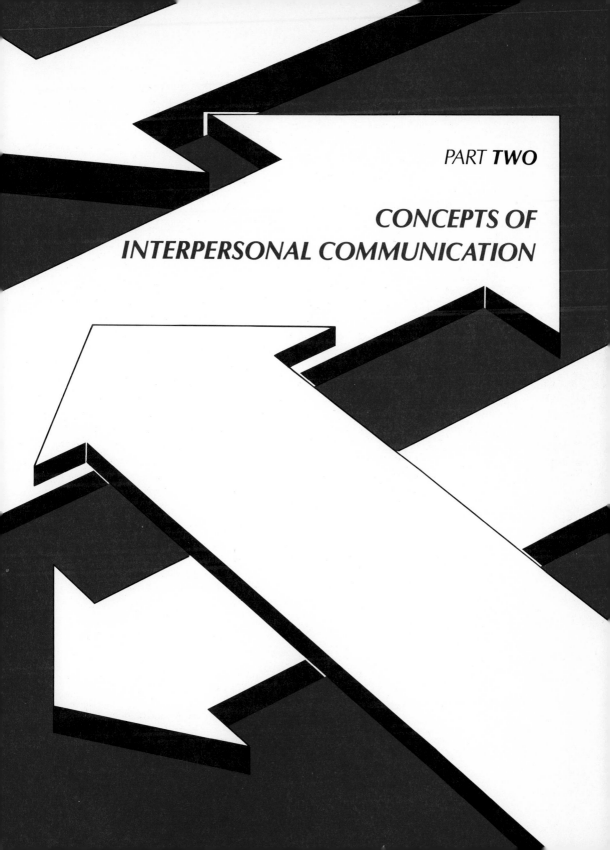

PART **TWO**

CONCEPTS OF INTERPERSONAL COMMUNICATION

HUMANS BEING HUMAN: WHY DO COMMUNICATORS REACH OUT?

STUDY OF THIS CHAPTER WILL ENABLE YOU TO UNDERSTAND

- *that part of being human is needing and wanting to communicate*

- *how humans are both alike and different*

- *that communication is both possible and necessary because of differences and similariti*

- *phatic communication*

- *specific goals of communication, related to: content, relationship, and norms or rules*

All humans communicate, but why? The question could be answered in a number of ways. Humans communicate to pass on information; to influence someone else; or to help one another secure basic needs—food, clothing, or shelter. Humans communicate in order to band together into communities or nations. And yet a more fundamental reason is that *humans communicate, in part, because they are human.* Let me explain this important idea.

To begin with, a human is both similar to and different from all other humans. By this I mean that there are certain basic characteristics shared by everyone. Still if we ignore the possibility of cloning, no two human beings are exactly alike. I might talk of someone as a "modern-day Lincoln," but I know that there will never be another person exactly like Abraham Lincoln. All I probably would mean is that this modern person shares many of the important characteristics that I identify with Lincoln.

Literary and social critic Kenneth Burke has created a way of explaining how people are (at the same time) alike *and* different from everyone else. He argues that the situations can be explained by three concepts: origin, placement, and action.[1] Let me use a personal example to illustrate each of these concepts.

My daughter Audrey and I, for example, are both alike and different in terms of *origin,* or ancestry. She and I both have characteristics of my parents even though we are of different generations. There are certain physical resemblances, as well as similar qualities of personality. And yet Audrey and I differ in many ways. She has some pronounced characteristics of her mother's side of the family. So while we are alike, we are also

---

[1] Kenneth Burke, *A Grammar of Motives* (Berkeley, Calif.: University of California Press, 1969), pt. 1, chap. 1. I have altered the terms somewhat for the purpose of clarity.

different. In the same way, each human shares certain physical and psychological characteristics of the being *homo sapiens:* two legs, an opposable thumb, an enlarged brain—for an animal our size—and so forth. Yet each human has a distinctive set of qualities that has to do with genetics, culture, upbringing—personal experiences. So while all humans are alike, all are different . . . based on origin.

Furthermore, Audrey and I are both similar and different in terms of *placement.* We live in the same city and house, the same nation and world. We share certain characteristics because of our environment: a general orientation to our house and life-style. And yet we can never exactly occupy the same physical space at any given moment. As a 5-year-old, she can try on my shoes—but not while I'm wearing them (even though she has tried!). Similarly, all humans exist on the same physical earth—except for space travel. We may all live in different countries, cities, or villages, but we are all earth people. As humans, we are bound by the pull of gravity and must live and function on something like solid ground most of our lives. Yet much of the earth is different from the rest; seldom are environments identical for a large area, and even if the environments were identical, again humans could not occupy the same space. While humans are alike in terms of placement, they are also different because of it.

Finally, Audrey and I are alike and different because of *action.* As residents of the same house in West Lafayette, Indiana, we do many of the same kinds of things. We engage in some similar activities such as going to the same stores and restaurants, but there are vast differences in our actions from day to day. She pets her guinea pig frequently; I seldom do. I write articles and books while she colors and draws. I earn a living, while she receives an allowance. In the same way, all humans tend to engage in the same *sorts* of behaviors. They eat, sleep, seek shelter from rain or snow or heat and use some sort of language. Despite all these general similarities, the differences are overwhelming. The human variations on eating, sleeping, and seeking shelter—not to mention language use—are amazing. So while all humans are alike in their action, they are also very different.

The simultaneous differences and similarities among humans are important in understanding human communication. This situation is true for two reasons: (1) it makes the existence of communication *possible* and (2) it makes communication *necessary.* Let me expand and explain each of these ideas.

Communication is possible because of differences and similarities

First, *communication is only* possible *because of the differences* and *similarities between two people.* Try to picture two people who are completely alike; there are no differences between them. Figure 4-1 shows what these two people would look like. Note that they . . . are really only one person. They share everything, so there is nothing that makes them separate. Is communication possible? Consider the definition used earlier: Communi-

If they were completely different, no communication could occur. [Malave, Stock, Boston]

cation is the symbolic transaction aimed at recreating similar meaning. In the diagram there is no possibility that one person has a "meaning" that the other does not already know. So there is no possibility of *re*creating similar meaning. "Each"—since they are identical—already "has" the meaning. No communication is possible.

Now try to picture a situation in which two people have *nothing* in common—there is no "overlap" of anything between them. Figure 4-2 illustrates this situation. The two "people" in the diagram would share no common language, interests, actions, or backgrounds. Again, such a situation is impossible; it cannot exist among earthly humans. But if it could, no communication would be possible. Even people who speak different languages can begin to communicate because they use similar gestures, make familiar sounds—*something*. In order for communication to exist, *some* sort of similarity *has* to exist.

What actually is the case, as Burke has pointed out, is that all humans are both alike and different. If they were totally similar, no communication could occur. If they were completely different, no communication could occur.[2] But when people are *both* alike and different, communication can occur. Figure 4-3 shows two people who can begin to communicate. There is enough difference for communication to make sense and enough similar-

[2] Kenneth Burke, *A Rhetoric of Motives* (Berkeley, Calif.: University of California Press, 1969), p. 25. Burke speaks specifically of rhetoric, but the point is essentially the same.

ity to make communication possible. As these two people communicate—sharing certain things one with the other—the amount of similarity
seems to grow. And so the amount of difference decreases, as shown in Figure 4-4. As the interpersonal relationship deepens and broadens further, the
relationship approaches what I have called the communing relationship: In
some ways and at some times the two people almost seem to be one. Consider Figure 4-5. In essence, communication is first made possible by both
the differences and similarities between people.

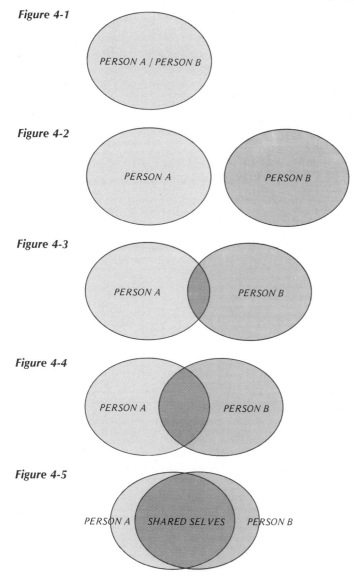

Figure 4-1

PERSON A / PERSON B

Figure 4-2

PERSON A

PERSON B

Figure 4-3

PERSON A

PERSON B

Figure 4-4

PERSON A

PERSON B

Figure 4-5

PERSON A   SHARED SELVES   PERSON B

Second, *communication is* necessary *because of the differences* and *similarities between two people.* If I were totally like anyone else, I would have no need to reach out to him or her. That would be like reaching out to myself. Yet if I were totally different from everyone else, I might not need to reach out to people at all. I would not need anything that another human could provide. But I am neither of these; I am simultaneously joined with and separate from another person. And what seems to happen is that I reach out for others somewhat similar to myself.

Humans do not tend to enjoy being separated from others for long periods—sometimes even for short periods—of time. Not everyone is like Henry David Thoreau who "escaped" to Walden Pond. But even then, he returned to civilization after two years, two months, and two days—and during that time had talked with other people. Solitary confinement—being completely away from contact with others—traditionally has been one of the most effective means of human torture. Everyone is a separate person but at some time he or she needs to establish ties between him- or herself and others.

That urge to reach out seems to be one of the strongest human desires—part of being human is the need to communicate with other humans. We use communication to get closer to others, to conquer the feeling of being more separate than we want. Communication, then, is one of the ways that we have of proving how basically human we are.

A term often used for this kind of basic communication is *phatic communication*—the label for communication that does not seem to have much of a purpose.[3] See if the following sounds familiar:

Hey, long time, no see.
Hi! How are you?
Fine. How's yourself?
Gettin' by. What do you know?
Not much.
Nice talkin' to you.
Yeah. See you around.

Scenes such as this are enacted countless times during a day by probably millions of people. Phatic communication is often viewed as "throw away" communication. Not much was said. Nothing was accomplished—or was it?

A conversation such as this might have followed the previous one.

I saw Larry today.
How was he?

[3] A. Craig Baird, Franklin H. Knower, and Samuel L. Becker, *General Speech Communication*, 4th ed. (New York: McGraw-Hill, 1971), pp. 32–33.

Fine. I hadn't seen him for months.
I haven't either.
It sure was good to see him.
Yeah. I wish I had been with you.

Something obviously occurred in the earlier conversation. No great decisions were made, and no large amount of information was transmitted. Still the two people had reestablished contact with one another. Even the highly ritualized "How are you-I am fine-How are you" communication may be important to humans. Such *phatic* communication may be the purest example of humans communicating because they are human. Making contact with others is not unimportant.

Specific goals of human communication

Still, of course, there are countless specific reasons for humans communicating with one another. In this section I shall describe and illustrate some of the more common goals—or reasons that people communicate.

Goals with a content focus

Often the reason for communicating has to do with some "content." *By content, I mean factors such as information, beliefs, attitudes, opinions, values, and behaviors.* Each of these may be the central idea or focus for communication between people. Let me briefly define each:

information. What people refer to as knowledge, news, or factual material; for example, "The earth is rather round."
belief. What someone thinks is the case, or thinks is accurate; for example, "Blue is prettier than red."
attitude. A predisposition or readiness to respond to something in a set way; for example, a negative view of politicians and politics.
opinion. A *stated* expression, which may or may not be consistent with an attitude; for example, "I think all politicians are crooks." (Notice the frequent similarity to belief.)
value. A general view of the world or some quality held to be important; for example, friendship.
behavior. An overt and observable action—verbal or nonverbal; for example, gambling.

Any one of these factors can be the focus for communication during a discussion between almost any two people. Any one of these might be the *content* of the communication.

When one of the content areas is the focus of the conversation, the specific *goal* might be one of several. In relation to the six content areas, taken one at a time, the goal might be to:

ask about information, beliefs, attitudes, opinions, values, or behavior
tell about information, and so on
exchange information, and so on

	INFORMATION	BELIEF	ATTITUDE	OPINION	VALUE	BEHAVIOR
TO ASK ABOUT	"Where are you going?"					
TO TELL ABOUT					"I admire honesty more than anything."	
TO EXCHANGE						"I went to the game...." "So did I...."
TO SEEK CONFIRMATION		"What do you think about my stand on cheating?"				
TO CONFIRM				"You don't think he's guilty, do you?"		
TO SEEK TO INFLUENCE			"You ought not be so hard on Harry...."			
TO SEEK TO BE INFLUENCED	"Can you tell me if I have been wrong in thinking that..."					

Note: Each of the squares could be filled with a somewhat different comment or event.

Figure 4-6

seek confirmation about information, and so on
confirm information, and so on
seek to influence information, and so on
seek to be influenced concerning information, and so on

I do not pretend that these are all of the possible content-related goals of human communication. Still each of the six major content areas could be related to each of the seven goals. Even this modest survey of content-related goals multiplies to 42 fairly different human goals. Figure 4-6 provides an example of how each of the 42 are related.

Why, then, do humans specifically communicate? You have just been introduced to 42 reasons. Any one of which—or several—may be involved in one of your conversations today. And yet these are only "content goals." There is another special category—"relationship goals."

Relationship goals concern how one or both people may be trying to influence the relationship between them. Several major characteristics that people can attempt to influence include:

liking. The affection or feeling for someone
distance. The social or physical space between people[4]
dominance. The power of someone over another[5]
status. The relative higher/lower roles played by people[6]
similarity. The likeness or parallelism between people[7]

Each of these factors in a relationship may be affected in different ways. In other words, there are several possible goals for each of these factors.[8]

Your goal in an interpersonal situation may be one of the following:

1   A wish to *increase* the amount of liking or the status differences—or any of the other factors.
2   A wish to *decrease* the dominance of someone "over" you or to *decrease* the amount of liking (e.g., "We're getting too serious; I think we should stop seeing one another.")
3   A wish only to *maintain* (but neither increase nor decrease) the similarity or the distance between you and another

All of these first relationship-related goals have to do with affecting the "amounts" of some of the factors.

4   A wish to *modify* (in whatever way) the "quality" of the relationship. So you might wish to change a physical distance into a psychological one: "Like me for my mind, instead of my body."

At one time or another, you probably will want to increase, decrease, maintain, or modify one of the following factors in a relationship: liking, distance, dominance, status, or similarity.

It is possible that your goal in a relationship may be complementary with the other person's goal. In that case the conversation may flow smoothly: You wish to become closer (distance, and perhaps liking), and so does the other person; you may wish to increase the amount of similarity,

---

[4] For a relevant discussion of liking and distance, see Wayne Brockriede, "Dimensions of the Concept of Rhetoric," *Quarterly Journal of Speech* 54 (Feb. 1968): 2–4.
[5] See Paul Watzlawick, Janet Helmick Beavin, and Don D. Jackson, *The Pragmatics of Human Communication* (New York: Norton, 1967).
[6] Status may be based on virtually anything, from social position to expertise to economic position. Status may or may not relate to the factor of power.
[7] The writings of Burke, cited in footnotes 1 and 2, are relevant here.
[8] This and the following lists of specific goals are meant to be suggestive, instead of exhaustive.

and so may the other. In relation to status and dominance, the complementary situation is reversed. In order for things to happen smoothly, one of you must *want* to be more dominant (or of higher status) and the other must *want* to be less dominant (or of lower status). But the point is the same. When interpersonal relationship goals are complementary, each wants something that "fits" well with what the other wants.

Often, however, the goals will be conflicting. Both of you may wish to be more dominant—or both of higher status. Or you may wish to increase liking, while the other person wishes to maintain, modify, or actually decrease the amount of liking. Conflicting goals simply mean that two people want to affect the relationship in different ways. Figure 4-7 illustrates all the various possibilities for these factors in a relationship.

Again, I shall not argue that these are all of the possible goals related to relationships. Still the numbers are impressive: each of the five factors, multiplied by each of the four goals, multiplied by two (each could be conflicting or complementary) equals 40 goals related to relationships. Why do humans communicate? There are many reasons—at least 40 are related to the state of the relationship.

Goals with a normal or rule focus

Other goals are neither related to content nor to the relationship directly. A third and final category of goals relates to the norms or rules of the social situation. "Norms" may be viewed as those *unstated expectations* about appropriate behavior. Interrupting conversations, for example, violates what most of us expect from someone. "Rules," on the other hand,

Figure 4-7

	LIKING	DISTANCE	DOMINANCE	STATUS	SIMILARITY
TO INCREASE	"I love you, and in time maybe..."		"Just for that, no cookies for a week."		
TO DECREASE			"Sit down. Relax. Consider yourself free to do what you want."		
TO MAINTAIN		"Mom, I think it's best if I just keep my apartment over here..."		"I am so happy working for you..."	
TO MODIFY					"I wish we had more in common. All we ever share is..."

Note: Each of the squares could be filled with a somewhat different response.

Conflicting goals simply mean that two people want to affect the relationship in different ways. [Herwig, Stock, Boston]

are more obviously *stated guidelines* for good behavior.[9] Courts of law, of course, have rules. So do sports events and children's games. But interpersonal relationships can also be affected by rules. A rule that has become a cliché is "No kissing on the first date." I will not argue the merits of—or the adherence to—such a rule, but it is a potential rule. Rules and norms in interpersonal relationships are seen by contemporary communication researchers as being very important. The survival of a relationship may well depend on how well people "follow" the norms and rules. Most of us are seldom conscious of the rules or norms, but they are there in specific situations: Are there certain things not talked about in this setting? Are certain acts of kindness expected in this situation? Is obscenity outlawed here—or expected? Since norms and rules are an important part of human relationships, they are important in communication.

Also, these rules or norms can be the focus for communication. Instead of concentrating on content or the relationship, two people may focus for a

[9] Burke argues, for example, that rules are created when norms lose their ability to influence behavior. For a discussion see Richard E. Crable, "Ethical Codes, Accountability, and Argumentation," *Quarterly Journal of Speech* 64 (Feb. 1978):23–32.

time on the rules or norms that help their relationship "work." When these become the focus, either one of the people (or both) may wish to:

confirm the rule or norm (e.g., I think no kissing on the first date is good, don't you?)
create a rule or norm (e.g., Listen, let's don't kiss goodnight, okay?)
modify the rule or norm (e.g., Hey, let's not even kiss on the second date!)
tell about the rule or norm (e.g., I don't kiss on the first date.)
ask about a rule or norm (e.g., Can I kiss you on the first date?)
violate a rule or norm (e.g, *****SMACK*****)

In all these situations revolving around the proverbial kiss, the emphasis is the same. A rule or norm is the object of the conversation. In each case, however, the specific goal is different. Humans communicate for all kinds of reasons that relate to rules and norms.

Of course, the emphasis on rules and norms has been just one focus. Other human goals relate to content (information, etc.) and the relationship between two people. For all of the reasons – or goals – stated in these three sections, humans communicate. And yet they communicate for a general reason that serves as an umbrella for all the specific purposes: Being alike and different from everyone else, humans communicate because they are human – and *need* to reach out to others.

CHAPTER SUMMARY

The basic goal of communication among humans seems to be to reach out to other human beings. In other words, communication occurs partly because humans are humans—who are both similar to and different from all other humans. This simultaneous similarity and difference include factors relating to origin, placement, and action.

There are, of course, other and more specific goals of human communication. Included in such goals are communication efforts with a content focus, a relationship focus, and a norm or rule focus. An understanding of the goal in communicating is necessary in order to understand communication in interpersonal relationships better. Only then can we comprehend specifically why humans are reaching out—"one to another."

LEARNING
BY APPLYING

1   *Try to envision someone who has absolutely no similarity to you. That would have to be, I think, a creature from some other planet or galaxy since the being could not eat, dress, look, talk, and so on. How could you com-*

municate? (By the way, you cannot rely on mental telepathy since that would presume that you shared some mental similarities.) If you "give up" — and I suspect sooner or later you will have to — you have confronted the issue that everybody shares something with you. That means you can communicate at some level with anyone!

2   Recall your last "phatic" communication. Since it probably did not occur long ago, try to recall how you felt — what you thought about — and what you thought the other person was thinking and feeling. Was this "phatic" communication really meaningless?

3   Select a novel or a nonfiction book that has examples of a two-person conversation. Try to analyze each statement made by the people by using Figures 4-6 and 4-7 and the material relating to rules and norms. Notice that in any lengthy conversation, several or many of these communication "goals" or purposes may be illustrated. How does a concentration of one or a few of these goals help you identify what kind of conversation is taking place?

LEARNING BY DISCUSSING

1   Discuss how communication seems to be needed and wanted by everyone (use both text and your own experience).

2   Explain your understanding of how people are both alike and different from everyone else.

3   Explain how you react to the idea that communication requires both differences and similarities among people.

4   Discuss the nature and use of "phatic" communication.

5   Discuss differences between and among communication that focuses on content, relationships, and norms or rules. Can you think of situations in which a single transaction might involve all of these? Explain.

NEGOTIATED MEANINGS: HOW DOES COMMUNICATION OCCUR?

NBC correspondent and reporter, Edwin Newman, has become one of the chief fighters against the abuse and misuse of language. He argues against jargon, "legal-ese," "social science-ese," meaningless slang, and other language problems. Plainly speaking, he wants people to speak plainly – and accurately. He is one of the more recent people to urge others to "say what they mean."[1]

Newman speaks and writes as a person who pays attention to vocabulary and grammar. And clearly, he is right that there is no reason to call a cow a "ruminating, quadruped bovine." There is no reason to say, "That statement and explanation are no longer operative," when you mean that you have either changed your mind – or that you lied in the first place. There is no reason for everything to be "super" or "fantastic," when some things are merely mediocre. People, then, should be clearer and more precise in what they say.

The problem with this advice, however, is that it often is given without an understanding of how "meaning" occurs. This chapter discusses the various beliefs about meaning and how it occurs.

There is a common belief that meaning is in the words we use. When we want to say something, we simply select the appropriate words – and when others hear or see the words, the meaning will be "transferred." The only way that the transfer of words will result in the automatic recreation of meaning is if meanings are in the words themselves. Newman's phrase is important: "Say what you mean!" The only way that this makes sense is to assume that the meanings are somewhere in words. If you mean "goat," say "goat." If you mean "fireplug," then say "fireplug." All that may seem to

[1] Edwin Newman, *Strictly Speaking: Will America Be the Death of English* (Indianapolis: Bobbs-Merrill, 1974).

Will saying the
word "love"
result in someone
knowing what
you mean? [UPI]

make sense. It makes communication seem a fairly easy task of selecting the appropriate word, sentence, or paragraph.

But the idea that meanings lie in words has some problems. What do you do in the situation where you *mean* "democracy"? Will saying the word automatically result in someone else knowing what *you mean*? No, of course it will not. Will saying the word "love" result in someone knowing what you mean? But take a less abstract task: Will the word "goat" result in the other person knowing what you mean? "Goat" might mean a four-legged animal that is reputed to eat tin cans. It might also "mean" a person who is sacrificed for others. It might "mean" someone who accepts all blame. It might also "mean" an animal that is either large or small, dead or alive, female or male, wild or domestic. . . . This list of possible meanings does not end there. The point, however, perhaps has been made. You and I cannot "say what we mean" because there are various meanings for any one thing we might say.

The only way in which meanings could be expressed in words would be for there to be one — and only one — meaning for each word. A look at a dictionary will show that this is not accurate. A survey of your recent conversations with others will reveal instances of "misunderstandings": You used what you thought were the right words, and still the other person did not "know what you meant." A rose by some other name would smell the same, but what we might mean by "rose" would vary greatly.

Are meanings in people? If meanings are not in the words themselves, then where are they? In recent years it has become popular to suggest that *meanings are in people*. "Words don't mean, people mean" has become a cliché.[2] The expression of that phrase may be fairly current, but the roots of the expression go back to some of the early work that resulted in the study of semantics. The basic issue is the relationship among thought (or meanings), things, and words (or symbols).[3]

To begin with, study the illustrated sequence:

DOG ――――― BELOVED PET ―――――

(SYMBOL)   (MEANING)   (THING)

Notice that "meaning" lies in the middle of the sequence. This means three important factors: (1) *There is a direct connection between "things" and the "meanings" we have for them.* In this case we see a dog, which brings a thought, conception, or meaning about the dog. (2) *There is a direct connection between "symbols" and "meanings."* As you say "liberty" a certain set of thoughts or ideas will be what you "mean." The reverse is accurate also. You may see the people of a country living freely, contentedly, and with some control over their own destiny. With these "meanings" in mind, the symbol that comes to mind might be the word "liberty." (3) *There is no direct connection between "symbols" and "things."* The animal that we

---

[2] For an interesting discussion, see Dean Barnlund, "Toward a Meaning-Centered Philosophy of Communication," *Journal of Communication* 11 (Dec. 1962), 197–211.
[3] See, for example, Charles K. Ogden and I. A. Richards, *The Meaning of Meaning* (New York: Harcourt Brace Jovanovich, 1964), chap. 1.

often call a "cow" could be called a "television"—if everyone agreed to it. There would be nothing humorous about "going out to milk the television" or "tuning in the cow" if there was an agreement to switch labels. While there is a direct connection between symbols and meanings, and between things and meanings, there is no direct connection between things and the symbols we use for them.

But if meaning is the only connection between symbols and things, then where *is* "meaning"? How does it arise and occur? The preceding discussion is used as a way of arguing that "meaning lies in people." Let me explain by expanding the earlier example of the dog.

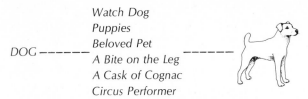

DOG ------
- Watch Dog
- Puppies
- Beloved Pet
- A Bite on the Leg
- A Cask of Cognac
- Circus Performer

Notice that we are dealing with the same four-legged animal. Let's say that there is a dog immediately visible. We both agree that the word-symbol "dog" is an adequate description. Yet any of the "meanings" in the middle could be what you or I "meant" by "dog" as the thing seen. The meaning that each one of us attaches to the animal has *little* to do with the symbol "dog." It has *more* to do with the animal in front of us, the thing we see. A poodle, for example, will hardly ever bring the idea "watch dog" to anyone's mind. But the meaning attached to the dog has *most* to do with who we are and what we have experienced.

The meaning of the dog, therefore, is mainly in us—at least according to this explanation. If you were a stereotyped mail carrier in a stereotyped environment with stereotyped dogs, the thing in our view might mean a bite on the leg. If you have had experience with guard dogs for protection, "watch dog" may come to mind. If you were once injured on a Swiss mountain, cognac and help may come to mind. If you are the average American with no extremely bad experiences with dogs, "beloved pet" might be associated with the animal and symbol. The dog as an animal, then, does not mean anything; the symbol "dog" does not mean anything. People make things and terms mean something—by their training, their biases, and their experiences. Meanings are in people and not in words.

This discussion explains why there can be so much confusion when we try to "say what we mean," for what we mean is inside us. When we try to explain what we mean, we have to search for some verbal or nonverbal symbol that will help someone else see what we mean. Symbols are things on the outside of us, which are used to show what we mean—inside us.

*Intra*personally, then, it makes considerable sense to talk about meanings being inside people. The intrapersonal process involves the attachment of meaning to symbols so that we better understand how we feel, what we think, and what we have done. Then, we hope to recreate the meanings that we have in the minds of other people and that their meanings will become similar to ours. But in this step of *inter*personal communication, something interesting seems to take place. Meaning occurs apparently in a more complicated way.

Meanings are negotiated

Inter*personally, meanings seem to be created in a process that appears to be "negotiation."* Negotiation is a familiar concept to most of us. Teachers and school board members negotiate a contract by bargaining. School boards generally provide more salary support than they say they can afford. Teachers usually accept contract terms below their "absolute and final offer." The same thing occurs when unions and managements conduct negotiations. Similar "compromises" are worked out in law between prosecutors who accept guilty pleas to "lesser" crimes. Instead of "going for all or nothing," they plea bargain with defense attorneys and court systems. Negotiation occurs when two people need a family automobile at the same time. Some sort of bargain or compromise may be accepted that gives each person as much as possible of what he or she demands.

Negotiation, in general, implies terms such as "compromise:" a middle ground on which agreement can be struck; "bargaining:" the give and take that results in compromise; and initial demands: the starting points from where bargaining begins. These same terms are helpful in understanding how meanings are negotiated in *inter*personal communication.

In the last section I discussed the idea that, intrapersonally, meanings are in people. These intrapersonal meanings are the *starting points* for in-

Meaning, it seems, is a product of interpersonal negotiation. [Hayman, Stock, Boston]

terpersonal communication. You *know* what you mean and you are prepared to use symbols to help me see what you mean by means of the process described in Chapter 2. You made a choice about a meaning you wish to share; you begin the process of encoding—of symbolizing "what you mean" and of transmitting it to me with verbal or nonverbal symbols. As I receive your transmission of symbols, I attempt to interpret them. But how does this interpretation occur?

The interpretation of the meaning seems to be created by the feedback you and I exchange as the discussion unfolds. You try to explain—nonverbally, as well as verbally in different ways—what you mean. I shall feed back to you verbal or nonverbal symbols that help you understand how well I am understanding you. You may think I am misunderstanding you, and so you try again. I begin to think I understand, but I feel you do not realize I am understanding. It can be a confusing process of *bargaining.* You have your meaning and I begin to get mine. These are our starting points for negotiation. Then, in the give and take provided by the original message and feedback, we finally arrive at what appears to be a commonly understood meaning. To arrive at this agreement, you and I may have altered part of what we meant and tried to say at first. In the end, the interpersonal meaning seems to be to some degree a compromise between what each of us started out to mean. I have some new meaning, and your own meaning may have been altered or modified. Let me illustrate this point by relating the following case.

Ivan	Claude was on my back again today.
Ben	What do you mean?
Ivan	You know how he is . . . never ever satisfied with anyone's work.
Ben	You mean he's been as demanding as ever.
Ivan	Exactly. That's what I meant. He was at it again. This time, he didn't like the Ferguson account ideas. I don't know what to do. I have to start all over.
Ben	Oh, man! That's a lot of work. From the very beginning?
Ivan	What?
Ben	Do you have to start from the very beginning?
Ivan	Well, no. He liked some of it. But a lot of it needs revision.
Ben	How did our group do with the other thing—the Kattleman account?
Ivan	More revision.
Ben	Then, he's on everyone's back?
Ivan	Yeah, I guess so. I didn't mean he was *just* after me. . . . Well, you know what I mean.
Ben	Yeah.

The meaning of this exchange—and I would argue all interpersonal communication—was created by the negotiation of meanings between the people. Ben began to see what Ivan meant. But then, Ivan also began to see more clearly what he himself meant. He may have *intra*personally known what he meant, but the *inter*personal transaction allowed him to see more exactly what he actually meant.

The meanings of symbols do not lie somewhere buried in the word. Intrapersonally, meanings are in the people who use words. Yet interpersonal communication demands that people attempt to recreate their meanings in someone else. When that happens the meaning of symbols probably becomes a process of starting points, of bargaining, and of final compromise for understanding. Meaning, it seems, is a product of interpersonal negotiation.

CHAPTER SUMMARY

In this chapter we confronted the general problem of "meanings" in communication. If communication is seen as a process in which meanings are recreated, then there must be some understanding of how meanings occur.

The chapter surveyed briefly the idea that meanings "are in words" and indicated the weaknesses of that belief. Next, the notion that "meanings are in people" was examined. This very popular belief was contrasted with the idea that "meanings" actually occur as a process of negotiation between and among people. In most interpersonal communication the individuals create and react to messages—and eventually "negotiate" what is meant. The meaning may be somewhat different from the originally conceived message, but some changes may be necessary in this process of meaning creation.

LEARNING BY APPLYING

1 Take a list of commonly used words and let a group of several people— perhaps your class—tell you what they mean. You can create your own list or use the following:

> petting
> democracy
> business
> beautiful
> good

Discuss the various "meanings" given to each of these words. What you are discovering is that, wherever meaning may lie, it does not lie in the words that someone uses.

2 Take at least three of the words from the list in exercise 1 and create a sentence using other words with them. What do you think you are communicating? What meaning do you think you have? Present the sentence to a

friend or classmate; allow him or her to ask questions or to make observations. Do you find that you may have really meant something a little different from what you thought? Perhaps, there was more of a different "meaning" in the sentence than, or from, what you thought. If so, you have just witnessed how "meaning" is negotiated between people.

LEARNING
BY DISCUSSING

1   Discuss the nature and the weakness of the belief that "meanings are in words."
2   Discuss the nature and limitations of the belief that "meanings are in people as individuals."
3   Discuss the idea that "meanings are in the negotiation between and among people."
4   Does this last conception help you to understand communication better? Why or why not?

LEARNING
BY READING FURTHER

Bois, J. Samuel, *The Art of Awareness*, 2d ed. Dubuque, IA: Brown, 1973.
Condon, John C., Jr., *Semantics and Communication*. New York: Macmillan, 1975.
Hanneman, Gerhard J., and McEwen, William J., eds., *Communication and Behavior*. Reading, MA: Addison-Wesley, 1975.
Youngren, William H., *Semantics, Linguistics, and Criticism*. New York: Random House, 1972.

6

VERBAL AND NONVERBAL SYMBOLS: HOW DO COMMUNICATORS REACH OUT?

STUDY OF THIS CHAPTER WILL ENABLE YOU TO

- *understand the nature of signs*
- *understand the nature of symbols*
- *understand that signs and symbols are differentiated by the reaction to them*
- *understand types of symbols*
- *understand specific areas of nonverbal study*
- *understand the complex question of the "meaning of symbols"*
- *understand the factors that help people attach meanings to symbols*
- *use an understanding of the preceding factors to more sensitively attach meanings to symbols*

Chapter 5 dealt with the general nature of meaning and how it is created in communication. This chapter will discuss the types and functions of the symbols that explain how communicators transact with one another. Interestingly, perhaps the best way to begin is to describe how symbols can be confused with something called "signs." Then, the explanation of verbal and nonverbal symbols will be clearer.

Symbols, signs, and signal responses Symbols virtually surround us. The words we say, the flags we fly, our bumper stickers, and on and on. Anytime we attach meaning to a stimulus of some sort, we are engaged in the use of symbols. Anytime we try to put into words or action what we mean, we are using symbols. Yet there is an easily made confusion between symbols and "signs."[1] Symbols themselves can be better understood once the nature of signs is understood.

"Signs" are things that produce an immediate, unconsidered, and single reaction to something present. Let me explain this definition by examining how a traffic "stop sign" functions. When you or I come to a stop sign, we stop. There is the *immediate* response. It is as if someone has just shouted "Stop!" In the same way, our stopping is *unconsidered.* Normally, we do not pause to decide what to do. Without any consideration, we simply stop. Next, the stopping is the only acceptable response. The stop sign normally produces *only one reaction*, and that is stopping. Finally, the stopping behavior is to something that is immediately *present:* the octagonal sign itself. Signs, then, are things that produce an immediate, unconsidered, and single reaction to something present.

Usually, "signal behavior"—the response to something as a sign—is explained in terms of animal behavior. When, for example, other crows in a

[1] For an interesting discussion, see Wallace C. Fotheringham, *Perspectives on Persuasion* (Boston: Allyn and Bacon, 1966), pp. 52–73.

tree hear the warning cry of a "sentry" crow, they will all fly. They do not pause to wonder why the caw was made. They simply react to the presence of the cry—immediately, without consideration, and with a single response. In humans, objects such as stop signs are usually used as an example of how humans sometimes respond "signally." But all this only tells us that both humans and lower animals can respond signally. What, though, can be a sign and can produce a signal reaction?

The answer is that *almost anything can be responded to as it if were a sign.* Flags, for example, are usually treated as symbols: people attach meaning to the object whether or not it is actually present, consider how or if they want to have a reaction, and choose which of various reactions will be theirs. Flags, then, seem like symbols. And yet flags can be responded to as signs. The Nazi flag, for example, can produce an immediate, single, and unconsidered response. To most people, this object produces a strong response of hatred—even though the swastika was once an ancient religious symbol. Words that seem to be symbols such as "communist," "liberal," "Uncle Tom," and "Jew" are often responded to signally. Among certain people, these words produce the automatic, unthinking response that characterizes signs. Signs, then, can be almost anything. The question is not "What is a sign?" but "What can people respond to as a sign?" The response to the thing determines whether something that appears to be a symbol will be responded to as a sign.

The reverse is also true. *Things that are usually regarded as a sign can be responded to as though they were symbols.* Let's take the example of the stop sign. Suppose you have just had the experience of someone failing to yield the right-of-way at an intersection that included a "four-way" stop. As you approach the four-way stop after the accident, you do not automatically respond to the sign. You are thinking of the accident. You hesitate, you think, you have new meanings for the stop sign. You are responding to it as if it were a symbol, and for you, it has become one. Instead of an accident involving violated stop signs, let's suppose you are taking a child to the emergency ward after an injury. You approach an intersection where the traffic light has just changed to red. Normally, you would stop with a signal response. But maybe you would not this time. With a child bleeding in the car and no traffic, you might pause and consider the value of stopping. Whether or not you decide to violate the traffic signal, the sign has become a symbol for you. You have not responded with an immediate, unconsidered, and single reaction to the thing present. Signs produce the automatic response. When those same objects give rise to consideration about how to respond, they are no longer serving as signs. For you, they are symbols.

Symbols and signs, therefore, are defined by how people respond to them. When I place an emphasis on symbols in communication, I am trying to highlight the idea that people reach out to others by using words, things, and behaviors. Those words, things, and behaviors should not normally be responded to as if they were signs, but should be reacted to as if they were symbols. Symbol, not signal, reaction provides the best approach to understanding the recreation of similar meanings.

Types of symbols

The human use of symbols provides a wealth of material for study. Basically, as we have seen before, *symbols are either verbal* (meaning that they are words) *or nonverbal* (meaning that they are not words). That is the basic division of human symbol use, but there are other divisions. *Verbal symbols can be subdivided into oral (spoken) words and written words.* In actuality, the familiar phrase "verbal agreement" could be *either* oral or written, but it generally is misused to mean only oral.

Similarly, *nonverbal symbols can be subdivided into a number of fairly separate "types."* The study of these various types is how the types themselves are identified. Just as verbal scholars might focus on oral, but not written, symbols *the nonverbal researcher might focus on kinesics, proxemics, haptics, oculesics, objectics, chronemics, vocalics, environmental factors, or physical appearance.*[2] A brief description of each of these will provide a basic understanding of the types of nonverbal symbols.

"Kinesics," for example, is the study of how people use bodily movements to express what they mean. Included in this study are head movements, posture, hand movements or gestures, facial expression, and movements of the arms or legs. "Proxemics" involves the study of how humans use or interpret the space around them. Personal space seems important to people, and many of us get uncomfortable when we are crowded together on elevators or at lunch counters. We stand or sit close to people we like, or to people we wish to intimidate. "Haptics" is the study of touching behavior. Some people caress to show love, while others hit to show anger; some people enjoy touching and to be touched, while others become nervous or irritated by it. Whatever the exact situation, touching is a way of trying to communicate. "Oculesics" has to do with eye movements, blinking, the amount of eye contact, and so forth. We look directly at someone, we avoid eye contact and look away, or we "blink back tears." In these instances the eyes are used for nonverbal communication. "Objectics" is the study of how humans use "things" to communicate. Sports cars, smoking pipes, diamond rings, and so forth are objects that can be used to mean something to someone else. The study of how humans use time is called "chronemics." We may arrive early for a date, keep someone "cooling his heels" in an outside office, or arrive "fashionably late" for a party. However we do it, we can

---

[2] Many of the labels here, including chronemics, objectics, haptics, and oculesics are suggested in James C. McCroskey, *Introduction to Rhetorical Communication*, 2d ed. (Englewood Cliffs, N.J.: Prentice-Hall, 1972), chap. 6. Some of the terms (not noted in McCroskey) have been developed over a period of years by various scholars.

be said to be using time for communication. "Vocalics" has to do with the use of the voice to give special emphasis or interpretations to what we are saying. Vocalics includes the study of loudness, pitch, rate or speed of speech, utterances such as "uhms" and "ers" (nonfluencies), and even the pauses incorporated into speech. "Environmental factors" include parts of the human surrounding such as neighborhoods, office furniture and arrangement, the degree of warmth or cold in a room, open doors, and telephone interruptions during a meeting, which may be used to symbolize or mean something. "Personal appearance," obviously, has to do with those factors relating to dress, makeup, and general cleanliness and grooming. Humans can manipulate their appearance in order to express what they mean.

Indeed, there are many types of nonverbal symbols. In addition, there is the category of symbols called verbal—either written or oral. Together, verbal and nonverbal symbols are the tools of human communication.

What, then, do symbols "mean?" On the basis of Chapter 5, the answer seems obvious: Symbols mean what the negotiation between people determine them to mean. And yet, particularly in relation to nonverbal communication, there exists the temptation to think the nonverbal symbols must *mean something.* Doesn't moving closer to someone mean you like him or her? Doesn't the avoidance of eye contact indicate someone is being evasive or dishonest? Doesn't a mellow, low-pitched, well-varied male voice indicate manliness? Doesn't keeping someone waiting outside an office mean that you are trying to play a superior role? Doesn't . . . In all these situations, the answer is the same. *Each of them* may *mean what is suggested, but none of them* necessarily *mean anything of the sort.* Moving closer to someone can be used to intimidate, not charm, the other. Avoidance of eye contact simply may mean that a person is trying to think precisely how to phrase what is said. A mellow, low-pitched, and well-varied voice may mean nothing besides a mellow, low-pitched, well-varied voice. The wait outside an office may mean only that the person in the office is busy with someone else. Just as with words, the meaning of nonverbal symbols depends on the interpersonal negotiation of meaning between the two people.

It may well be that for a given individual, a particular nonverbal symbol would mean one and only one thing. But then, that is also true of verbal symbols. Each of us probably equates some words with only one possible meaning. That single-meaning assumption means that the person is responding to the symbol as if it were a sign. In the same way, the assumption that a nonverbal cue has only one meaning is to regard it as a sign, and not a symbol. There are certain commonly assumed meanings for smiles, frowns, particular touches, and so forth. But these are only common assumptions. In any specific situation a nonverbal symbol might mean almost anything—much the same as a verbal symbol. Special caution, though, needs to be used in the interpretation of nonverbal communication. The study of nonverbal cues is fairly young, and the temptation is greater to assume that any one symbol has one meaning.

Factors in the meaning of symbols

All this discussion may make communication—the recreation of similar meanings—seem to be difficult indeed. If so, I have achieved my purpose. Communication is difficult, partly because of the complexity of symbol use. There are, however, certain factors that can help you to determine the meaning that is intended to be recreated and that can help you to understand the meanings of symbols in specific situations.

One of these factors is *"culture."* Culture pertains to the environment and social forces in which you were born, raised, and educated. The meanings of symbols can vary with the culture—a national, regional, or more specific culture. Certain phrases in American urban "street talk" that mean no offense in the city might be highly offensive to rural-living individuals or to people other than Americans. Nonverbally, the "okay" sign with thumb and forefinger touching is regarded as obscene in other parts of the world. The specific influences of culture on the communicator can provide a key to the intended meaning of verbal and nonverbal symbols.

Second, the nature of the *specific situation* can provide a clue to the intended meaning. A wink at a bar may not be intended to mean the same thing as the same wink on the job. A wink could mean a variety of things partly because of the influence of the situation. Similarly, the word "gold" takes on different *probable* (not positively accurate) meanings when the situation varies from gold field, to dentist office, to jewelry store, to the international money market. The precise situation can help you interpret the verbal or nonverbal symbol more easily in the desired direction.

A third factor is the *relationship* between the people involved. What seems a gross insult may actually be the accepted way that two particular friends greet one another: "Hey, worthless, did they finally let you out of jail?" In the same way, a touch between lovers and a touch between employee and employer may have very different meanings. The point is simply that the relationship helps form a context within which you need to try to understand the desired meaning of symbols.

The final factor to be discussed—although there are no doubt others—is the *relationship between verbal and nonverbal symbols*. It has become the traditional comment in the field that nonverbal symbols and verbal symbols usually occur together.[3] That is the primary reason I have chosen to treat them in the same chapter: They need to be considered in relation to one an-

---

[3] See, for instance, Mark L. Knapp, *Nonverbal Communication in Human Interaction* (New York: Holt, Rinehart and Winston, 1972), pp. 8–9.

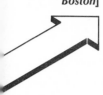

other since there are several specific ways in which verbal and nonverbal symbols interrelate.[4]

For one thing, verbal and nonverbal symbols sometimes simply *repeat* one another. The calmly answered "No" accompanied by a shake of the head is an example. Neither one really adds any new shades of meaning to what is being transacted. Often the verbal and nonverbal symbols *complement* one another. In giving oral directions, most people point fingers, turn heads, and change bodily position. The verbal instructions add to the nonverbal meanings; the nonverbal cues help the understanding of the verbal symbols. Sometimes the verbal and nonverbal cues *accent* one another. Telling someone gruffly to sit down while you literally push him or her into a chair is an example of accenting. The strong meaning of each set of symbols magnifies the effect of each.

Two other special cases of the verbal and nonverbal relationships

[4] The following is based mainly on Paul Ekman and W. V. Friesen, "The Repertoire of Nonverbal Behavior: Categories, Origins, Usage, and Coding," *Semiotica* 1 (1969):49–98.

occur. Either verbal or nonverbal symbols may *substitute* for the other. A finger up to the lips may be a way of saying, "Be quiet!" without actually uttering any words. Less obviously, it seems, do verbal symbols substitute for nonverbal symbols. The phrase "I love your truly" may be used to substitute for a kiss, a caress, or other more intimate forms of touching. And finally, verbal and nonverbal symbols may *contradict* one another. A person can confuse another by smiling and saying, "I hate you." "I'm telling you the truth" uttered without eye contact may not be believed: *When nonverbal and verbal cues contradict one another or conflict, the nonverbal symbol*

From the contradiction of verbal and nonverbal cues, we get specific events like humor, sarcasm, and irony. [John Michel]

NEATNESS
IS A
VIRTUE

is usually (but not always) believed. From the contradiction of verbal and nonverbal cues, we get specific events like humor, sarcasm, and irony.

In essence, there are several ways in which nonverbal and verbal symbols interrelate, and these interrelationships form just one factor in clues to the meanings of specific messages. Other factors include the culture, the situation, and the relationship.

CHAPTER SUMMARY

The chapter began by examining symbols and how they may be confused with signs and signal reaction. With the emphasis on symbols, we explored the types of symbols, the question about what symbols mean, and the factors in the meaning of symbols. Both verbal and nonverbal symbols form the tools for communication. Together, they help explain how people are able to reach out to one another through communication.

LEARNING BY APPLYING

1   One of the central themes in the chapter is that symbols are given meaning by the negotiation of the people involved. As an exercise in understanding the relationships between verbal and nonverbal symbols, you can react to the following "meaning games"—and then create your own examples of such word games:

What does the phrase "I love you" mean?
Try saying the phrase orally . . .
    with love in your voice
    with hatred in your voice
    with surprise in your voice
    with doubt in your voice
    with frustration in your voice
    with conviction in your voice; etc.

"I love you"—and phrases you can create—mean mostly whatever your voice "says" it means.

2   From across the room you see a man stroke a woman's arm. What does that instance of touch "mean"? How do the following overheard conversations change the "meaning"? She says,

    "If you ever see him again, I'll break this."
    "I would like to be this close forever."
    "My, that's smooth skin."
    "I'd like you to see my etchings."

71

"I've never seen anyone with such hairy arms!"
"If you forgive me, I'll never . . ."
"I think it may be broken about here, but I won't know till we X-ray."
"Gosh, you have a long life line. . . ."

The "meaning" of the touch will depend partly on the relationship between the people. What clues do you have about the relationship in each of the preceding comments?

3   Meanings of symbols depend in part on the situation or context. Consider the word "fire." What do you think it probably "means" in the following situations?

> a crowded and old theatre building
> an interview between a superior and her employee
> a battlefield
> a campsite
> a Fourth of July celebration
> a church

Be careful. The word *fire* might have several meanings depending on other factors: a campfire as well as the command to fire a gun could occur at a battlefield; arson could be committed during an interview between two people; and so on. The point is, though, that the situation often gives clues to the most likely meaning negotiated.

4   Verbal and nonverbal symbol interactions often give clues to the meaning of messages. How do the following verbal and nonverbal symbols interrelate (e.g., complement, contradict, etc.)?

> *"Go ahead,"* he said sticking up a huge fist.
> *"Go ahead,"* she said waving her hand past her.
> *"Go ahead,"* she screamed, slamming the door behind her.
> *"Go ahead,"* the officer said, signaling for right-hand turns only.

LEARNING
BY DISCUSSING

1   Discuss the differences between signs and symbols. Is (are) the distinction(s) helpful to you in understanding communication?
2   Describe and discuss the various sorts of symbols.
3   Discuss how you now react to the phrase "the meaning of symbols."
4   Discuss the nature and importance of the factors that influence the meanings that may be attached to symbols.
5   How can a knowledge of symbols and interpretation help you to use communication as a tool in building better relationships?

LEARNING
BY READING FURTHER

Bois, J. Samuel, *The Art of Awareness,* 2d ed. Dubuque, IA: Brown, 1973.

Condon, John C., Jr., *Semantics and Communication.* New York: Macmillan, 1975.

Knapp, Mark L., *Essentials of Nonverbal Communication.* New York: Holt, Rinehart and Winston, 1980.

Knapp, Mark L., *Nonverbal Communication in Human Interaction.* New York: Holt, Rinehart and Winston, 1972.

Koneya, Mele, and Barbour, Alton, *Louder than Words.* Columbus, OH: Merrill, 1976.

7

PEOPLED ORGANIZATIONS: WHERE DOES COMMUNICATION OCCUR?

STUDY OF THIS CHAPTER WILL ENABLE YOU TO

- *understand that communication occurs nearly everywhere*
- *understand that "organizations" are basically simply "organized humans"*
- *understand the ways in which organizations affect interpersonal communication*
- *avoid some of the problems that arise when organizations affect interpersonal communication*

Kelly begins his day by rolling over in bed and kissing his wife good morning. They discuss their schedules for the day to decide how to do what best.

Shortly before 8:00 A.M., Kelly's mother calls—before the rates go up—and assures the family that she and Kelly's father returned from vacation safely the night before. Also reported are the health conditions of most of the relatives. They are all fine except Floyd who is divorcing his third wife . . . well, maybe it's for the best.

Over breakfast, Kelly, Jr. and Peter are aglow that this is the last day of school—and a variety of end-of-year activities are planned.

On his way to work Kelly leaves his wife Pat at the office, and then listens to the car radio. Fair, warm, and sunny, with a high of 74°F. Traffic is heavy on the inner belt, and there is an accident involving personal injury on Holly near 58th. He arrives at the construction site and puts on his hard hat.

He is met by his foreman and the contractor for whom he works. They discuss the delays in shipping, the need for hiring summer replacements, and the state of the economy in general under the present administration.

On his way home that evening Kelly picks Pat up at the office. They discuss plans for the cookout and Pat's decision to be a United Way volunteer. Kelly confides the problems he is having with the local union representatives and explains the status of the new project.

They are almost home. Silence. Pat and Kelly are engrossed in their own thoughts. They pull into the driveway and the guy next door asks if he can borrow the lawnmower since his doesn't seem to want to work. . . .

Where does communication occur? Where does communication occur? A better question is: Where *doesn't* it occur? Symbolic transaction that is aimed at recreating similar meanings occurs so frequently that it is tempting to say it occurs everywhere. Sometimes it is successful, and sometimes it's not. Sometimes we enjoy it and sometimes we don't. Sometimes we are prepared for it and sometimes we aren't. Still communication occurs almost everywhere.

In the example of Kelly, his efforts to communicate involved a wide range of individuals and a variety of topics. But such a general observation does not seem to justify an entire chapter. Even if communication occurs nearly everywhere, isn't there something more helpful to be said? I think there is, but it has to do with the nature of "organizations."

The nature of organizations and organized life

In one sense, an organization is a collection of buildings and offices, inventories and equipment, account books and profit statements. This view focuses on the nonhuman factors that make up an organization. In a larger sense, an organization is mostly human; it is a collection of people who have *formal* roles to play, *specified* tasks to perform, and a *structured* chain-of-command. This concept of organizations is becoming more popular in studies of organizational management. No matter what the inventory, buildings, or account ledgers look like, *people* are the primary ingredient in organizations. Organizations can exist without buildings and inventories, but they cannot exist without people.

A better phrase for organizations might be "organized people." They are recruited, hired, trained, and then perform certain tasks. *Only with the*

Figure 7-1
Organizations and the "self"

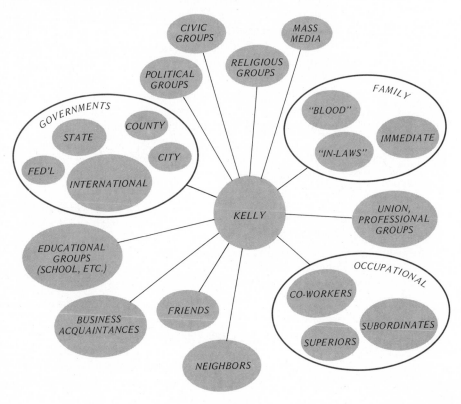

existence of people in the organization do account books, buildings, and equipment make sense. And so a major oil company claims that "we got together to do it better"—didn't everybody? A local bank in Lafayette, Indiana, calls itself the "bank with real people"—are there any other kind? Today's army "wants to join you"—whether or not you want them to. The point is that our highly organized society's organizations want you to appreciate their basic element: people.

But if people are the basic ingredient in the organization, maybe the "larger view of organizations" just discussed is still too narrow. Perhaps we need to think of organizations as a collection of people with *informal* roles to play, sometimes *unspecified* tasks to perform, and often *unstructured* chains-of-command. This view obviously allows many other "things" to be considered "organizations." And that, it seems to me, is an asset in communication studies.

Kelly, in the example, when asked to list the major organizations to which he belonged might state the company, his local religious group, and his political party. Yet Kelly might more accurately start to realize that those were just the beginnings of his membership in organizations. With organizations defined more broadly, he belongs to or interacts with many other "organizations": his immediate family, his blood relatives, his "in-laws," his neighbors, his circle of friends, his union or professional group, his set of superiors and subordinates—even various levels of government. Kelly lives amid a wide variety of organizations—formal and informal; Kelly, like the rest of us, is an organizational human. Study Figure 7-1, which merely hints at his organizational ties.

In recalling the account of Kelly's day, you will realize that his communication occurred in relation to most of these organizations or their representatives: his wife, his children, his blood relatives, his local school, the mass media, his subordinate, his superior, a civic or charity group, his wife's company, his own company, the local union, the national government, and his next door neighbor. Clearly, he did not personally communicate with all of these. Yet his communication was affected in several ways by them all. Let's examine further how communication is affected by organizations.

Communicating "in" organizations

Interpersonal communication is affected by organizations, first, because *organizations create a context or "backdrop" for communication.* Chapter 6 described how verbal and nonverbal symbols are interpreted differently based on context: crying at a wedding does not "mean" the same thing as crying at a funeral—probably. But even that generalization can be affected by context: If you are convinced your younger sister is marrying "the wrong man,"—if that is the context—your crying at a funeral and crying at the wedding may mean much the same thing. Context has a tremendous effect on interpretation and meaning recreation.

Organizations provide their own kind of context. At work you may be happy, cheerful, and relaxed; at home, you may engage in very different kinds of communication—and vice versa. Yet even when you are not physically "inside" an organization, the organization can continue its influence. "Shoptalk" at a "social gathering" is sometimes a terrible bore. It occurs because an organization provides a context for communication although the people are obviously away from that organization. The reverse can also happen. The company can suffer inefficiency if a troubled home situation is the context for a worker's communication at work. Similarly, a supposedly religious meeting can be ineffective if your thoughts are shrouded with fears of final exams, a troubled relationship, or the "world situation." So organizations, even when you are not actually *in* them at the present, can provide a context that affects your communication in another situation.

Second, *organizations can affect communication by setting the agenda—or topics of likely discussion.* Listening to the mass media can turn your attention to thoughts of famine, political graft, natural or man-made disasters, and so forth. The context of family can turn your thoughts toward finances, interpersonal problems, or house maintenance. Talking with a subordinate in an organization—as Kelly did—can bring to mind ideas about union problems, worker dissatisfactions, and so on. A church or synagogue may push spiritual thoughts to a much higher priority than, say, a golf match with friends might. The topics of most concern can be affected *by* the organization.

Third, communication is affected by organizations because *organiza-*

When a child confesses to a violated family rule, will you respond more as a parent, or more as a friend? [Herwig, Stock, Boston]

tions provide some sort of membership or role expectations.[1] How you "act"—or are expected to act—may vary from situation to situation. Communication that may be entirely appropriate on the tennis courts with friends may be less appropriate at work. How you converse with blood relatives may not be the same as how you communicate with your spouse's family. Your communication toward subordinates at work may or may not be similar to your communication with superiors. Your communication as a union representative may not be similar to how you approach an audit with the Internal Revenue Service. How you act in your role of parent may not be the same as how you act as a "friend" to your child. Different organi-

[1] See also, Richard E. Crable, *Using Communication* (Boston: Allyn and Bacon, 1979), pp. 204–206.

zations will provide different norms or expectations about what is appropriate communication. Virtually any organization can provide you with a sense of membership—even something as informal as a neighborhood cookout. That sense of membership can provide certain role expectations about your communication.

Fourth, *organizations affect communication by providing the possibility of numerous role or membership conflicts.*[2] Formal memberships in organizations, obviously, sometimes put people in conflicting situations. For example, you may be a loyal supporter of the company and a union representative. How will you respond to a union demand that the company says will bankrupt it? Which organizational "pull" will more strongly affect your communication? When a young employee with two children "has to be fired," will the role of superior or considerate mother be more influential? When a child confesses to a violated family rule, will you respond more as a parent, or more as a friend? The possible role conflicts are nearly endless. When there appears to be no conflict in your role expectations, no problem exists. However, when the situation involves conflicting role expectations because of your various organizational connections, the problem can be serious. There are no easy answers to these dilemmas. But we do know, though, that you as a member of many organizations will often find your communication affected by conflicts in role expectations.

CHAPTER SUMMARY

The chapter began with an illustration of a not-so-unusual person. His communication involved a number of people, topics, and situations. The central theme that communication occurs within an organizational context was developed. People belong to numerous formal and informal, structured and unstructured organizations. These organized people—these peopled organizations—provide a context that acts as a backdrop for interpretation and the recreation of meaning. This context helps set agendas, helps create role expectations, and provides the distinct possibility of role and membership conflicts. Where does communication occur?—almost everywhere—and the shadow of one or more organizations is never out of sight.

LEARNING BY APPLYING

1   *Make a list of the "organizations"—formal and informal—in which you are involved. Make a contrasting list showing activities during your day that are not related to some kind of organization. What do the varying sizes of the*

[2] Ibid., p. 205.

lists tell you about the importance of understanding organizations in your life?

2 Search through a local or school newspaper to find an issue of importance to you — a problem, a difficulty, or a conflict. Now decide how that problem, difficulty, or conflict affects you in various ways because you are a member of several organizations. For example, off-campus student parking might affect you as a student, you as a local taxpayer, and you as a member of the community who drives a car. A proposed nuclear power plant might affect you as a member of the local community, you as a utility bill payer, you as a stockholder in area companies, and you as a parent of young children. Not all these "you's" will want the same thing from an issue: Sometimes our membership in one group conflicts with membership in another. What is the issue you found, what are your relevant organizations — and which role will most affect your position on the issue?

3 Recall any recent disagreements you have had with another person. Have any of the problems been related to the fact that the two of you "represent" different organizations? Explain. (After you begin thinking in these terms, you will find more and more of these instances).

LEARNING
BY DISCUSSING

1 The text argues that communication occurs nearly everywhere. Can you think of any situation in which people exist, but in which no communication is important?

2 Discuss "organizations" as explained in the text. How does this differ from other conceptions of the term that you have studied? Does the conception here help you see yourself as a member of dozens of different organizations?

3 Can you think of anytime in which you are not — at least partly — communicating as a member of some organization (as defined in the book)?

4 Discuss the various problems that organizations prompt in communication. Which of these do you think is or are the most common? most important? most difficult to overcome?

5 How can knowledge of this chapter make your communication a better tool for building relationships?

LAYERS UPON LAYERS: WHAT CAN BE COMMUNICATED?

STUDY OF THIS CHAPTER WILL ENABLE YOU TO UNDERSTAND

- different "levels" of communication
- that the different levels of communication are really levels of language use
- that the layer of meaning attached to communication depends on the "context"
- the factors that comprise the interpersonal context

Not every use of symbols results in the recreation of similar meanings. So not all symbol use is successful communication. In the same way, not every recreated meaning results in people forming a deeper, more intimate relationship. Therefore not all communication furthers the development of communion.

The creation and recreation of meaning happens, as seen in Chapters 5 and 6, when people understand what is "meant" by symbol use. Still there are different ways in which this understanding occurs. This chapter deals with two main topics: different levels of communication and different layers of meaning in communication. From the discussion you should gain insight into the rich possibilities for using communication to develop a communing relationship.

Levels of communication

For years, people have realized that language can be used for the discussion of both superficial and intimate communication. One of the popularizers of this view, John Powell, has provided a useful way of analyzing how language is used.[1] He speaks of these uses as "levels of communication." Let's examine each, beginning with the "lowest" level.

The lowest level is what he and others call "cliché communication" – or what we called "phatic" communication in Chapter 4. *"Cliché communication" is generally considered "throw away" statements and questions* such as "How are you?" "Whatcha been doing?" "How's the family?" "Long time, no see" and "Nice seeing you again." None of these comments are eloquent, deep in meaning, or necessarily seriously stated. We use such phrases with slight acquaintances, strangers, or someone not truly close to us. Most of these questions or statements do not really require an answer or a response. They are simply stated when there seems to be little else to say.

[1] See John Powell, *Why Am I Afraid to Tell You Who I Am?* (Chicago: Argus Communications, 1969), pp. 50–85.

Cliché language, while it may be a way of establishing contact with others, is also a means to talk without seriously engaging in conversation. [Franken, Stock, Boston]

Cliché language, while it may be a way of establishing contact with others, is also a means to talk without seriously engaging in conversation. Cliché communication does not require any personal risk for either the person speaking or the person listening. Such communication could be carried out by robots: no particular thoughts or feelings are necessary. When this sort of language use occurs between mere acquaintances, there may be no problem. What else would there be to talk about except matters of little consequence? The problem occurs when cliché language use comprises most of the conversation between two people who are supposedly friends, family members, or lovers. Such relationships can only be developed by personal risk and fairly intimate communication, which is the opposite of what cliché communication demands. For this reason, cliché communication – generally discussed first – is the "lowest" of the five levels of communication.

Level four can be termed *"reporting communication": statements about other people, events, and nonpersonal situations.*[2] In a conscious or unconscious effort to avoid cliché communication, people frequently

[2] Powell uses the term, "Reporting Facts About Others," which seems a bit too narrow.

discuss what is happening to others—especially mutual acquaintances, events reported in the world, latest gossip, and a never-ending barrage of "shoptalk." A party is one of the best situations—but not the only one—where reporting communication can be observed easily. Listen, as cliché communication gives way to reporting communication and then emerges again:

A   Hi, I haven't seen you in days. How've you been?
B   Fine, thanks. You?
A   Never better. Nice party, huh?
B   One of the best. Harvey always throws a good party. I knew him in Chicago.
A   Oh, really? Well, they think a great deal of him at the plant. Real go-getter, they say.
B   That's important, the way they talk about the economy.
A   Yeah. . . . I just heard on the news that there was a big loss in the stock market.
B   Yeah, folks are worried, I guess. . . .
A   Yes, I guess so. . . .
B   Yeah, a good party. . . .
A   Yeah. . . .
B   Think I'll go and get some of that dip. . . .
A   Okay, nice seeing you.
B   Yeah, we'll have to get together over lunch. . . .
A   Oh, yes, real soon. . . .

At this level no personal contact was established. Once they got past the opening clichés, they freely engaged in reporting communication. In neither case did one learn anything about the other. With no investment of themselves in the conversation, not much was accomplished.

Level three communication can be termed *"intellectual communication": statements that express evaluations, judgments, and observations.*[3] Intellectual communication consists of expressions based on what people themselves think or how they reason. This requires more personal commitment than either cliché or reporting communication. Here the speaker takes a certain amount of risk and "opens" him- or herself to some limited extent. Some people are fairly reluctant to reveal their thoughts and ideas:

Page   Well, Mildred, you've been awfully quiet. What do you think of the new school board?

Mildred   I . . . Me? . . . Well, I guess I think that . . . Well, they said in last night's paper that . . .

In contrast, some people are very anxious to share their intellectual selves:

[3] Powell uses the term, "My Ideas and Judgments." I use the term "intellectual communication" to get at the common observation that people "intellectualize" so much of what could be reported as feelings.

85

Mildred	. . . The new school board, huh? . . . Well, . . .
Page	I'll tell you what I think. The board should have been made up of more professional people. Imagine putting people on the board who don't even have a high school diploma. . . . Have you ever heard of such a thing? Besides that . . .

Communication about thought and observations are simply easier for some people than others.

Yet the temptation to stereotype should be avoided. Depending on the topic or the situation, even the most eager intellectual communicators may become reluctant:

Mildred	Now that we've heard what you think of the elected board members, what do you think about the budget issue in the schools?
Page	I . . . Uh, well, I think . . . You know, it really goes back to the election. Yes, if better people had been elected . . .

Stating thoughts and observations, then, calls for some personal investment—some giving of yourself. For that reason, cliché and reporting behavior is often easier to accomplish.

But intellectual communication does not require the ultimate personal risk. Many people are quite willing to "intellectualize" things as a way of avoiding having to state how they *feel* about those same things. *"Personal communication,"* the second highest level of communication, *has to do with feelings, values, "gut-level" comments.*[4] To see the difference between intellectual and personal communication, let's continue the dialogue between Mildred and Page.

Page	And so, I think the whole question is a matter of voter education in such matters. . . .
Mildred	I guess I don't know so much about it as you do. All I know is what I read in the papers. . . . But, I do feel confused . . . and, I guess, a little afraid. I so much want the kids to get a good education. . . .
Page	We're back to the voting. . . . I think. . . .
Mildred	Excuse me, but how do you feel?
Page	I just told you how I felt. . . .
Mildred	No, you told me what you thought. . . .
Page	Oh. . . . Well, I guess I think—sorry—feel . . . Oh, I don't know. . . . For one thing, I guess I am hurt that I put all that effort into Jake's election, and he lost. I thought he would make a much better board member. . . . I am bitter, I guess. I also am angry at people who don't follow what is really going on—people who rely on the newspaper and don't try to . . .
Mildred	People like me, you mean?
Page	Oh, no, I didn't mean that. . . . Well, yes, I guess I do mean it. . . . You know, I think I've been taking my hostility out on other people. . . .

[4] The term that Powell uses, "My Feelings (Emotions)," does not seem to connote value judgments which I think are also important.

Mildred	On people like me?
Page	Yes, I'm afraid so. . . .

Intellectual communication and personal communication are very much related. Page and Mildred began to get to know something about one another the moment that personal communication about feelings started to emerge. The difference is sometimes explained by the difference between "belief" and "attitude." Belief is the more intellectual statement, while attitude carries an expression of favorableness or unfavorableness.[5] Even this simplistic explanation is helpful: Two people can have the same intellectual belief about something, but very different personal reactions.

Ellen	Smith will be elected, I think, and I'm thrilled!
Sue	Smith will be elected, I think, and I'm leaving the country!

If Sue and Ellen communicated only at an intellectual level, very little would be gained. They would seem to be in agreement. Once they begin to express their feelings and attitudes in personal communication, they can begin to understand one another better.

Personal communication is not always easy, as we shall see in the chapters that deal with feedback and self-disclosure. Personal communication is more difficult because it requires a risk: There is always the chance that someone will disagree with you. It is more difficult because it requires you to share something about *yourself*—not clichés, reports from others, nor merely intellectual statements. Interpersonal relationships cannot develop when one person always thinks, "Well, she agreed to go, but I don't know what she really *felt* about it." Deeper interpersonal relationships develop on the basis of honest personal communication.

There is, though, an even higher level of communication that can be labeled *"peak communication": communication that approaches the state of communion.* Peak communication occurs more rarely than other levels. It occurs when you and the other person seem "in tune" with one another: when you seem to know what each other is thinking and feeling even without much conversation. "Yes, yes, I know what you mean," "Go no further. I understand." and "Yes, we are on the same wavelength," are all comments that express those peak moments. At times like this the relationship may be at its highest and "talk" may not seem necessary at all. The difference here between intrapersonal and interpersonal communication seems truly to be blurred. You and the other seem to be creating and recreating meanings almost simultaneously. During times of peak communication the communing relationship seems more of a reality than a vague goal.

---

[5] This will be an obviously basic understanding of the terms. The topic of beliefs and attitudes has been a subject of innumerable articles, essays, books—and professional discussions.

87

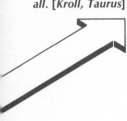

And so communication can be analyzed in terms of the different levels. Beginning with level five—cliché communication—the levels require more and more risk, and more and more personal input. The higher levels require more commitment, but they also offer greater rewards and the greatest hope for interpersonal communion.

Layers of meaning

The major problem with the discussion in this chapter so far is the temptation to think that there is something magic in these five levels of communication. Will statements of your personal feelings always result in a closer, deeper relationship? Can everything that is "sayable" be classified as one of the five levels? The levels of communication must be understood realistically.

First, *the levels of communication are really levels of language use.* The use of language, as we have seen, does not always result in the desired meaning recreation. Our concern must be for how language helps meaning recreation, and not for language itself. Let me give you illustrations that point out how these levels of communication are not so easily distinguished on the basis of language.

"How *are* you?" he says as he kneels by her bedside? The nurse brings the evening medicine and quickly leaves. "Are you better?" he asks taking her hand. "Yes, much better." As they sit in silence, looking at one another, we can ask whether this is cliché – or peak – communication. On the basis of language use or "levels of language use," the conclusion is obvious: This is classic cliché communication. The "How are you?" "I am fine" comments simply reek of cliché. And yet I suspect you have trouble believing that this is communication without deep and intimate meaning. The kneeling, the touch of a hand, the silent look – all mean that something more intimate is occurring. There seems no need here for an "I love you" or for a "I am so concerned about you." There is no need because what seems to be occurring is an experience in peak communication. Words have become unnecessary in this very personal and intimate situation.

What may sound like cliché communication can be something very different for the people involved. But the situation can also be reversed:

R-r-r-i-n-n-g!
Hello.
Hello, Bernie? This is Larry.
Oh, Hi, Larry. What can I do for you?
Well, I just called to ask you how you think the meeting went? Was I too pushy, do you think? You know, I sometimes feel that I'm too dominating. Maybe it was the influence of my old man. . . . Anyway, what did you think?
I told you last night, Larry, that I thought everything went well. . . . We got the job done. . . . That was what was important. . . .
Yeah, I know, but you know how much respect I have for you. Did you think I fumbled the ball when Hal asked about the Murdock proposal?
No, Larry . . . Well, I have seen you more articulate, but I . . .
You think I did okay, then? I was really nervous – with the boss man there and all. . . .
No, Larry, fine. You did just fine. Hey, I have to run. . . . Saturday morning errands, you know.
Well, Bernie, you were the one person I needed to hear from.
Bye, Larry.
Bye, Bernie.
R-r-r-i-n-n-g!
Hello?
Hello, Ned, this is Larry. . . . I just wanted to see how you felt about the meeting. . . . I have so much respect for you. . . .

Without Ned's response, the point perhaps has been made. Intellectual communication – even personal language use – can become a game played by people who pride themselves on being "intimate communicators." In the example Larry displayed his supposed knowledge of intimate and personal communication like a badge on his shirt. He said all the right things and used all the appropriate language levels. And yet his associates could detect his efforts as being hollow and false. True, he wanted personal reinforcement and compliments. He may have needed them in fact. But he was not accomplishing anything much by his language habits. The habit of using just the right language level is not the main issue. What sounded like personal communication had, for Larry, become cliché communication. Superficial knowledge of "levels of communication" is perhaps more dangerous than none at all. Without concern for meanings and recreated meanings the various levels of *language use* may have little to do with levels of *communication.* In all communication there are layers of meanings that may have little to do with levels of language use.

First of all, the "levels of communication" described are really "levels of language use." But how are different layers of meaning actually decided? To look at communication realistically, we must realize, then, that *the layer of meaning depends on the* context *of communication.* The context of communication, as discussed in earlier chapters, can be anything that provides a background or environment for the communication. In this case the context that determines the meaning of communication can be one or more of several factors: the "situation," the complement of nonverbal symbols, the status of the relationship, and the interpretation of the other person. The examples of the people in the hospital and telephone conversations can be used to explain how these influence the layers of meaning — and so the actual level of communication.

First, *the situation itself affects what layer of meaning will be attached to the communication* — that is, what "level" of communication is occurring. A chance meeting in the street between two people is very unlike the scene in the hospital. On the street the "How are you?" would seem like a "throwaway" phrase. In the hospital it may communicate all the love, dreams, hopes, and concern that one person can feel for the other. So it is the situation — not the language itself — that partly results in different layers of meaning. Both cliché and peak communication could be embedded in one comment. The situation helps determine which layer of meaning will be recreated.

Second, *the layer of meaning attached will be affected by the nonverbal symbols that complement the verbal symbols.* Personal communication seems harder and rarer over the telephone, as when Larry wanted to ask about the meeting. The gazing, the touching, and the nearness of the people in the hospital seemed to communicate more than words could possibly express. Just as nonverbal symbols generally affect the interpretation of the word, the complement of nonverbal symbols does the same thing here. The "How are you?" was much less important than the nonverbal communication. The telephone conversation and hospital talk might have been either cliché or personal. But the nonverbal cues helped determine that the hospital was the scene of peak communication. The telephone was the medium for well-rehearsed clichés that were meant to sound like personal communication.

Third, *the relationship between two people helps determine the layer of meaning* and thus the level of communication. Bernie was so well respected by Larry. On the other hand, Larry also respected Ned – and probably anyone else who happened to be within view. On the other hand, the hospital was the setting for the meeting of two very close people. For Larry, relationships that seemed close were a substitute for really close relationships. In the hospital the relationship seemed much stronger and deeper. Peak communication – and even personal communication – does not tend to occur between casual acquaintances. When the language seems very personal and the relationship seems weak, the words may sound hollow indeed. When the relationship is deep, even the most hackneyed words can have deeper significance. The layer of meaning actually attached will depend more on the relationship than on the language used.

And finally, *the layer of meaning attached to communication depends on the interpretation of the other person.* The importance of receiver interpretation has already been discussed. Here again, it is crucial. No matter how you *wish* communication to be interpreted, you are still at the mercy of the receiver. What you intend as personal communication can be interpreted as self-serving clichés. Larry found that out with Bernie – and perhaps Ned. A casual "You are beautiful" can be considered as either a cliché, a personal bit of communication, or somewhere in between. Again, there is no magic in the words. They are simply one of the ways we have of trying to recreate meaning and may not, however, be recreated as we would wish. When that happens, what we intended as a high level of communication can be entirely ignored. The interpretation of the other person plays a role in deciding what layer of meaning will be attached.

What we have seen, then, is that these various levels of communication are also levels of language use. The extent to which you succeed in using communication to build toward communion – and peak communication – will depend on the context: the situation, the relationship between verbal and nonverbal symbols, the relationship that exists between the people, and the interpretation of the other person. How can peak communication be more frequently attained? In the rest of the book we attempt to answer that question – to show a path toward attaining interpersonal communion.

CHAPTER SUMMARY

The chapter began with a discussion of what are called "levels of communication." Cliché, reporting, intellectual, personal, and peak communication can describe the various levels of how people transact. Still these are overly simplistic labels. In fact, they are labels for language use, which does not always dictate how layers of meaning will be attached. Almost anything can be cliché communication—even things that appear to be personal or peak communication. In contrast, almost anything can be personal or peak communication. These layers of meaning exist in almost all language use. Also discussed were some of the factors that help determine what level of communication will occur. These included the situation, nonverbal cues, the relationship, and the interpretation of the other person. The factors—more than the exact language used—decide at what level the communication is occurring.

What can be communicated? Practically anything, if we include the nonverbal symbols that can help establish peak communication. Yet peak communication does not occur easily. It takes place when the situation, the nonverbal cues, the relationship, and the interpretation of the other are all favorable. All that is likely to occur infrequently. And so peak communication and the state of communion are also likely to be infrequent. However, peak communication is worth pursuing. Honest and open communication—not tricks in using language levels—is a key to using interpersonal communication to seek communion.

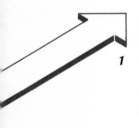

LEARNING
BY APPLYING

1 *Chapters 5 and 6 were discussions of meanings and symbols, respectively. The "meaning" of a phrase is not necessarily the same as the "level" of communication. The same phrase, for example, may mean somewhat the same—and yet the level of communication may vary greatly. To understand this idea better, discuss the differences between the following by using the terms cliché communication, reporting communication, intellectual communication, personal communication, and peak communication:*

a. *"My dear," said the matronly lady as she swept through the crowd of guests, "we must get to know one another better."*

b. *"Wow," he said looking deeply into her eyes, "we have to get to know one another better. I think I may love you."*

c. *"Clearly, with our interests being so similar," he said, "we must get to know one another."*

d. *"Oh, yes," he intoned, "everyone says we must get together."*

e. *"Francine, I could stay here like this forever—feeling you close and getting to know you."*

I would label these (respectively): cliché, personal, intellectual, reporting, and peak communication. Yet the layer of meaning to be attached depends on perception. In what ways do you agree and disagree with my perceptions? Explain why you agree or disagree.

2   Choose a novel or a nonfiction book that has ongoing conversation between
    two people who have just met, but who either fall in love or develop a deep
    friendship as the story unfolds. Analyze how their conversation develops.
    Do you see a change in their conversation as the relationship develops? If
    their relationship deepens, and then deteriorates, do you see changes back
    toward less intimate conversation? Discuss how the communication seems
    to vary with the state of the relationship.

3   Keep an informal record of conversations you have during, for example, a
    morning's activities. At what level is most of the communication? What is
    the relationship you have with these various people? Does the communica-
    tion seem to vary with the nature of the relationship? Explain.

LEARNING
BY DISCUSSING

1   Explain what you think the "levels" of communication are.
2   Discuss how these levels of communication actually refer to language use
    and interpretation.
3   Explain the importance of "context" in helping explain various levels or lan-
    guage use interpretations in communication.
4   React to the various factors that make up the "context." Which of these
    seem most common? most important? most difficult to control?
5   How can your understanding of this chapter help you to use communication
    as a tool in a relationship?

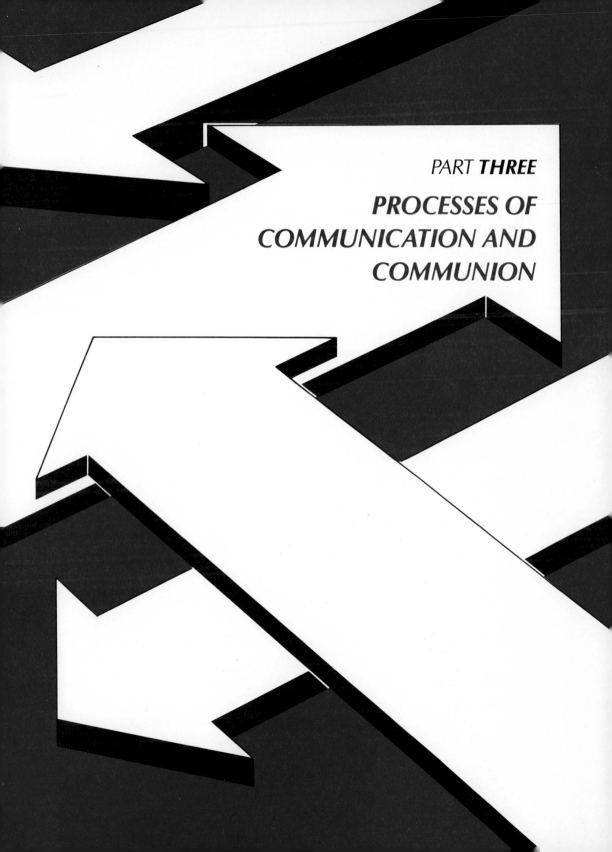

PART **THREE**

PROCESSES OF COMMUNICATION AND COMMUNION

SHARING: THE HEART OF COMMUNION
(AN INTRODUCTION TO CHAPTERS 10, 11, and 12)

STUDY OF THIS CHAPTER WILL ENABLE YOU TO UNDERSTAND

- *the relationship between sharing and communion*
- *the relationship of the self to others*
- in general *how the sharing self is based on* decreases *in the naïve, unknown, and undisclosed selves*

At the heart of "communion" is the ongoing process of sharing. That certainly seems simple enough: To commune, we share, right? Unfortunately, the situation is not that simple. The problem is that "sharing" can have all sorts of meanings—most of them unrelated to communion between individuals.

The meanings of sharing "Sharing," for instance, can mean no more than two people having the same things. Here the term means that I "share" with perhaps millions of other people a number of things: brown eyes, brown hair, and a beard; a two-story house, a teaching job, and a station wagon; or a boat, two children, a cat, a dog, and a turtle. While I may share these with a vast number of other people, I have no necessary communion with any or all of them.

Similarly, "sharing" can mean a giving of things between people. I might share a story with you. As a child, I was taught to share candy or cookies with others. This interpretation of sharing comes closer to the idea of communion, partly because these shared things are not accidents: someone has *chosen* to give something to another. In that sense, people have things "in common" because they have decided to give to and receive from one another. Still the exchange of things does not necessarily mean that there is any sort of communion. I have even given candy to people who were mere acquaintances. So communion and this second sort of sharing are not necessarily related.

The kind of sharing that is most significant here is the sharing—not of things—but of one's self: the exchange, for example, of bits of you for bits of me—the exchange of intimate feelings, thoughts, fears, ideas, doubts, and hopes. The sharing of self does not lessen who you are or what you are. The self can be given over and over again. When someone else reciprocates, the result is that neither of you loses anything, and both gain a great deal.

98

The "self" is truly a me/us concept. The relationship between two people is a product of both the people as a pair and the persons as individuals. [Ullmann, Taurus]

I don't want this discussion to sound terribly abstract and idealistic. As discussed in Chapter 3, intrapersonal and interpersonal communication should not be discussed separately. People develop themselves greatly by the influence of and by influencing others. The "self" is truly a me/us concept. The relationship between two people is a product of both the people as a pair and the persons as individuals. Let me illustrate what I mean.

The process of sharing

At this point in the relationship between you as the reader and me as the author I have already shared with you some of my thoughts and feelings about communication and interpersonal relationships. Still you know very little about me, and I know almost nothing about you. I have the urge to tell you more about myself and would wish to speak with you in person. If you were a student in my office or a friend sitting in the union with me, we would have an obviously better chance to "get to know one another." By telling you about myself, I would start a whole process of happenings: Probably I would feel closer to you, and this contact could affect how I felt about people in general. At the same time, your newfound relationship with me could affect in some way your own feelings about yourself, and our relationship itself would begin developing. In essence, by sharing our thoughts and feelings and information about ourselves, *I* grow as a person, *you* grow as a person, and our *relationship* continues to develop. Communion, then, is the sharing of each of us—one to another.

Let me try to explain this visually. The diagrams I use are original, but they are refinements of the Johari window — a graphic model used extensively in communication classes.[1]

First, you should understand that while communion is based on sharing, not everything about you is easily shared with a second person. Some parts of you are known to you, but not known to this other person; I shall call this the "undisclosed" you. These parts of you are not necessarily hidden purposely or concealed. For any one of dozens of reasons, you simply have not shared them with the other person. I have not shared with you, for

[1] The refinements I have attempted in the Johari window are easily explained. The original graphic appeared in Joseph Luft, *Of Human Interaction* (Mayfield Publishing, 1969). The original design was a box separated into four equal sections, giving it the appearance of a window. The window sections could change to show progress in the developing self, but no section could expand *infinitely* or change *independently.* In addition, what I call the "undisclosed" self was originally called the "hidden" area — a term that seems (erroneously) to mean things intentionally kept from the other person. What I call the "shared" you was called the "open" you. I prefer "shared" since it implies something "open" only to a selected person — not just generally "open" to the world. What I call the "naïve" self was termed the "blind" or "repressed" self — terms that seem less accurate than "naïve." Finally, one of the advantages of the intersecting lines (rather than the window design) is that the selves of both parties can be studied simultaneously.

Figure 9-1
You

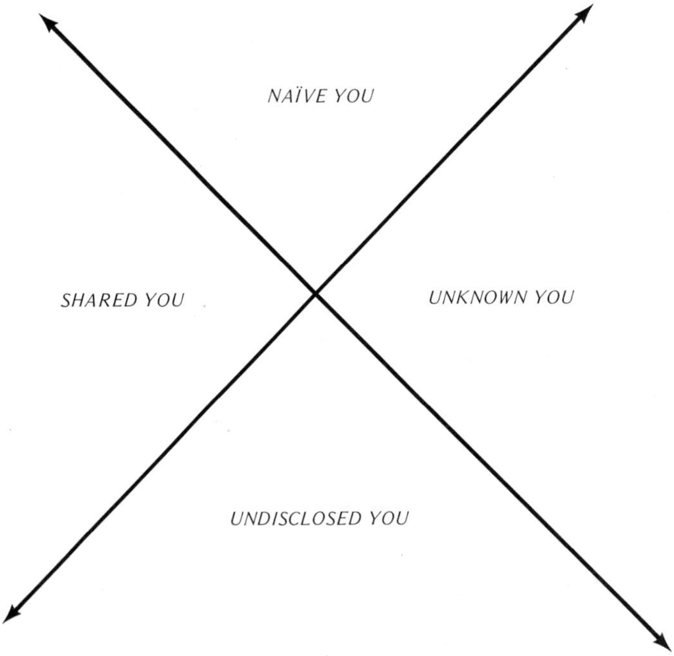

NAÏVE YOU

SHARED YOU

UNKNOWN YOU

UNDISCLOSED YOU

Figure 9-2
You at the start of
a relationship

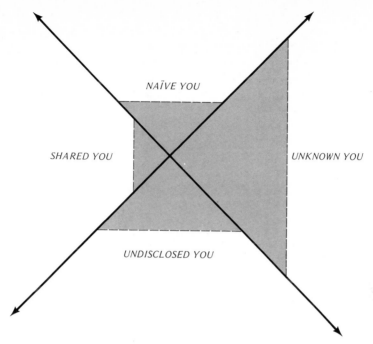

NAÏVE YOU

SHARED YOU

UNKNOWN YOU

UNDISCLOSED YOU

example, my feelings about premarital sexual relationships, my voting preferences in the last election, my favorite color, or my goals for the future. That does not mean that I am trying to hide these parts of what makes up "me"; it means only that—given the state of our relationship—there has been no strong reason to relate this information. Some parts of "you" will be undisclosed in any relationship. Parts of who you are, however, are obvious—or at least known—to the other person, but not necessarily known to you. I shall call that information the "naïve" you. It is not that you are incapable of knowing these parts of you, but that, for whatever reason, you do not now know them. You may consider yourself to be quite an athlete even when your coach knows that your ability is limited. Or you may assume that you are inefficient while your boss (secretly or openly) is amazed at your productivity. These are examples of the naïve you. Third, there are parts of you that neither you nor the other person recognizes. This "unknown" you means simply that both you and another fail to see or to appreciate something about you: an artistic ability, a streak of meanness, or a capacity for caring greatly. Finally, there are parts of you that are known to both you and the other, which I shall call the "shared" you. These various parts of "you" are illustrated in Figure 9-1.

This basic diagram can be used to illustrate all sorts of occurrences between two people. Figure 9-2, for example, shows that at the beginning of a

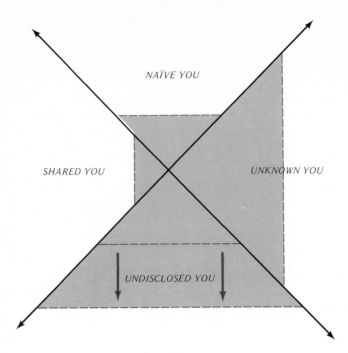

Figure 9-3
Events occur,
unshared by you

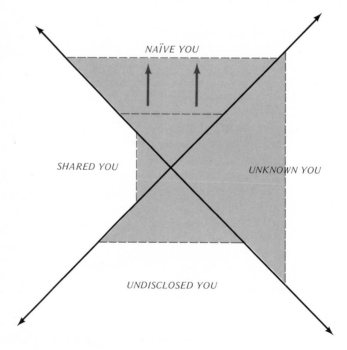

Figure 9-4
Events occur,
unknown or
unperceived by
you

relationship the naïve and shared area of you may be quite small, but the undisclosed and unknown areas may be rather large. This means that interpersonal contact has been limited or nonexistent, so the chances for sharing are as small as the chances that the other knows much about you (which you fail to see). Much of you, of course, is as yet undisclosed; and a great deal of you may be unknown by both of you.

All kinds of things, though, can happen that affect how the "you" in the diagram should be described. You may take a vacation, have a new spiritual insight, learn a new concept, or discover in yourself a quality you didn't know existed. Figure 9-3 shows this situation by illustrating how the undisclosed you can become large as you experience things not shared with the other.

In a different situation Figure 9-4 might better describe the change in you. In a relationship the other may discover things about you—qualities, characteristics of which you are unaware. If that happens, the naïve you expands.

Also, at times you may experience new feelings, enjoy new experiences, or have new things happen to you. If neither you nor the other is aware of these changes, then Figure 9-5 describes the new you. The unknown you has increased.

Figure 9-5
Events occur,
unperceived or
unknown by
either person

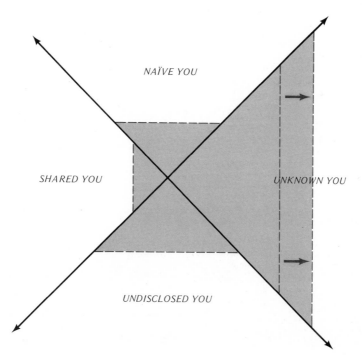

NAÏVE YOU

SHARED YOU

UNKNOWN YOU

UNDISCLOSED YOU

*You might feel
pain and grief
such as you had
never felt before.
If unshared, those
feelings increase
the undisclosed
you. [Holland,
Stock, Boston]*

In Figures 9-3, 9-4, and 9-5 I have shown how parts of you might increase as events in your life unfold. In real life, of course, two or three of the areas might increase at the same time. Figure 9-6 shows what might occur during a traumatic time such as the death of a close family member. You might feel pain and grief such as you had never felt before. If unshared, those feelings increase the undisclosed you. A close friend might see in you more courage than he or she thought possible. If you are unaware of that courage, your naïve self has also expanded. And finally, both you and the friend might be unaware of some more profound changes taking place within you. If so, the unknown you also enlarges. Figure 9-6 illustrates the changes that might occur in such a situation.

The preceding discussion of the diagrams leads to a very important point: *communion occurs*, not when these first three areas enlarge, *but when they become smaller and* more *of you becomes shared with another.* Figure 9-7 illustrates what happens to *you* as you take steps toward the communing relationship.

However, "you" are only one-half of the necessary ingredients in the communion process. It is necessary that we visualize a second person in the situation—someone who will come to share with you what you share with

Figure 9-6
Various events
affecting "you"

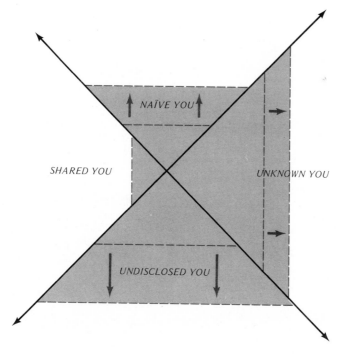

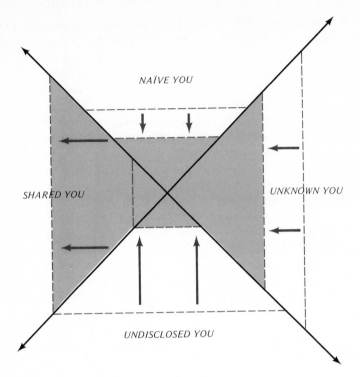

Figure 9-7
The goal in
sharing

NAÏVE YOU

SHARED YOU

UNKNOWN YOU

UNDISCLOSED YOU

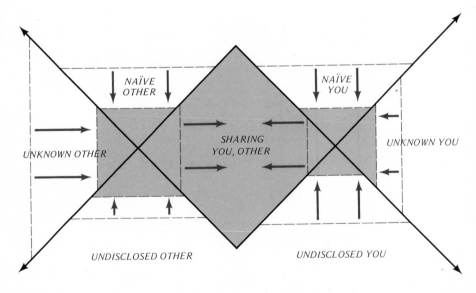

Figure 9-8
One to another

NAÏVE
OTHER

NAÏVE
YOU

UNKNOWN OTHER

SHARING
YOU, OTHER

UNKNOWN YOU

UNDISCLOSED OTHER

UNDISCLOSED YOU

him or her. Figure 9-8 illustrates the essence of communion: the making of "commonness" between people through sharing.

CHAPTER SUMMARY

I hope that Figure 9-8 helps you to see what I mean by communion . . . and the role of sharing in communion. The shared you (each of the you's) enlarges as the other areas become smaller. But understanding this doesn't mean that you see how the naïve you, the unknown you, and the undisclosed you "become smaller." These areas become smaller and the shared you enlarges in three related processes which I shall discuss in each of the next three chapters: Chapter 10, "Laundering, Self-Disclosing, and Sharing . . . Selves," deals with how the undisclosed area can be lessened; Chapter 11, "Doctoring, Giving Feedback, and Sharing . . . Feedback," describes how the naïve area can be modified; and Chapter 12, "Doing, Experiencing, and Sharing . . . Discoveries," discusses how the unknown you can be reduced.

Together, these three chapters form the basis for understanding how sharing is at the very heart of human communion.

LEARNING BY DISCUSSING

1   *Explain what you now think about the relationship between sharing and communication.*
2   *Explain how the development of self depends so much on interactions with others.*
3   *Explain—perhaps using the diagrams in the chapter—how sharing (and ultimate communion) is based on decreasing the naïve, unknown, and undisclosed self.*

LAUNDERING, SELF-DISCLOSURE, AND SHARING... SELVES (ON DECREASING THE UNDISCLOSED YOU)

STUDY OF THIS CHAPTER WILL ENABLE YOU TO

- *understand the concept of "laundering"*
- *understand the characteristics of laundering*
- *understand the concept of "self-disclosure"*
- *understand the differences between laundering and self-disclosure*
- *use self-disclosure appropriately in the interpersonal situation*
- *understand the concept of "sharing selves"*
- *understand the qualitative differences in sharing in the communal relationship*

The plane was rising in the early morning clouds over Chicago. I was on my way to Minneapolis and was tired from the preparation for the trip. I settled back and gazed absentmindedly at the back of the seat before me.

Nice day, isn't it? *(came a voice from beside me.)*

(I turned, mustering a smile,) Yes, not bad for the Midwest. *(I turned my gaze from the gentleman sitting next to me, and continued staring at the seat.)*

My boys lives in Minneapolis. That's where I'm headed.

(I could sense him looking at me, waiting for a response.) I'm going to Minneapolis, too. Business. *(Actually, I was to deliver a paper at a conference, so that was business of a kind.)*

My boy just got married. About time. He'd been living with that girl for three years. She's pregnant, you know.

(I smiled uncertainly,) No, I didn't know. *(The back of the seat was looking more and more interesting.)*

You'd think they'd be smarter than that, wouldn't you?

Yes, I guess so, *(I said shifting my gaze to the window view.)*

It didn't help.

Well, his mama and I had to get married, so I guess things like that can happen, huh?

(I sighed deeply—and thoughtfully,) Yeah, I guess.

I kept looking out the window, even though there was nothing there but clouds.

What do you do?

I beg your pardon?

(He spoke slowly—I suppose to make sure that I understood him:) What . . . line . . . of . . . work . . . are . . . you . . . in?

I'm a professor of communication at Purdue, *(I said—knowing that that would not end the discussion.)*

You work with telephones?

No, I teach things like interpersonal communication and argumentation.

Man, my ol' lady and I argue all the time. The other day, we really got into one. She hit me with a pan. . . .

There was a long pause. . . .

You mean you teach people to argue with each other?

I had to respond more fully to that one.

Not exactly, *(I said.)* I teach people — among other things in my course — to argue with one another constructively. I try to get them to see that differences can be solved by listening and . . .

Well, believe you me, I listened to her after she hit me with that pan.

I try to teach people that differences can be handled without using pans and things. The differences between people . . .

(He chuckled.) I already know the difference between us. They were clear after the wedding ceremony. . . .

Eventually — sometime after he told me about how he pads his expense account at the office — we arrived at Minneapolis. I never saw him again.

Laundering Scholars and researchers in communication have become aware that scenes such as I've just described occur fairly frequently. Trains, planes, and so forth seem to be the most likely spots for such transactions to happen. Yet they also happen in places other than the seats of public transportation. What they are and why they occur make an interesting study in human nature.

Basically, the scene on the plane can be called "laundering": *the revealing of personal, even intimate, details about one's self, friends, or relatives to strangers.* The laundering act gives meaning to the old cliché of "doing one's dirty laundry in public." The personal — better yet, sordid — knowledge that someone has is "hung out" for everyone to see. The process of laundering is far more than merely casual conversation — although it may begin with an innocent, "Nice day, isn't it?" No, laundering is a specific sort of communication with a number of recognizable characteristics.

First, laundering *arises from the common — and positive — desire to establish intimacy.* The goal is to reach out, to confess, or simply to share something known or felt with someone — anyone. None of that seems to be a problem. Reaching out to others may help with those common feelings of isolation and loneliness. Confession, in fact, may be good for the soul. The problem is not with the characteristic goal of laundering; the problem is with how laundering relates to other interpersonal concerns.

For example, a second characteristic of laundering is *a lack of apparent concern for the other person as an individual or as one member of a relationship.* The launderer on the plane may have received some *intra*personal gains from the process, but clearly this specific other person did not. How or whether this other person is affected is virtually irrelevant to the conversation. In laundering there seems to be little or no *inter*personal concern. This is why, third, laundering so often *involves strangers or at least casual acquaintances. Who* the other person is or *whether* a relationship exists is unimportant. There is just a need for someone who will listen.

That *who*, of course, could be a close friend, relative, or co-worker. The problem that launderers would have with such people is that revealing intimate or personal information about themselves or others would involve what they might consider a "risk:" "What would Aunt Helen (or dad, the rabbi, the boss, etc.) think if I told them . . . ?" Whether or not the risks are real is not the point. What *seems* real can be important. Fourth, laundering, then, implies *a lack of willingness to take risks.* When friends, relatives, or co-workers share intimate knowledge or feelings, there is always the risk that one or the other will be offended, hurt, or shocked by the information. The relationship could be helped, but it *might* be damaged. With strangers, there is little risk. The two probably will never see one another again. There is no chance of hurting a relationship that does not exist. So the launderer picks a stranger — any stranger will do: the possession of an ear is the only quality needed.

While none of these characteristics seem particularly harmful, why should anyone avoid laundering? That is especially a good question if the lack of harm is balanced by a gain for the launderer. Why not forget about it? The answer, I think, lies in a fifth and final characteristic. Laundering *does not necessarily have to relate to the launderer personally.* In the airplane conversation some of the material related to the man's thoughts and feelings. That may have been therapeutic for him, to some small degree. Most of the information, though, had to do with others. That is simply "gossip" — and the therapeutic value of gossip has always been debatable. The launderer, then, is not simply "letting it all hang out," but can be interested in nothing more than rather clumsily reaching out.

Yet there are better ways of reaching out. Studies from a variety of social sciences and humanistic perspectives have provided an alternative approach to the natural human tendency to "launder" at varying degrees. That approach is called "self-disclosure."

Self-disclosure   "Self-disclosure" is the term used to describe a more constructive means of fulfilling the urge to launder. So self-disclosure and laundering stem from the same human impulse to reach out and establish contact with others. Self-disclosure, however, is *the process of sharing information, thoughts, and feelings about one's self in ways that contribute to the growth of a relationship.*[1] Many of the differences between laundering and self-disclosure are implied in that definition.

---

[1] See, for example, Robert Monaghan, "Self-Concept: Through the Communication Looking Glass," in *Small Group Communication: Selected Readings,* ed. Victor Wall, Jr. (Columbus, O.: Collegiate, 1977).

In self-disclosure the emphasis is on decreasing the "undisclosed" you—on sharing the known self with others. [Rogers, Monkmeyer]

First, self-disclosure involves a *revealing of information, feeling, and thoughts*—parts of one's *"self"—with another*.[2] Laundering may involve information about nearly anyone. The laundering process can go on for hours without there being any truly personal self-revelations. This is not the case with self-disclosure. In self-disclosure the emphasis is on decreasing the "undisclosed" you—on sharing the known self with others. The disclosure of information about others is only relevant if it somehow contributes to an understanding of the person disclosing. Self-disclosure, then, involves a more narrowed range of information and thoughts.

Second, self-disclosure involves *a concern for the other and the relationship*. The launderer will talk to anyone about anything. The person engaging in self-disclosure will focus on those parts of the self that are relevant also to the other person—and their relationship. The self-disclosure is not meant simply to be self-therapeutic, but to be helpful to both people in their effort to understand one another. So there is not necessarily any value in simply saying something intimate about yourself. Self-disclosure assumes that the information revealed will be important in increasing the "shared" area of the relationship.

Relatedly and third, self-disclosure is *best when it is appropriate to the stage in the relationship*. Even the closest friends once were strangers. Does that mean that one does not self-disclose to strangers? No, self-

[2] For an excellent discussion, see David W. Johnson, *Reaching Out: Interpersonal Effectiveness and Self-Actualization* (Englewood Cliffs, N.J.: Prentice-Hall, 1972).

disclosure is appropriate *if* the other person is considered, *if* a relationship is being sought, and *if* the disclosure is appropriate to the level of the relationship. I would urge you not to have your second sentence to a stranger be something like, "Did you know, I just had an abortion?" or "Did you know that sometimes I fantasize that I . . . ?" That, I think, is laundering. In the same way I would expect self-disclosure among close friends to be something more than, "I have always liked tulips, did you know that?" Virtually anything about the self can be disclosed. The important thing is whether the relationship has developed to the point where whatever is shared is appropriate. This is a fundamental difference between self-disclosure and laundering.

Because of the stress on *self* (and not information about others) and the concern for the other and the relationship, self-disclosure involves *a willingness to take* appropriate *risks*. This final characteristic means that the revealed parts of the self can affect the relationship. If the information had no potential effect on the relationship, it would not be self-disclosure as defined. True self-disclosure involves the question about whether the information will help or hurt the relationship. The self-disclosure *might* imply some risk to the relationship but, more importantly, it may increase the

Self-disclosure involves an awareness of—and an acceptance of— appropriate risks. [© Marjorie Pickens, 1977]

113

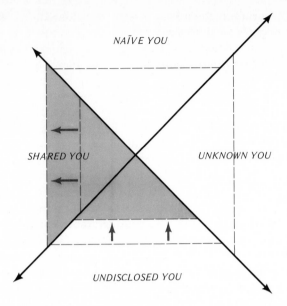

Figure 10-1
The goal of self-disclosure

NAÏVE YOU

SHARED YOU

UNKNOWN YOU

UNDISCLOSED YOU

chances of deepening the relationship. The appropriateness of the disclosure is important here. Newly acquired friends may be shocked by too intimate a disclosure. Old friends may never become close friends without intimate disclosure. The risk in revealing the information should be weighed carefully, for if it seems too great, the disclosure might better be postponed. But that will always be a guess. The amount of probable risk depends on factors such as the nature of the information disclosed, the stability of the relationship, the stage in the relationship, and so forth. Self-disclosure involves an awareness of—and an acceptance of—appropriate risks.

Again, as discussed in the last chapter, the overall goal of self-disclosure is to decrease the "undisclosed" parts of the self. The result of such a decrease should be an increase in the shared area of two people. Figure 10-1 reviews the situation.

Study the following illustration which makes clearer how self-disclosure can have a positive impact on a relationship. Fred and Ethel are leaving a class where midterm exams have been returned.

How did you do, Fred?
Got an "A." How 'bout you?
A "C," and I really studied for that test.
Yeah.
How much did you study?
Only . . . well, not too long.
You must be smarter than I am.
Not really.

You have to be. . . . I've known you for two years and you always set the curve. What do you have, a photographic memory?

No. . . . Listen, do you want a soft drink?

No. I don't understand it. . . . I study so hard.

Will you stop?

What's wrong?

Ethel, I had help on the exam. That's all.

You mean a tutor or something?

I mean a little bitty sheet of paper that knew all the answers. . . .

You mean . . . *(She stops walking.)*

I mean I cheated a little.

This is a joke, right?

Look, I can't handle all the pressure I get from home. I have to do well here to keep up the family image. So I do what I have to to get by.

You mean you cheated.

I already told you that. I didn't want to tell you, but I couldn't handle you always comparing your grade with mine. . . .

I see. . . .

No, I don't think you do. I'm not basically a dishonest person. Everybody cheats at something. . . . I just do it a little bit more consistently.

I see. . . .

I wish you could think of something else to say. We're honest about almost everything else. . . . I don't like to have you think you're so dumb. . . . Haven't you ever been tempted to get a little extra help on an exam or a paper . . . something?

I don't know what to say. . . .

While Ethel is thinking of a response, let me interrupt. Fred was not engaging in idle laundering. He was disclosing something about himself completely unknown to Ethel. In addition, he claims he was disclosing in order to increase the honesty between them. He seemed to be genuinely interested in her and their relationship. But even more important, he reluctantly chose to risk their relationship as a way of trying to deepen it. He undoubtedly hoped that their relationship was strong enough to withstand the disclosure. He hoped to be fair to Ethel and to improve their relationship. He balanced the real or imaginary damage that could be done to the relationship against the chance for improving it.

Though we cannot predict how Ethel would respond, a point needs to be reiterated: self-disclosure is a potentially valuable tool for the improvement of interpersonal relationships. It is hard to argue that the two people would have been "closer" interpersonally if the cheating remained part of Fred's undisclosed self. Fred took what he felt was a reasonable risk to help the relationship. Still my basic concern is with how human communication can help people toward communing relationships. In a relationship aiming toward communion, self-disclosure is important, but the sharing of selves is even more so.

The most basic distinction between self-disclosure and sharing selves is that the disclosure is *mutual*. In the example of Fred and Ethel the disclosure was basically a one-way process from Fred to Ethel. A relationship aiming toward communion depends on the idea that *both* people will disclose — according to characteristics for self-disclosure. Disclosure seems to increase when the people reciprocate. Both of their undisclosed selves will decrease and the area of the shared selves will increase. Figure 10-2 repeats this idea graphically. As the relationship deepens, more and more can be disclosed by both parties. Eventually, the "undisclosed selves" of the two people will shrink further. As they do, the shared area will become more of a stabilizing factor in the relationship. The point is fairly simple: A constructive giving of self by two "me's" can be a profitable investment in a more satisfying "me/us" relationship.

There are some other more subtle, more *qualitative* differences between self-disclosure by one person and sharing selves in a communing kind of way. To begin with, self-disclosing involves a weighing of risks — and a decision to disclose. Yet as the relationship deepens, the act of disclosure is less a matter of conscious choice: *It becomes a natural result of communion.* Just as you would freely "talk to yourself" about your thoughts and feelings, communing individuals would disclose to one another just as freely. Conscious choice? Not really; it would simply be the natural thing to do.

Figure 10-2
The goal of
sharing selves

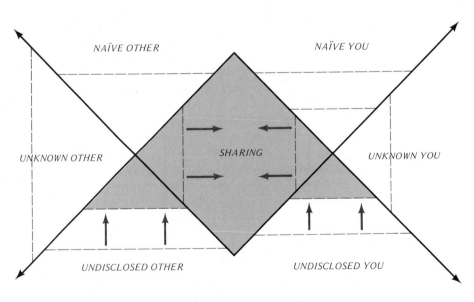

Similarly, disclosing by communing individuals would *become less concerned with how "appropriate" the disclosure would be*. Given the depth of the relationship, virtually anything would become appropriate disclosure for the communers. The trivial as well as the extremely intimate would become equally appropriate in more and more situations; factors of timing and appropriateness might eventually become irrelevant.

Finally, communing individuals would go beyond a concern for reciprocity. Certainly, each would disclose, just as a matter of course. But they would *come to disclose habitually,* perhaps even almost simultaneously. The technique of self-disclosure assumes almost a "turn taking": I disclose, then you do, now I will again, and so forth. Such "turn taking," though, would be of little concern for communing individuals. Disclosure of an ongoing nature would be nearly as common—and unconscious—as thinking and feeling. This would be true sharing of selves.

To emphasize particularly how the sharing of selves is mutual in relationships aiming toward communion, let's return to Fred and Ethel and see how Ethel responds. Ethel has just said:

I don't know what to say. . . .
I suppose you think I'm evil. Right?
No.
Then what do you think?
I think . . . Look, you're not unique. Yes, I have been tempted to cheat before. . . . I
    didn't think someone as smart as you would ever . . .
Yeah, well . . . *(He starts walking.)*
I'm not finished. . . . I have cheated on a test before . . . my senior year in high
    school. I got behind in studying. . . .
You? Really?
What do you mean by that?
Oh, I just meant . . . you seem so . . .
Straight?
Does that sound like an insult? I meant it as a compliment, you know.
I know. Look I'm not proud of what I did. I'm also not proud of what you've
    done. . . .
Listen. . . .
Do you mind? . . .
Sorry.
I feel better about telling you. I don't like the . . . what? guilt you're feeling?
You know what?
What?
I like you.
Good. . . . Where's that soft drink you promised me? Let's go somewhere and talk.

The case is not meant to condone cheating on tests but *is* meant to illustrate how the sharing of selves can become a help in developing an ongoing relationship.

The step beyond self-disclosure – sharing – is, of course, an ideal step. I suspect that no me/us relationship actually achieves complete communion. That, however, does not mean that the discussion of sharing as communion is unimportant. Human relationships can certainly progress beyond laundering; they can even progress beyond self-disclosure as usually discussed. Human relationships – *your* human relationships – can become very much a matter of sharing as I have described it. When this happens, you have taken a step beyond communication: You have begun to approach communion with a special other person.

CHAPTER SUMMARY

The chapter focused on ways of increasing the "shared you" by decreasing the "undisclosed" you.

The chapter began by illustrating what I call "laundering": the revealing of personal, even intimate, details about one's self, friends, or relatives to strangers. The process of laundering arises from the goal of establishing intimacy, but there are some major factors that keep laundering from being the best response to that desire.

A better approach is what is called "self-disclosure"—a process of revealing parts of one's self to another in an appropriate way and at an appropriate time. Self-disclosure can help in reducing the undisclosed self, of course, but mutual self-disclosure is even more productive. This "sharing of selves" is an indispensable part of the relationship building toward the level of communion. One major way of increasing the shared "you's" in a relationship is by mutual self-disclosure.

LEARNING BY APPLYING

1   *Consider the following:*

Ulla   George, this is Harvey; Harvey, George. Oops, someone else is at the door. Will you excuse me?

George   Sure, Ulla, Harvey and I will get acquainted.

Harvey   So, how are you, George?

George   Not bad. Just got married, again. Caught my wife with another man – so I divorced her and married my mistress. I guess I showed her, huh. . . .

Harvey   . . . Ah, yes . . . well, I . . . say, where's the punch bowl?

Explain George's comment by applying the characteristics of laundering. Why do George's comments differ from what we can call self-disclosure?

Can you think of a time, and a state in the relationship, when George's comments might have been appropriate self-disclosure? Explain.

2 *Think about your own relationships with other people. Make a list of several of these people. Now make a list (even mental) of some parts of the un-disclosed self that you might share at some time. Which of these things on the second list would you be comfortable sharing with people on the first list? Discuss what such a "matching" tells you about the importance of en-gaging in thoughtful self-disclosure.*

3 *What is (are) the person(s) in your life from whom you have no secrets? If there is one or more, explain the difference between disclosing yourself to this (these) person(s) and disclosing to fairly good friends. If there is no one with whom you are free to disclose everything, explain how you feel about disclosing parts of yourself to (a) family members, (b) acquaintances, and (c) your best friends.*

4 *Think about the people with whom it is easiest for you to self-disclose. Are they also the people who freely self-disclose to you? Discuss the importance of mutual self-disclosure.*

LEARNING BY DISCUSSING

1 *Give your own interpretation of laundering. Why is laundering not just a matter of "letting it all hang out"?*

2 *Discuss the differences between laundering and self-disclosure.*

3 *Discuss ways of communicating that will help in making self-disclosure an effective interpersonal tool.*

4 *Explain your understanding of "sharing selves"—and how that differs from self-disclosure.*

5 *How can the process of sharing selves make it easier to build and maintain better interpersonal relationships?*

LEARNING BY READING FURTHER

Culbert, Samuel A., *The Interpersonal Process of Self-Disclosure: It Takes Two to See One.* New York: Renaissance, 1968.

Jourard, Sidney M., *Self-Disclosure: An Experimental Analysis of the Transparent Self.* New York: Wiley, 1971.

Pearce, W. Barnett and Sharp, Stewart M., "Self-Disclosing Communication." *Journal of Communication* 23 (1973):409–425.

Rogers, Carl R., *Carl Rogers on Encounter Groups.* New York: Harper & Row, 1970.

Tubbs, Stewart and Baird, John W., *The Open Person: Self-Disclosure and Personal Growth.* Columbus, OH: Merrill, 1976.

Worthy, W., et al., "Self-Disclosure as an Exchange Process." *Journal of Personality and Social Psychology* 13 (1969):59–63.

DOCTORING, GIVING FEEDBACK, AND SHARING ... FEEDBACK (ON DECREASING THE NAÏVE YOU)

STUDY OF THIS CHAPTER WILL ENABLE YOU TO

- *understand the concept of "doctoring"*
- *understand the characteristics of doctoring*
- *understand the concept of "giving feedback"*
- *understand the nature of constructive feedback*
- *use constructive feedback in interpersonal situations*
- *understand the concept of "sharing feedback"*
- *understand the nature of shared feedback*
- *share feedback—with the help of another—in the interpersonal situation*

Joan had just completed a two-hour meeting with her supervisor. The meeting involved Joan's work on plans for a new approach for the screening and training of new employees. Some of Joan's plans had been rejected because they were too expensive; others were rejected because they did not "fit in with" company tradition. Joan feels that she is "back to the drawing board." Gloomily, she sits having a sandwich and a cup of coffee for lunch. Her friend Mary approaches.

Hi, Joan. Can I sit here—or are you expecting a party of eight?

(With a weak smile) Oh, hello, Mary.

Do you mind if I join you?

Oh, no, I'm sorry. No, I'm not expecting anybody. . . . Actually, I'm not sure what to expect.

(Sitting down) Wow, what's wrong with you? Did you lose your job—or your boy friend?

Joan simply looks at her, expressionless.

Sorry. I guess something is really wrong, huh?

No, I'm the one who should apologize. I am feeling down in the dumps. . . .

Well, with food like this . . . *(She looks at her tray)* . . . What do you expect?

Yeah.

Can I help do anything, Joan?

I don't think so. I just had a meeting with Helen about the plans for trainees. She . . . let's say . . . wasn't wild about them. I feel like I just got nailed to the wall. I can think of better ways to start a career.

Well, you know how she is. Look, she's my supervisor, too, and I've known her for years. She was a lot less picky about things before she became personnel director. It's gone to her head—the promotion, I mean. At any rate, don't let it get you down.

Yeah, but . . .

Listen, her bark is worse than her bite. I know. She's barked at me for months now. . . . But I haven't got bitten, yet.

That's easier for you to say. You've been here longer, and . . .

That's not the point. The point is that you can't let a thing like this affect you. Take what she said today and change your plans accordingly. Nobody gets fired for coming up with unacceptable plans for a training program. *(She finishes a salad.)*

But, there are good reasons for doing it like I planned. Helen just didn't want to listen to any new ideas. . . . It's against tradition around here to listen to untraditional plans.

Say, you *are* upset. *(She continues eating.)*

Yes, I thought you knew that! . . . I'm sorry. I'm just a little edgy about the whole thing.

And I'm telling you it isn't all that bad. Just change the plans and everything will be okay. Forget all this and get back to work. . . . Don't you want your sandwich?

Here. It's yours. I guess I'm not hungry.

(Joan rises to leave.) I guess I'll go back to the office.

Good idea. Get back in there and get busy. Best thing in the world for you. You see if I'm not right.

Yeah, I guess.

Listen, any time I can be of help, you let me know. Don't you want your drink? . . .

Doctoring The preceding discussion is an illustration of what I shall call *"doctoring"*: *the effort by one person to "fix" the problems of others.* Obviously, there are all sorts of familiar kinds of doctors. Veterinarians, medical doctors, dentists, and psychiatrists are the more common types. Regardless of their specialties, all of these kinds of people offer their services as a way of helping other people. Each specialist is trained to "fix" problems of a particular kind.

"Doctoring," however, can be of a different sort. From time to time all of us "play doctor" as we attempt to help friends and acquaintances "fix" whatever is wrong with them. Call it "helping," "being a friend," or playing amateur psychologist. Whatever, it involves the human impulse to help others. There is nothing wrong with this. And yet the illustration of doctoring just related appeared to be of little real help to Joan and her situation. Why might this be so, even though Mary seemed sincerely interested in helping? To understand the weaknesses of (untrained and unspecialized) doctoring best, let's look at its major characteristics.

First, doctoring is characterized by *a genuine and sincere desire to help*. This healthy characteristic is perhaps why doctoring attempts are so common among close friends and relatives. You probably will not find it difficult to get well-meaning advice from those around you. It may not be valuable, may not be based on any special training, and may not be something you would want to do. Still the advice probably is there when you ask for it — sometimes even when you don't ask.

This healthy characteristic of desiring to help, though, is more than off-

set by certain less healthy characteristics. For doctoring, also, is characterized by *the assumption of complete understanding*. Specially trained and
educated doctors such as dentists and psychiatrists make an assumption
that they understand or learn to understand what is bothering you. This is
(hopefully) a well-founded assumption. Yet amateur interpersonal doctors
can make the same assumption – whether or not it is accurate. In the case
discussed, Mary assumed that she understood exactly what Joan was experiencing. She told Joan how well she knew Helen and how often she herself had heard her "bark." "I know exactly what you're going through,"
Mary seemed to be saying. But it had been a long time since Mary was a
new employee. She was not present during the two-hour meeting. Just as
important, Mary's assumption that she understood everything so well
seemed to be a way of minimizing Joan's problems. Joan may have sensed
Mary was actually saying: "We've all gone through this – Why do you think
your problems are so unique?" At the very least, Mary's assumption that
she understood everything did not seem to help Joan.

Third, doctoring implies *the role of expert or final authority*. Special-
ists often view their observations and conclusions as final. After all, they
have training and experience; they should know – or so the assumption
goes. In the same way, Mary felt that her experience on the job and with
Helen placed her squarely in the role of expert. Helen's "bark was worse
than her bite"; no one ever got fired over a matter of training plans. Joan
was uncertain about herself, but Mary wasn't. Mary had all the necessary
insights and knowledge. So as doctoring implies, fourth, Mary placed an
emphasis on prescription. The cliché about medical doctors is "take two
aspirin and call me in the morning." That is prescription: the specifying of
what will help or the statement of what the other person *should* do. Mary
gave prescriptions without any sort of license. Forget about it; don't let it
bother you; get back to work. All these were meant as prescriptions that
would help Joan. All were meant to be statements about what Joan should
do.

But the prescriptions are even more than statements. Fifth, doctoring
means *an attempt to* bind *the other to follow the prescription*. Dentists or
podiatrists would expect that their prescriptions would be followed. "Doctor's orders" is a cliché that is supposed to justify everything from jogging
to a glass of wine with a meal to increase milk production in nursing
mothers. Similarly, Mary was giving more than a prescription. She expected Joan to follow her advice. She was trying to bind, informally force,
Joan to the prescription. For Joan to have ignored the advice might have
seemed an insult to Mary. After all, Mary would reason, "I know the
problem and the cure. Surely, she will follow my advice."

And yet Joan didn't seem to be helped much by what Mary said. Mary
assumed that she knew exactly what Joan was experiencing; she assumed
the role of expert; and she had freely given (her best) advice. If none of that

seemed to help, what *could* Mary have done? The answer lies in what inter-personal scholars and researchers call the process of "giving feedback."

Giving feedback   In general, feedback is a set of responses. There are more specialized defi-nitions than this, which will vary with the sort of feedback being described. This chapter focuses on *feedback* as *a set of responses to a message, situa-tion, or event.* Joan's problem provided Mary with an opportunity to provide feedback. That is, Mary had the opportunity to:

show that she understood what Joan was saying
explain her reaction to Joan's situation and statements
provide input into Joan's thinking about her situation

Each of these is a major goal or purpose in giving feedback.

In some respects Mary provided feedback since she did respond to Joan and her situation. She tried to show that she understood and explained her reaction. She certainly provided input into Joan's thinking. Yet there are more *constructive* ways of providing feedback than Mary used. Mary's— and your feedback—can be better if some basic guidelines for giving con-structive feedback are followed. As we shall see, Mary seemed to have little knowledge of these.

Essentially, constructive feedback is aimed at allowing the "naïve self" to decrease and the "shared self" to expand. Your giving of constructive feedback enables someone else to know things about him- or herself that he or she had not known before. Figure 11-1, which was seen in Chapter 9,

*Figure 11-1
The goal of giving
feedback*

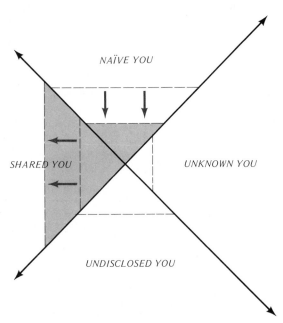

NAÏVE YOU

SHARED YOU

UNKNOWN YOU

UNDISCLOSED YOU

Make sure that the other person is interested in or at least receptive to your opinions. [Hamlin, Stock, Boston]

shows the goals of constructive feedback. To ensure better that the goal is reached, the giver of feedback can concentrate on several factors.[1]

First, the *feedback should be solicited*. Make sure that the other person is interested in or at least receptive to your opinions. Advice – or even observations – seemingly forced on an unwilling person will probably have no impact. Worse yet, unwelcome feedback can be irritating. In the long run, unsolicited feedback may damage the relationship. If you are not sure whether feedback is desired, ask about it. You may feel "compelled" to provide feedback and be tempted to give it, whether or not it is desired. What is important to know is that you cannot force the other's "naïve self" to decrease. Solicited feedback means that the person is at least entertaining the idea of seeking information that he or she might not already know.

Second, *feedback should be well timed*. By this I mean several things. It may do little good to provide feedback about experiences in the distant past. What someone did when both of you were children may or may not still

[1] Much of the material in this section is based on suggestions in Howard W. Polsky, "Notes on Personal Feedback in Sensitivity Training," *Sociological Inquiry* 41 (Spring 1971):175–82. The treatment is also consistent with the material in Richard E. Crable, *Using Communication* (Boston: Allyn and Bacon, 1979), chap. 10.

be relevant. If past situations and actions are irrelevant, the feedback about them probably will be just as irrelevant. In addition, it is generally unproductive to discuss "what a person *always* does." Saying "You never clean up your room" or "You always take things too seriously" may be unwelcome and unhelpful. Treat the situation in the present, that is, *this* failure to clean a room or *this* thing being taken too seriously. Make the feedback focus on one time at a time whenever possible. And finally, make sure that the physical and emotional *timing* is right for your feedback. In times of stress or anger or fatigue, feedback may be harder to accept. If difficult to accept, it may be impossible to use. Your feedback, then, should be well timed for a variety of reasons.

Third, your *feedback should be* descriptive *of feelings and thoughts.* In contrast to the "doctor" who acts the role of expert, constructive feedback is simply what you as a person observe or believe. In most interpersonal situations you will not really be the ultimate authority. But you have the ability to state what you believe or what you see occurring. Because of this, you can state an opinion *without prescribing* an ultimate cure. Your perception is simply your perception. The person can do with it what he or she thinks best.

Yet even descriptive comments can be less than helpful. Fourth, *feedback should be specific.* Even something like "John, it seems to me that you try too hard," may not be useful. Something that vague and general may leave John at a loss about what to do. How does one try "less hard"? Be specific: "John, it seems to me that you put too many hours in at the office." That *may* be what "trying too hard" means. It may also mean that you think John wasted energy worrying about a particular thing, that he attended to too many details, or something else. Whatever you mean, try to explain as specifically as possible.

Fifth, relatedly, *feedback should concentrate on modifiable things.* Telling John that in your considered opinion he would be a better salesman if he were taller probably will not help. Telling him you think he failed a test because he thinks too slowly may be just as useless. Feedback that is constructive will focus on things that John can do or knows can be changed.

Giving constructive feedback, as we have seen, is far different from "doctoring." To illustrate this, let me reconstruct the opening case study. I will pretend that Mary knew and used the strategies of giving constructive feedback. Compare this Mary's comments with the first.

The situation is the same, and Joan's friend Mary approaches.

Hi, Joan. Can I sit here, or are you expecting a party of eight?
(With a weak smile) Oh, hello, Mary.
Do you mind if I join you?
Oh, no, I'm sorry. No, I'm not expecting anybody. . . . Actually, I'm not sure what to expect.

(Sitting down) Wow, what's wrong with you? Did you lose your job—or your boy friend?

Joan simply looks at her, expressionless.

Sorry. I guess something is really wrong, huh?

No, I'm the one who should apologize. I am feeling down in the dumps. . . .

Oh, do you want to talk about it?

No, I don't think so.

Okay. . . . Your sandwich looks good. Wish I'd bought one like that. . . .'' *(Mary munches on her sandwich.)*

I guess I would like to talk about it. You've been around here longer than I have.

Well, Joan, I'm willing to listen.

I just had a meeting with Helen. She rejected most of my plans for new trainees. I feel like I got nailed to the wall. I can think of better ways to start a career.

Well, I know she can be picky. It seems to me she has been worse since her promotion. I know her bark's worse than her bite. She's barked at me a time or two.

You've had a run-in with her?

Let's say at least several.

Maybe I'm not all that unusual, then. . . . I mean, maybe she just acts like this with everyone.

All I can tell you is the way she acts toward me.

But you've been around a while. I thought maybe she was just rejecting me when she threw out the plans. *(Mary continues to eat.)*

My plans for things have been thrown out, but I'm still here.

Maybe I'm just taking this too hard. It was my first stab at doing anything like this. What do you think, Mary?

You really want to know?

Yes.

I think you are upset about an upsetting thing. I think you are nervous about the job —and all that. And I think that Helen treats everyone about the same. She's tough, but fair.

Maybe I'm overreacting.

That's understandable. But this is not the end of the line.

Maybe I ought to just work on the changes she suggested.

You could.

Would you, Mary?

I probably would. You know best for you, I guess, Joan. Aren't you going to eat your sandwich?

It's yours. Here . . . Hey, this thing is not going to get me down. I can make those changes. I might even be able to convince her she's wrong in a coupla places. . . .

Joan, do . . .

I'm going back to the office and get on it. . . . I'm sorry, what were you going to say?

Do you want your drink?

No, have it. Hey, thanks a bunch. You've been a big help.

The change in Joan may have seemed a bit dramatic . . . but then the change in Mary was dramatic too. This time Mary *made sure that Joan wanted the feedback*—several times. She *timed* her feedback and made sure that it focused on *specific descriptions* of *modifiable* things. In essence, Mary was not doctoring; she was providing constructive feedback. In ways similar to the first situation Mary tried to show that she understood and was direct in explaining her reaction—two of the goals of feedback. But she also simply supplied input to Joan. It was Joan who was then able to prescribe for herself—who was the expert on how she felt and what she should do. The guidelines for giving constructive feedback are easy to learn. They are, however, difficult to apply at first. Practice can make you more aware of whether you are doctoring, or giving constructive feedback. Practice can make the giving of feedback an important part of your interpersonal skills.

In the situation we analyzed, Joan was helped by Mary giving constructive feedback. In many situations the emphasis is not on one person, but on two: two people who aim toward a communing relationship. In those situations a slightly different approach is desirable.

Sharing . . . feedback

In the previous section the emphasis was on feedback as a way of decreasing one person's "naïve self" with information from the other. When the focus is on the communing relationship, the emphasis shifts. In the communing relationship the goal is to have *both* "naïve selves" decrease with information from each person. Figure 11-2 illustrates this emphasis. The

Figure 11-2 The goal of sharing feedback

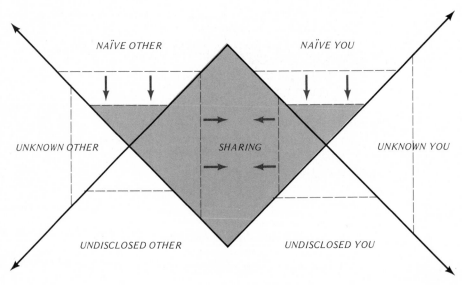

NAÏVE OTHER   NAÏVE YOU

UNKNOWN OTHER   SHARING   UNKNOWN YOU

UNDISCLOSED OTHER   UNDISCLOSED YOU

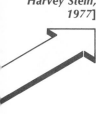

diagram shows that the interest is in both people learning by the feedback of the other.

Sharing feedback is basically an extension of *giving* feedback. To begin to share feedback, you will want to make sure the comments are solicited (or at least welcome), well timed, descriptive, specific, and focused

129

on modifiable factors. There are, however, three factors that make sharing feedback something more than just giving feedback.

First, the process of sharing feedback means that there is *a concern for each of the two people, and their relationship.* In the case discussed neither Mary nor Joan was very interested in Mary or in Mary and Joan's relationship. Joan had a problem. Feedback seemed to offer a way of helping. But notice that the emphasis was on Mary trying to help her friend. Nothing was done that particularly would be helpful for Mary. Nothing about the conversation specifically helped or affected the relationship between them. Mary was trying to give feedback; the two were not *sharing* feedback.

Second, because of the emphasis on both people and their relationship, sharing feedback involves *mutual feedback.*[2] In other words, feedback is given by and given to both people. In order for their relationship to aim toward a communal level, each can benefit from being less "naïve." Some mutual feedback will occur as they almost simultaneously comment to one another. Some will occur as they seem to "take turns" giving feedback. However it occurs, and it will vary from time to time, both individuals give and receive feedback. They will share what the one observes, thinks, or feels about the blind spots of the other.

Third, the sharing of feedback means a *willingness to take risks to help the relationship.* When two people aim toward a communal relationship, some of the feedback will probably involve intimate or highly personal — perhaps even potentially insulting and hurtful — observations about the other person. To tell another person things that are meant to help (but may hurt) the relationship involves a *risk.* But risks are taken best in an atmosphere of mutual *trust.* And interestingly, trust grows *because* risk taking has not met violent reaction in the past.[3] This is known as the "trust-risk" cycle. Such a cycle exists most easily in a communing relationship. Two people trust one another so much that they can say virtually whatever is on their minds. When each grows as a less "naïve" self, other responsible risks can be taken. And so it goes. Mutual feedback between two people who are willing to take risks to continue improving their relationship — all those factors help describe and further the communing relationship.

Clearly, not all interpersonal situations will free you to emphasize the relationship and both people. Also, not every interpersonal relationship will permit taking the risk to say constructive, but potentially damaging things. But then, not every relationship is one that you want to be communal. Still when you are interested in developing a communal relationship, you can focus on both of you and the relationship. You can engage in mutual and risk-taking feedback.

[2] The need for mutual feedback is developed in Polsky, "Notes on Personal Feedback," ibid.
[3] For an interesting discussion of trust and risk see Gerald M. Goldhaber, *Organizational Communication* (Dubuque, Ia: Brown, 1974), pp. 78–80.

In the situation experienced by Joan the *giving* of feedback seemed completely appropriate. Joan had a problem and Mary was in a position to help. In a different context the importance of *sharing* feedback may have been more obvious. Consider the following discussion.

Joan and Mary have met one another at the water cooler a few days after their earlier exchange.

Hi, Joan.

Oh, hello, Mary.

How are you?

Much better thanks to you, Mary. I think I have the plans for the new training program well in hand. Helen even likes the plans now.

Well, I wasn't much help. But I'm glad things are better for you.

Yeah. . . .

Well, back to work. . . .

Mary, . . . Oh, never mind. . . .

What?

Well . . . I have been wondering what you meant when you asked about me losing my boy friend.

Just a joke. . . . Hey, I have to leave. . . .

Mary, I have to tell you that it seemed to me you meant more than that. . . . How do you feel about George?

George is your man. . . . Off limits to friends. . . .

But you seem to like him. . . . It seems that when he and I are together . . . that you, well . . . look at him a lot.

Look, Joan, I have my own man. . . . You seem to be thinking that I'm after your guy. . . .

I just meant . . . that. . . . Well, I was just wondering if you like him more than you think you do, that's all.

Well, he is a hunk . . . but I don't think. . . . You know, you sound to me like you have a case of the jealousies, Joan. . . . Have you listened to what you've said?

Oh, no, I'm not jealous, Mary. . . . I was just wondering. . . .

Whether I was after him? . . . Sounds to me like the basic case of "Is my best friend after . . ."

Oh, no! . . .

Maybe I do think he's all right. But I don't think I'm *after* him. . . . Now, if you two split up, that might be a different story. . . . I don't know, maybe I have been drooling a little. . . . I really haven't done it on purpose. . . . I just. . . . Well, he is something special. . . .

I'm sorry, I didn't mean to make a big thing out of it. I really like George. . . . I guess I felt a little competition. . . .

Maybe jealousy, Joan . . . ?

Yeah, maybe that too. I guess I've been wanting to talk about this for a week or so now. . . .

Well, I'm not . . . consciously trying to move in on him. . . .

131

I'm sorry. . . .

No, I'm glad we talked. . . . I'm glad we *can* talk. . . .

Me, too, Mary.

This may not be the end of the conversation—or the feelings that each had. The illustration, though, involves a concern for both people and their relationship. It involves mutual feedback and a willingness to take risks for the good of the relationship: Mary and Joan each said things that *might* have been insulting to the other. In an atmosphere of considerable trust, they took those risks. Having survived what was probably a difficult conversation, they both came to some new knowledge about themselves, their thoughts, and their feelings. Sharing of feedback allowed them to decrease the "naïve" self and to expand the shared parts of themselves, resulting probably in an improved relationship. They might continue to build toward a communing relationship.

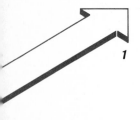

CHAPTER SUMMARY

The chapter was built on the previous emphasis on mutual self-disclosure by indicating a complementary way of increasing the "shared" you. This chapter involves approaches to decrease the "naïve" you.

In contrast to more helpful approaches, the chapter began by describing "doctoring"—a kind of help offered that may do more harm than good in the interpersonal situation. A more helpful approach, called "giving feedback," was given as well as the detailed ways in which people can make their feedback more acceptable and more helpful.

Still in order for two people to build their relationship, each can benefit from the feedback of the other. "Sharing feedback" is a powerful factor in any healthy, growing relationship. With mutual feedback, each person can help decrease the naïve area of the other and at the same time can help increase the area of their "shared you's." The result can be a closer, deeper relationship—"one to another."

LEARNING BY APPLYING

1   *Consider several people with whom you are close friends. If you had a problem with which you needed help, which of these would come to mind? Does this preference have anything to do with whether they "doctor" or "give feedback"? Do you know anyone who specializes in "doctoring" interpersonal and intrapersonal problems? Use the characteristics of doctoring to describe what he or she does.*

2   Giving constructive feedback is much more difficult than it sounds. In order to prepare yourself for giving feedback about truly important matters, practice giving feedback in terms of the criteria in the following situations:

   a.   A co-worker comes into the office wearing a bright red, pink, and yellow (ill-fitting) sweater and saying, "Hey, what do you think of this designer special?"

   b.   Your spouse has just purchased what you think is a beautiful, but too expensive new coat. What do you say?

   c.   A fairly boring, unenthusiastic professor has just completed the first half of the course. She or he asks for feedback about the course—oral feedback. What do you say when she or he asks you to make a comment?

3   At least one of the following criteria for giving constructive feedback has been violated. Can you identify it or them?

   a.   A small child has just finished a "scribble" picture and asks you (a complete stranger) what you think. You answer: "Give it up, kid. You'll never be able to draw."

   b.   Man to wife: "Helen, if I've said this once, I've said it a thousand times, you always look okay to me!"

   c.   "Look, so your father just died. He's better off than being in pain, and you're not helping by crying for hours."

   d.   Student comment on a class paper: "Try to do better next time!"

   e.   "Listen, I know what I'm saying. Give up on him. There never was a decent man to come out of Zeffle County."

4   Think about recent situations in which you and another have engaged in mutual feedback. Were there times when the second person's feedback seemed to be "retaliation" for the first feedback (e.g, "Yeah, well, you're not so good in math either")? Were there times when the mutual feedback seemed much more constructive. Discuss the differences to get an idea of how the constructive sharing of feedback can help build toward a communing relationship.

LEARNING BY DISCUSSING

1   Explain the concept of "doctoring" and the problems it poses in interpersonal relationships.

2   Discuss the differences between doctoring and giving feedback constructively.

3   Discuss what you feel is or are the most important factor(s) in giving constructive feedback.

4   Explain how "sharing feedback" goes beyond simply giving feedback.

5   How does a knowledge of sharing feedback help the chances of building better relationships?

LEARNING
BY READING FURTHER

Crable, Richard E., *Using Communication*. Boston: Allyn and Bacon, 1979, chap. 10.

Gibb, Jack R., "Defensive Communication." *Journal of Communication* 11 (1961):141–148.

Giffin, Kim, and Patton, Bobby R., *Fundamentals of Interpersonal Communication*. New York: Harper & Row, 1971.

Polsky, Howard W., "Notes on Personal Feedback in Sensitivity Training." *Sociological Inquiry* 41 (Spring 1971):175–182.

Rogers, Carl R., *Carl Rogers on Encounter Groups*. New York: Harper & Row, 1970.

Wiener, Norbert, *The Human Use of Human Beings*. Boston: Houghton Mifflin, 1950.

12

DOING, EXPERIENCING, AND SHARING...
DISCOVERIES (ON DECREASING THE UNKNOWN YOU)

STUDY OF THIS CHAPTER WILL ENABLE YOU TO

- *understand the concept of "doing"*
- *understand the characteristics of "doing"*
- *understand the concept of "experiencing"*
- *understand strategies for "experiencing"*
- *use strategies of "experiencing" better*
- *understand the concept of "sharing experiences"*
- *understand techniques of "sharing experiences"*
- *share experiences—with the help of another—in the interpersonal situation*

Hi, Lana. I bet I'm early, huh?

No, not at all. C'mon in, David.

Okay. *(He sits on the sofa.)* Well, what'll it be tonight? Bowling, the movies, just dinner out—you name it.

Oh, I don't know. I'm kinda tired tonight. Do you just want to stay here?

Hey, that's a good idea.

Good. I really don't feel like going out. . . . Maybe we could just sit and talk.

Anything you like. Do you want to watch TV or listen to the stereo, or what?

Well, I thought we could just talk . . . you know.

You got it. Nice sofa. Mind if I turn on the stereo, Lana? . . . A little music might be nice.

(From the kitchen) Go right ahead. I'll be in in a minute. I thought some drinks and snacks might be good.

You bet. . . . Ah, the new *Time*!

What?

I said, "*You bet. We got time.*"

(Entering the room) There. Ah, this will be nice. . . . What are you reading, David?

Huh?

I asked what you were reading. Do you want one of these?

Yeah, that'll taste good.

Well. . . . How did your day go, David?

Fine. . . . Did you read this article on . . . What's the matter?

Oh, nothing. I thought I'd just sit over here.

Ah, I can read this some other time. You want a back rub—or a pizza later?

No, not really.

Which?

What?

Not to which, Lana—the back rub or the pizza?

I'm fine. Really. I don't want anything except to be with you, David.

136

Great. C'mon over here.

That's not what I mean. . . .

Oh . . . Maybe later?

David, . . . Oh, never mind. . . . Say, what do you think of the new apartment?

Nice.

I thought about doing some painting. . . .

Hey, I'll help you. I can do a room like this in an afternoon. . . . Looks like that
  Danish modern chair could use a little repair. . . . I'll bring my tool case next
  time. . . .

David, I didn't ask for a remodeling estimate. . . . I was just trying to talk with
  you. . . .

You do want a pizza, right?

No. . . .

Tacos?

No . . . David. . . .

Well, what do you want? Name it.

David, I want you. . . .

You said "later."

Yes, I know. . . . No, I didn't. . . .

Now?

DAVID!!!

Okay, I'll go.

I don't want you to go.

Make up your mind. . . . What do you want me to do?

Doing As a child, David probably was described by his early teachers as "hyperactive": someone in perpetual motion. Hyperactive children frequently suffer
so much from the uncontrollable impulse to be active that they become discipline problems. The attention spans may be short, the craving for attention may be strong, and the classroom may experience its first "class
clown." Special diets and mild tranquilizers may be prescribed for such
children. Interestingly enough, hyperactivity in adults may be considered
more of an asset than a curse. Part of the American experience has been
created by the restless movement to unchartered areas of the frontier. The
giants of business and industry are often described as "hustlers," "movers
and shakers," . . . as "doers." High degrees of activity in humans, then, can
range from being considered a severe problem to being a tremendous asset.

Whatever the explanation for David's behavior, his actions did not help
his relationship with Lana. In interpersonal terms he can be considered a
"doer" — a mildly negative term as I use it here. There are several characteristics of "doing," the first of which is entirely positive.

First, *"doing" is based on the healthy desire for joint activity.* Surely,
to be alive is to want to do things with other people: parents, siblings,
friends, and lovers. I remember clearly how I enjoyed events such as fish-

137

ing weekends with my father. I loved to fish, but I also enjoyed just being alone with my father on a quiet lake at dawn. The desire for playmates is a perpetual one for children: "Can I go to Matt's house?" Later, the desire for joint activity turns toward members of the opposite sex. Dating becomes a sometimes bittersweet attempt to satisfy the need for people to do things together. As discussed in Chapter 4, one of the reasons people communicate is that they are human. Here the couple seems to want joint activity, which is a perfectly natural and positive force, because they are human.

Yet what I call "doing" has some other, less positive characteristics. Second, *doing can become activity for its own sake.* In the opening example David had acquired the habit of always needing to do something. He was prepared to read, to watch TV, to listen to the stereo, to go bowling, to go to the movies, or to go get takeout food. What Lana wanted was a quiet evening of conversation and togetherness — something not to be confused with "petting," "necking" or lovemaking. But conversation and togetherness did not seem like things to *do.* David was willing to *do* practically anything but was not willing to do what he considered nothing.

I do not think David's desire for constant activity was unusual. Probably every parent has heard a child complain, "I don't have anything to do." The parent probably responded just as impatiently as his or her parents did 20 or so years earlier: "You have games there, you have a radio, you have a room full of toys, you could take a walk, . . ." The answer is also a classic instance of ignoring the point: "But I don't have anything to do." Doing something — almost anything — can become a preoccupation. Contemporary observers know that most Americans find it hard to relax. Even a camping trip to the woods becomes a major project full of things to do to get ready. . . . Then a relaxing weekend can occur, with volley ball, tennis, fishing, hiking, and an outdoor movie for when there is "nothing to do." These same observers point to the growing problem of retirement: How can people adjust when they retire and have "nothing to do"? The emphasis in these examples is not that there are things that need to be done; the focus is on people who simply need to do things. Doing, for many people, seems a necessary end in itself.

A third, and again less positive, aspect of doing is that *doing often becomes a substitute for deeper human interaction.* In the example David was willing to do anything to avoid simple conversation and togetherness. Reading, television, and the rest provided things to do to distract his and Lana's attention. With activities such as these they would not have to focus on one another. David had no problem with shifting the focus away from his relationship with Lana. Even his thinly veiled interest in lovemaking would have provided, ironically, a substitute for interpersonal interaction with Lana. To Lana, none of this sounded especially appealing. She wanted to be with David, without having to *do* anything.

Again, I see the situation as being fairly common. The divorce courts are filled with people who either cooked good meals and stayed at home or helped bring in extra income, but who could not maintain a loving relationship with a spouse. The same courts—and maybe the same cases—contain those who provided a good income, three cars, a fine house, status in the community, but who failed ever to invest time and effort in a relationship. Juvenile court judges often hear cases involving children who had their own TV, a stereo, every possible toy and game, but no attention. Clearly, "doing" seems prompted by the desire for interaction. Just as clearly, doing things with and for others can become a substitute for that same interaction. David asked at the last, "What do you want me to do?" The answer, if Lana had been able to phrase it, probably would have been: "That's just the point: I don't need you to *do* anything. In fact, I wish you would *do* less"—an answer that would have confused David even more. He figured that there must be something he could *do* to help make Lana feel better.

Finally, *doing often is a method of debt creation*. David, for example, was willing to spend money, to run errands, or to serve as handyman. While he may not have realized it, these doings may have been ways of making Lana obligated to him. "After all," he could argue, "look at all I have done for you—you owe me friendship and warmth!" It may well be more blessed to give than to receive, but I suspect that refers to gifts without strings attached. When the giver feels that he or she is earning something or some response, then the doing is not a gift; it is a bribe. David's "What do you want me to do" might be better phrased as, "What *else* do you want from me? I have volunteered to do everything I can think of."

Is this characteristic of doing common? I think so. The best evidence lies in some relevant phrases that are so common they have become clichés: "After all I did for her!" "And this . . . this is how I am rewarded?" "I tried so hard—God knows I've tried!" and "This is what I get for my effort?" All these indicate the hurt, the anger, or the indignation of people who felt betrayed. The debts owed them by someone else were not payed. And after all, these people had done so much; they (felt anyway that they) deserved better debt payment.

We have discussed that doing stems from a natural and healthy impulse for human joint activity. Yet doing can become an end in itself; it can become a substitute for more intimate interaction and can be used to create obligation in others. Yet you, like David, may ask about alternatives to "doing." One better alternative is our next topic for discussion: experiencing.

Experiencing In Chapter 9 the focus was on "sharing" as the heart of communion. The question became, "What can one share and what effect can such sharing have on human relationships?" Using the basic diagram in Chapter 9, we saw in Chapter 10 how self-disclosure and the sharing of selves could decrease the "undisclosed you." Chapter 11 described how giving feedback

139

and sharing feedback could decrease the "naïve you" in a relationship. Each of these decreases could be expected to result in an expansion of the "shared you." But what of the part of you, and the part of the other, *unknown* to either of you? Events occur and changes take place that are not recognized by either you or the other. What of this "unknown" part of you? It is here that the concept of experiencing becomes important.

Simply stated, *"Experiencing" is being appreciatively aware of as many as possible of the countless stimuli that surround you.*

Having written that, I should warn you that "experiencing" is not nearly so simple and automatic as it may sound. Several basic strategies can help you decrease the unknown you by better experiencing what you sense and feel.

First, you should *be aware that you are bombarded by literally millions of stimuli every day.* By "stimuli," I mean all the sights, smells, sounds, tastes, things to feel, thoughts to think, and feelings. Humankind changes, but the existence of stimuli simply changes form. Where the cave people had roars of animals, we have the roars of cars, trucks, trains—and alarm clocks. Where they had damp earth (or worse) under their feet, we have carpeting or parquet floors. Where they had wind, rain, and blue sky, we have wind, rain, and skies of various colors. Where they had the roughness of animal skin garments, we have denim, suede, cotton, and silk. Clearly, of course, we have increased the variety of stimuli. We have created cities, amusement parks, and mass media—all of which may be mixed blessings, but which have added to the potential stimuli for humankind. And still, just as cave people did, we think, feel, "sense things," have hunches, and experience desires. Stimuli are all around us and within us. Once only death was considered an escape from stimuli, and now we are not even sure of that. The first step in experiencing is to be aware of the countless things ready to be experienced.

Second, *be aware, however, that humans naturally seem to "screen out" much of this stimuli.* As I sit writing, there is no way for me to experience everything that is a stimulus: the watch on my wrist, the smell (I call it the aroma) of my pipe, the sound of the air conditioner, the degree of lighting, the sound of the typewriter, the feel of the keys against my fingers (both of them), and so on. I *can* become aware of all these and others. But I have to stop, pause, and consider them. Normally, I am unaware of most of them. This ability to ignore stimulation is a necessary part of leading a normal life. Picture yourself beginning a conversation with a friend. Now *think* about the socks or hose you have on, the feel of the shirt, pants, dress, or shorts you are wearing, the jewelry you have on, the tightness of any undergarments you're wearing, and the fit and nature of your shoes. Now try to talk. In order to converse, some of these stimuli—and probably all of them—have to be ignored. And the ones mentioned have only to do with

things "felt" physically. Also screened out would be a variety of stimuli having to do with sights, sounds, smells, certain thoughts, particular feelings, and so on. For you to function as a human being, most of the stimuli bombarding you will have to be ignored. The natural tendency to pay attention to only certain things is made even more effective by training: "Oh, pay no attention to: A, Uncle Ralph; B, The *New York Times;* C, bad breath; D, religious fanatics; E, (fill in the blank)." Humans, by nature and training, screen out much of what they can experience. Experiencing things better depends in part on realizing this.

Third, experiencing means you *know that you can become more open to the stimuli around you.* Clearly, there are things around you and feelings and thoughts within you that you would rather ignore forever. Yet just as humans seem to be quite able to screen out things, they can learn to be

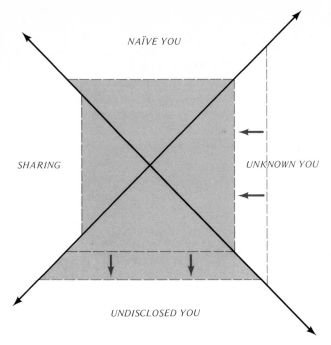

*Figure 12-1
Being
appreciatively
aware*

NAÏVE YOU

SHARING

UNKNOWN YOU

UNDISCLOSED YOU

aware of them. Time and effort are probably the critical factors here. Are you willing to spend the time and effort to become aware of your internal and external stimuli? A popular singer once sang of taking time to smell roses. That should be considered an analogy: No one I know spends much time smelling roses. Yet it does take time and effort for one to be aware of the pleasant, sometimes exhilarating, stimuli in the external environment: the sight of the first spring flower, the crisp cold of a winter day (where I live), the smell of the spring air when the gases begin to rise from the earth, the feel of sunshine on a wintered skin (also, where I live). In the same way, time and effort are required for you to "stay in touch with yourself." That is, there must be moments alone, or at least quiet moments, to "sort out" your thinking and feeling and how you are changing. The "doer" has no desire to take the time or to spend the effort in experiencing. He or she is too busy being busy. What Lana wanted in the opening case was a chance simply to sit quietly with David. He seemed unable to "do" this, because to him it seemed like doing nothing. True, no jobs would be done and no tasks would be completed. But something more important would have occurred. David might have begun to realize the love and warmth that Lana offered him and which he felt for her.

In describing the conception of experiencing earlier, I used the phrase "appreciatively aware." So far the discussion has focused on being aware. But finally, experiencing can be achieved best if you *learn to appreciate the value of these newly received stimuli.* Cloudy days are not necessarily without beauty, though I prefer sunshine. The "old man down the block" may also be appreciated as a person of quaint charm. The feelings of discomfort in a relationship can lead to a fresh awareness of who you are and what you want from life. Surely, it is easy to appreciate the more obviously pleasant things in your life. Just as necessary, though, is your ability to appreciate the value—whatever it is—in these new things reaching your consciousness. The direct result of appreciative awareness is that you open yourself to wider and wider circles of clearness about yourself and to things around you.

By being appreciatively aware, you have the opportunity of reducing the "unknown you." There is less that occurs around and in you that escapes your notice. Less of your world is unknown to you. The result is illustrated in Figure 12-1. Note that these changes in the "unknown" you do not automatically increase any of the "shared" you. The decreases in the "unknown" you lead only to an increase in the "undisclosed" you—unless, of course, you and another experience these stimuli together. And the process of "discovering together" is our next concern.

Sharing . . .
discoveries

Experiencing can lead to sharing of two somewhat different kinds. As just discussed, experienced stimuli can "move from" the unknown you and "into" the undisclosed you. When that happens you can share something of this new undisclosed you, making it part of the shared you. Experiencing, then, can *indirectly* result in sharing. Consider Figure 12-2. Yet a second and more direct way of sharing through experiencing occurs when two peo-

Figure 12-2
Being
appreciatively
aware, and then
self-disclosing

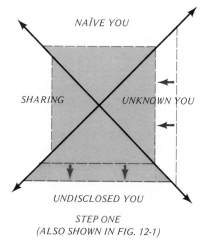

STEP ONE
(ALSO SHOWN IN FIG. 12-1)

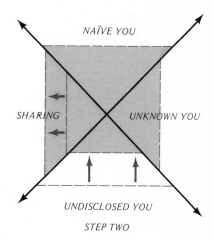

STEP TWO

143

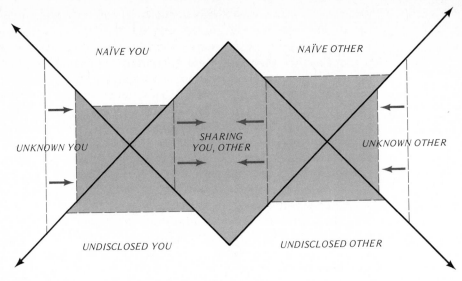

Figure 12-3
Sharing (directly)
discoveries

NAÏVE YOU

NAÏVE OTHER

UNKNOWN YOU

SHARING
YOU, OTHER

UNKNOWN OTHER

UNDISCLOSED YOU

UNDISCLOSED OTHER

ple experience or discover things together. Note the difference in Figure 12-3.

Sharing discoveries, then, *is nothing more than two people deepening their relationship by* jointly *experiencing feelings, sensations, thought, and events.* Notice that this is not the same as simply sharing joint activity. David and Lana earlier in the chapter were sharing the physical scene of the apartment, the seating on the sofa, and the activity of drinking. And yet David seemed unable to join Lana in actually experiencing what they could have shared together. He was willing to engage in all sorts of physical activity and diversions but was unwilling to engage in what Lana desired: the experience of a quiet, intimate togetherness. Together they could have shared the discovery of how good it was to sit on the sofa, to feel the closeness of each other, to be alone and quiet and relaxed, and to establish something approaching a communal relationship. When Lana tried to express her need for such mutual discovery, David misinterpreted it as sexual desire—and then was confused when that was obviously not what she intended to ask.

The techniques for better sharing of discoveries are mostly a modification of experiencing. Two people need to *be aware that there are countless stimuli that help define their relationship:* a touch on the arm, a knowing smile, a hint of frustration, a wisp of perfume, a special warmth. Second, however, they need to *realize that many of these stimuli can be taken for granted or ignored:* a perfume that goes unnoticed, a comment that hurts, the nonverbal request for tenderness. Third, it is important to *remember that both people can become much more aware of the stimuli that are part of the relationship.* Taking the time and making the effort to notice moods, feelings, new hairstyles, and so forth are not just ways of being overly romantic. In fact, romance has nothing directly to do with it. These same approaches can help relationships between friends, co-workers, family members — any two people — who are interested in establishing a communing relationship.

A direct result of sharing experiences or discoveries is that two people, simultaneously, decrease their unknown selves and increase the self they share with the other. They become closer to one another because they "have been there," "they know what (each) you mean," "they've been through it" together. There is a cliché that "experience is the best teacher"; it is also the case that joint experience and mutual discoveries are perhaps the best teachers about the relationship. The jointly experienced discoveries and the sharing of discoveries about each person become crucial in seeking a deeper and more satisfying relationship. The sharing of discoveries can become a key in the move toward communion.

To illustrate this, let's return to David and Lana. This time David begins to understand the need for the sharing of experiences. Toward the end of the original dialogue, David was saying,

. . . it is important to remember that both people can become much more aware of the stimuli that are part of the relationship. [Franken, Stock, Boston]

Okay, I'll go.

I don't want you to go.

Make up your mind. . . . What do you want me to do?

David, I don't want you to *do* anything. I really only want to enjoy the evening with you—not TV, records, or anything else. I want to be with you.

Oh. . . . I see. . . . Will you come back over here?

DAVID!

I'll be good . . . Scout's honor. . . .

(She laughs) I happen to know that you were never a Scout. . . . But I'll trust you anyway.

I don't think you ever said that before. . . .

I have never been able to trust you! Just kidding. . . . Well, not really. I guess I meant it, but I never thought of it before.

Silence.

You know, Lana, this doesn't feel too bad. The quiet, the soft sofa . . . you . . .

I don't feel so tired. . . .

Do you want to go bowling then? . . . Just a joke, Lana.

I hope, so, because, no, I do not want to go bowling. . . . I have never in my life wanted to go bowling less. . . .

Me, too. Ummmmmmmmm. . . . I could stay like this forever. . . .

Don't you want a taco, David?

Ha! . . . But, no, I don't care for a taco. . . . You *are* feeling better, aren't you?

I have never felt better. . . . I have never enjoyed us more, David. . . .

Even though we're willing to waste the entire evening doing nothing?

No, David, *because* we are willing to waste the entire evening doing nothing . . . except enjoying our time.

The change in David may seem a bit abrupt, and yet it may not be unrealistic. Children are taught how to read, write, play games—both child and adult games. Seldom are they taught how simply to enjoy the time with someone else, even when "there is nothing to do." And yet learning to discover and experience jointly is not difficult. The keys to sharing discoveries are awareness of the need and a mutual desire to share. The decision to take the time and to spend the effort is crucial in the establishment of a communing relationship.

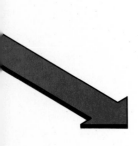

CHAPTER SUMMARY

As the third of three related chapters, this chapter explained how the shared self can be expanded by decreasing the area called the "unknown self." In order to decrease the unknown self, people must become constantly aware of what they are seeing, doing, and feeling.

A decrease in the unknown self does not come automatically from "doing" things. Being active, seeing new sights, reading new books, and meeting new people do not ensure personal growth—much less, a better relationship between two people.

Instead of "doing," which may actually increase the unknown area, the chapter emphasized "experiencing." Experiencing new activity, new sights and new books, and new people may all decrease the unknown area. But then, sitting alone in the sun may also decrease the unknown area if the person is truly aware of the surrounding stimuli.

In interpersonal relationships, sharing experiences or sharing discoveries is a way that two people can increase their shared selves by jointly experiencing themselves and each other. Sharing discoveries can be a tremendous help in building toward the communing relationship.

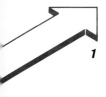

LEARNING BY APPLYING

1   In the mid-1970s many people became aware of the differences between "A"- and "B"-type personalities. The "A"-type personalities are people who seem to be driven to work, to achieve, to remain busy. Besides the fact that these people tend to be prime candidates for heart trouble, they are also people who may be "doers" as I use the term. Do you know anyone like this? Are you one yourself? Is it possible to be dynamic, busy, and highly competitive, and still have the capacity to experience? Explain your thoughts.

2   Take a small child you know for a walk, or at least observe very small children (3 to 5 years old) at a park or nursery school playground. Notice their tendency to find "magic" in pretty rocks, fallen leaves, dandelions or other weeds, bottle caps, and so on. You may find it more common for them to enjoy pure "experience," no matter how simple the experience. Thoreau, Wordsworth, and others constantly seemed to view the world through the eyes of an eager child. Can we all take lessons from children, and apply what we learn to our interpersonal relationships?

3   Contrast times when you have been walking with a friend discussing school, business, or other matters with times you have simply been walking with a friend. Notice how much easier it is to share random thoughts, feelings, and ideas in the second situation.

4   You are lying in the cool grass, under a tree or on a hillside. The sun is bright and the fragrance of spring is in the air. There is nothing special to do, or to talk about. With whom would you like to share such a moment? What does this tell you about the special importance of sharing . . . discoveries—even when there is nothing earthshaking to discover.

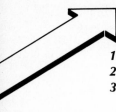

LEARNING
BY DISCUSSING

1 Discuss, in your own words, the meaning of "doing."
2 Explain important differences you see between doing and experiencing.
3 Explain how "sharing experiences" is different from two people simply doing something together.
4 How can an appreciation of "sharing experiences" help your efforts in building and maintaining better relationships?

LEARNING
BY READING FURTHER

Friedman, Maurice S., *Martin Buber: The Life of Dialogue*. New York: Harper Torchbooks, 1960.

O'Banion, Terry, and O'Connell, April, *The Shared Journey: An Introduction to Encounter*. Englewood Cliffs, NJ: Prentice-Hall, 1970.

Powell, John, S. J., *Why Am I Afraid to Tell You Who I Am?* Chicago: Argus Communications, 1969.

Rogers, Carl R., *On Becoming a Person*. Boston: Houghton Mifflin, 1961.

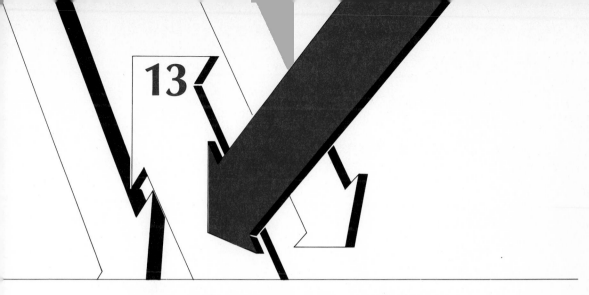

AUTHENTICITY: THE SOUL OF COMMUNION
(A CONCLUSION TO CHAPTERS 10, 11, and 12)

STUDY OF THIS CHAPTER WILL ENABLE YOU TO

- *understand "dialogue" as high levels of interpersonal communication*
- *understand "authenticity" as an interpersonal ethic*
- *understand the elements of authenticity*
- *adopt the ethic of authenticity as an approach to the development of communion*

In the preceding chapters the notion of sharing has been examined from three different perspectives. The mutual sharing of selves, feedback, and discoveries are vital in aiming toward a communing relationship with another. The communing relationship is not easy to establish. But good interpersonal communication can aid your efforts to share, and sharing is the heart of communion.

The relationship that progresses toward communion is a very special one; one that poses its own problems. For example, all relationships are affected by norms and "rules." What are the norms and rules of communion? All people seem to have some response to ethics, even if they deny that ethics are important. What would be an ethic, or code of behavior, for relationships aiming toward a communal level?

Contemporary writings about "dialogue"[1] can be used to create an ethic for communion that can be called "authenticity."[2] In its simplest form, authenticity is a code of behavior that calls for people to treat one another with the respect that human beings deserve. That seems very abstract, I suspect. Authenticity could also be compared to the "golden rule" in its best sense: treating others as you would have them act toward you. But authenticity goes beyond even the popular interpretations of the golden rule. Perhaps the best way to explain authenticity is to describe its characteristics, and then build a definition.[3]

---

[1] Much of the material on the characteristics of authenticity is based solidly on Richard L. Johannesen, "The Emerging Concept of Communication as Dialogue," *Quarterly Journal of Speech* 57 (December 1971):373–382.

[2] There is general agreement that all human interaction takes place within the concept of some sort of ethic — some formal or informal code of appropriateness and propriety.

[3] The material in this section is based on three primary sources: F. J. Murphy and James Otten, "The Golden Rule of Dialogue: A Philosophy of Ethics and Communication" (unpublished manuscript); F. J. Murphy, "Authenticity in Dialogue: An Ethic of Human Communication" (unpublished manuscript); and an untitled article-length manuscript by R. E. Crable and F. J. Murphy.

The first element of authenticity is what can be called *"unconditional positive regard": a valuing of the worth of people.* With an ethic of authenticity you regard the other person *and* yourself as special examples of creation.
It doesn't matter whether you or the other have particular problems, flaws,
faults, or hang-ups. Beneath these imperfections lies a human being—
whether you or the other. You do not have to approve or overlook the flaws
in both of you—nor do you have to dwell on them. You do not have to be so
optimistic as to think that all people are supremely wonderful. You only
have to regard them as people. Perhaps the greatest tragedies in history
have begun when some people thought a certain group was subhuman. The
results have been slavery, genocide, or senseless wars. In war it is commonplace to train soldiers to kill the enemy—an enemy not of people, but of
krauts, chinks, or pigs. Surely, most people never think of others as nonhuman. Yet all of us have been nasty to salespeople, children, grouches, or
bums--someone, who for an instant, was not treated as a human. Consider
the following.

Polly, pick up your things! Your room's always a mess.
Ah, mom. . . .
I said to pick up in your room. It looks like a pig sty.
But, mom. . . .
DO IT. AND, I MEAN NOW!
But I was trying to finish . . .
Do you hear me, I said straighten your room!
I just wanted to finish drawing you this picture. . . .
Oh . . . well. . . . Thank you. . . .

The ethic of authenticity reminds us that all human transactions involve *humans*—humans who generally deserve more respect than they receive.

Authenticity also implies a *"spirit of mutual equality": an avoidance
of attempts to control a perceived inferior.* Not everyone is equally talented, equally intelligent, or equally attractive. In some situations you may
well be tempted to control, mold, or "guide" the other person—or the roles
may be reversed. Still the communing relationship is built on mutual self-
control. Attempts at dominating or using power are *not* steps toward communion. You and the other person should be free to exercise your own
choices, and to make your own mistakes. This does not mean that feedback,
for example, is not appropriate, but simply that coercion, either physical or
psychological, is not desirable. The nagging wife, the man "who wears the
pants," the henpecked husband, the "weak sister"—usually a man—and
many others are stereotypes that can and should be avoided. In any relationship there will be some inequality. In a given situation one or the other
might, and perhaps should, dominate. The two people still can maintain an

"authentic" perspective. The specific opportunity to take charge should not lead to a general attempt to control:

> . . . and then he said, "Listen. . . ."
>
> I've heard enough. Laura, if you really want my advice, I'll give it. Drop him like a frog with a rash. He's no good, I tell you. . . . Lucky you came to me when you did. I've seen his kind before. Your father was like that . . . rest his nasty soul . . . and I should have divorced him long before he died. I'll tell you another thing: If you would just pay more attention to classes and less time mooning over every . . .

The communing relationship is built on mutual respect and individual worth. At no time should control become more important than a spirit of mutual equality.

A third characteristic of authenticity has to do with *"presentness": a constant focus on the present instead of the past or the future.* The relationship developing exists in the present. What it *was*, it can never be again. What it *will become* is not knowable. But what it *is* can be cared for and nurtured. There are great risks, and probably little chance of reward, in discussing past sins, old problems, or even the glories of the past. In the same way, speculation about the future can shift the focus from what is happening now. Focusing on either the past or the future can confuse perceptions of the relationship at present.

> . . . But, Katherine, she's simply a girl from the office. I hardly even know her.
>
> Yes, I know: She always calls perfect strangers "Buzz Baby."
>
> Oh, that. . . . That's just a kind of nickname—you know, kind of a friendly . . .
>
> Yes, she looked friendly, all right.
>
> I've had it, Katherine. If you are so concerned about innocent flirting, then why did you join your ol' high school boy friend for a carryon reunion?
>
> Carry*in*, Buzz; not carry*on*.
>
> You didn't seem to know the difference. . . .
>
> Are you saying that I . . .
>
> You are always flirting with someone, Katherine.
>
> And what about you, *Buzz Baby*? You always spend a lot of extra time at the company. Does your friend take shorthand, or does she just work there!?
>
> Hah! Really humorous, Katherine. What about Gus?
>
> Gus who?
>
> Gus our neighbor, Gus our, I-didn't-mean-to-bother-you-while-you-are-sunbathing-but-could-I-borrow-your-shovel neighbor. . . . That Gus. Remember him?
>
> I hardly ever talk to him.
>
> Just a matter of time, huh, Katherine? . . .
>
> Why you . . .

Notice that in this situation the entire focus of the discussion began on past doubts and future fears. That, of course, was not the only problem

The relationship developing exists in the present. What it was, it can never be again. What it will become is not knowable. [Collidge, Taurus]

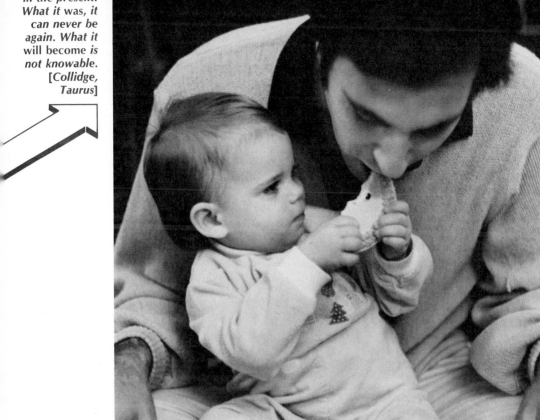

Buzz and Katherine had in communicating. Still a concentration on the present would have been helpful. In short, the people moving toward a communing relationship will focus on themselves at present, their relationship as it exists in the moment, and what they can do that will help the relationship and each other.

Fourth, authenticity has to do with *"genuineness": a basic honesty and an absence of interpersonal games.* Communing individuals—or ones who are seeking such a relationship seriously—do not need to play roles extensively with one another. There is no need to play "Look how macho I am!" "Come and get me, you brute!" "Look at me I ain't chicken!" "Aren't I cultured?" "I'm a laugh a minute!" or any other childish game. Some human situations perhaps call for games: you are invited to the family reunion ("My, how you've grown!"); you are seeking your first job ("Wow, I love to work on Saturdays!"); a friend asks you what you think of a new yellow, pink, and olive drab outfit that cost one hundred dollars ("Boy, that's something, all right—gonna wear that tonight, huh?"). But if those situations seem to call for game playing—dishonesty—it's because the individuals involved are not prepared to aim for a communing relationship. That's no problem. Not every relationship you have can be so intimate. But when the desire is for a communing relationship, genuineness is a vital factor. Consider the following:

What do you think of the new advertising campaign, Wellington?
Huh, gee, I hardly know where to begin. . . . It's so . . . original, yes, that's it. It's
    original.
How long have you worked with me, Wellington?
I've worked with you for five years, ever since my husband and I married. . . .
And do you know why I said "worked with me" instead of "for me"?
Uh . . . no.
Because I have always depended on you for an honest evaluation—straight from the
    shoulder—no holds barred.
I see.
What do you think of the campaign—*really*?
Well . . . I think it stinks. It has all the charm of a wet caterpillar and all the vitality
    of a wounded snail. . . . I just think the whole thing needs rethinking. . . .
Well, Wellington, I think you're absolutely right. And I want you to give some
    thought to it over the weekend.
Goodbye . . . *(sighs)* . . . The weekend? . . .

There may be a time and place for interpersonal game playing. But relationships growing deeper present neither the time, nor place.

Finally, authenticity is characterized most basically by *a modified version of the golden rule: Behave toward others as you would have them behave toward you—assuming you liked, respected, and valued yourself.*[4] As a factor in authenticity, this means that you treat the other as fairly, as lovingly as you possibly can. You actually envision yourself as the other person, and then decide how you would like to be treated. Sometimes the result

---

[4] Given the extremely poor self-image of some individuals, the rule is modified to *assume* positive self-images as a guide to behavior.

of this is a happy decision: Wouldn't *you* wish to be told how much you are loved by another, again and again, at precisely the right moment? Sometimes the result of this imaginary role switching is less happy: Wouldn't *you* wish to know if you had only a few months to live?

In actuality, this last element of authenticity – the enactment of the modified golden rule – is based on the other characteristics. The rule can only be applied if you, first, value yourself and the other person as human beings despite what you interpret as flaws. The rule can only be applied if you assume equality between you and the other. You can only pretend to switch places fairly if there is no perceived difference in status. The rule can only be applied when there is a concern for what is good *now* – not yesterday, and not next week. The rule can only be applied in a context of basic honesty and genuineness: after all, you may have to take risks. But the rule can be applied. You and another can treat each other as you would want to be treated.

From these characteristics of authenticity the term itself can be defined. *"Authenticity" can be considered the genuine application of the golden rule between perceived equals who value one another and their relationship with a sense of ongoing presentness.* Sharing may be the heart of communion. But it is the continuous sense of ethics that guides and directs the development of the relationship. In sum, an ethic of authenticity can be the soul of communion.

CHAPTER SUMMARY

The chapter is really a conclusion to Chapters 10, 11, and 12, as well as to Chapter 9, which introduces those chapters. The focus in those chapters is on the general importance of sharing and how mutual self-disclosure, mutual feedback, and sharing discoveries can help decrease the undisclosed you, the naïve you, and the unknown you. The result, almost automatically, is an increase in the shared self by both people involved.

This chapter created a code of behavior, or an "ethic" for that sharing. The elements of "authenticity" were described and illustrated. As a modification of the golden rule, authenticity means that you behave toward another as you would wish the person to behave toward you—assuming that you liked, respected, and valued yourself. Such an attitude toward behavior—such an ethic—can be the soul of the communing relationship.

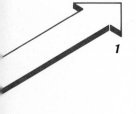

LEARNING
BY APPLYING

1 *What do you understand an "ethic" to be? Once in a small town a local elected official used official city stationery to write a letter of endorsement about a local insurance company. The letter was copied and sent to 2000 people as a way of soliciting stockholders. This official, it turns out, owns a small amount of stock in the company. No one in the city or county government could find a law that had been broken, so everyone concluded that the matter was closed. Discuss whether you think there was an ethical problem here, regardless of whether there was a legal problem. Is something "right" just because it is not legally wrong? Explain your position. Now, how does your position affect how you think two people ought to act toward one another?*

2 Recall any incidents in your life when you have felt "used," "misled," or "hurt" by someone else's actions. Would these actions have occurred if the other person had acted in a spirit of "authenticity"? Be specific.

3 Discuss the ideas involved in "authenticity." Are there other factors that you think ought to be added? If so, what are they? Are any of the factors unclear to you? If so, how could you clarify them?

4 Consider your relationships in general with other people. Do you think that your behavior and communication toward others tend to be authentic? Is it easier to be authentic with people whom you love, or is it more difficult? Explain. Are there things you can do to improve the authenticity of your relationships? Explain — if even to yourself!

LEARNING BY DISCUSSING

1 Explain the concept of dialogue as you understand it.
2 What do you mean by the word ethic? Do you see that an ethic can be a guiding principle in every form of human transaction?
3 Explain the nature of "authenticity."
4 Explain how a knowledge of "authentic" behavior can help your communication in building better relationships.

LEARNING BY READING FURTHER

Buber, Martin, *Between Man and Man.* Trans. Ronald Gregor Smith. New York: Macmillan Paperbacks, 1965.

Friedman, Maurice S., *Martin Buber: The Life of Dialogue.* New York: Harper Torchbooks, 1960.

Johannesen, Richard L., "The Emerging Concept of Communication as Dialogue." *Quarterly Journal of Speech* 57 (December 1971):373–382.

Rapopart, Anatol, *Strategy of Conscience.* New York: Harper & Row, 1964.

Rogers, Carl, *On Becoming a Person.* Boston: Houghton Mifflin, 1961.

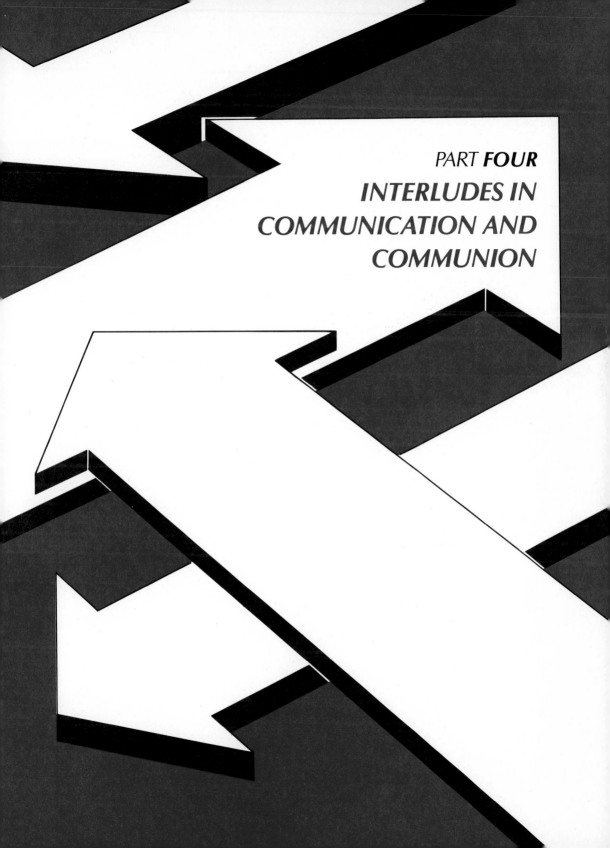

PART **FOUR**

*INTERLUDES IN
COMMUNICATION AND
COMMUNION*

LISTENING AT, LISTENING TO, AND LISTENING WITH

Hey, Dad, I'm back from the game. . . . Oops, I didn't know you were watching the
    baseball game. . . .
That's all right. . . . How did the game go? WOW! Did you see that error?
Yeah, who was that?
Rose—he doesn't miss many of those.
Yeah! . . . It went great. We won.
Won what?
The game. We played against Willie's Sports Center and Laundry. We beat them 34
    to 27. . . . Close game.
I'll say it is. Bottom of the eighth, one man on, two outs, and the score tied.
I meant ours.
Our what? Look at that. . . . He swung on a three–nothing count!
Not "ours" . . . MINE!
I'm sorry. Your what?
We won our game today against . . .
Great. You really have come along. You might even make it in the . . . Look at that,
    will you? Strike Two!
Yeah, I might.
Might what?
Play in the pros.
Yeah. What position did you play?
Pitcher.
Oh, the pitcher's doing okay. . . . He just needs . . .
I meant me.
You, what?
Never mind.
Strike three. That does it. Okay, now here's a commercial, Kile . . . Kile? . . . Hey,
    Kile, how did the team do today?
(From upstairs) Okay, I guess. We won.

162

Listening at　　Listening has been described as an "art." This means, I guess, that not everyone does it well; there is some kind of ability called the "ability to listen" that some people have and others do not. On the other hand, in communication, listening is usually viewed as a "skill," which means supposedly that everyone can listen if trained to do so. Perhaps the skill of listening can be taught, but the basic factor in listening is *interest*, not training.

In the case study the father may or may not have been a "born listener," nor have been educated in listening. Those two facts are not clear from the conversation. What is perfectly clear, though, is that he was not seriously *interested* in listening. The case may have seemed somewhat exaggerated, but I will argue that it is not at all unusual. People – and not only parents – frequently engage in much the same kind of behavior described here. They do not really listen; they *listen at* the person. Let me explain.

"Listening at" a person means, first, that the *two people can hear one another.* One of the traditional misconceptions about listening problems is that they frequently are *hearing problems.* Clearly, many people suffer from some degree of hearing loss. When that is the case, listening may be more difficult. But communication researchers agree that most listening problems are not at all related to hearing problems. So "listening at" another person means that some degree of hearing occurs but yet little listening is done. The father heard some part of what his son was saying, but yet he listened very little.

"Listening at" another person means, second, that *there is some pretense or effort to listen.* Sometimes people will make an effort to listen and somehow fail to do it effectively. In the case study the father seemed, at least, to be trying to listen even though he almost completely failed. At other times, a person will simply pretend to be listening. For whatever reason, the person does not want to listen but feels compelled to act as if listening is occurring. While this seems less sincere than the father's effort, the result is the same. Little listening actually occurs.

Third, "listening at" means that there will probably be *some verbal behavior that suggests listening is occurring.* People who pretend to listen – or who are failing in their effort to listen – may still use the verbal phrases that people use when they actually listen. "Go on," "I see," "Yeah, boy," and "What do you know?" are common examples. From the process of growing up and being with people, all of us know the standard things to say as we listen. But then, we can use the same phrases even when we are not listening. The father went even further, by asking questions as the "conversation" continued. Now he may not have been completely conscious of his questions nor have listened for the answers, but he said the kinds of things that people say when they are really listening. In the same way, the person who simply pretends to listen can take advantage of these phrases.

Finally, "listening at" means that there probably will be *some nonver-*

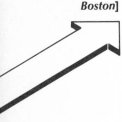

bal behavior that suggests listening is occurring. You are probably more familiar with this idea than you think. Let me give you a personal example. When I was a student, I was enrolled in at least my share of (what I considered) dull and uninteresting classes. Although it seemed usually dangerous not to listen, I just could not bring myself to do it. So I would give all the nonverbal signs I knew that said to the professor, "Hey, I am really interested!" I would furrow my brow, jot down notes every once in a while, nod seriously at times (hoping that it was appropriate), and smile when it appeared everyone else did. In essence, I played a game with the professor—a game which, as far as I know, I always won. I probably devoted more effort at pretending to listen than I would have if I had actually tried to listen. No matter. It was kind of entertaining for me.

But classrooms are not the only place where this happens. Anytime someone thinks listening is appropriate—if not possible—one can probably engage in some kind of nonverbal behavior that suggests listening. Though we do not have a visual description of the father and the young ball player, no doubt eyebrows were being raised and smiles and nods were evident. Little actual listening, however, was occurring.

"Listening at" another person, then, is an important part of the interpersonal situation. Poor listening can lead to serious interpersonal problems. Fortunately, people can learn to listen better. Certain attitudes and actions can help anyone become a better listener.

Listening to　"Listening at" another person means in general that you are hearing to some extent, but only "sort of" listening. In contrast, "listening to" another person means that you are *really* listening. The key to listening to another person lies with a factor we have discussed before: interest. In order to listen you must have some interest in listening. That may seem a little simplistic and idealistic, but let me explain. Sometimes you will simply be interested in listening because of your interest in the other person. On the other hand, sometimes you will listen because of your interest in finding out what the other person has to say. The difference between these two "interests" is important. It may be easy, for example, to listen to a close friend, a lover, or a member of your family – you simply care a great deal about them as people. I suspect that this will not always be the case. Sometimes you may not care much for the other, but you need or want to hear what he or she has to say. In this latter situation what is said is more important than who is speaking.

In still other cases you may be interested because you *have* to be. In a classroom, for instance, there may be rewards and punishments for different degrees of actual listening. In this instance, or when you are on the job, listening may be important whether or not you like the other person or think that what he or she has to say is important. In sum, interest, even if you have to force it a bit, is a key attitude for better listening.

The question remains: How can listening be improved in the interpersonal situation? There are several strategies that can be helpful.[1]

First, *search* – and it may take some effort – *for some good reason for listening.* The attitude of interest can be created most easily by finding something of value in what the other person has to say. Should you listen simply because this is a close friend? Should you listen because what she says might help you, even if the "she" is not a close friend? Is there *something* of value *somewhere* here? My personal experience is that almost anything someone says can be of value. I may learn a new idea, a different way of saying something, a new perspective on some matter, or just learn more about the nature of the individual. Admittedly, I do not always find value in what people say. Still I have found something of interest in some of the least likely conversations. Although it may take effort, communication

---

[1] Many of these strategies have become traditional bits of advice. One good early treatment of listening – and listening strategies – is by probably the leading expert in the field of listening. See Ralph G. Nichols, "Listening is a Ten-Part Skill," *Nation's Business* 45 (July 1957). Several of the strategies listed here are similar to those developed in Richard E. Crable, *Using Communication* (Boston: Allyn and Bacon, 1979), chap. 9.

scholars agree that listening can be improved by *searching* for some good reason for listening.

Second, *try to be in a physical and emotional state that allows listening to occur.* Being physically tired, too hungry, or sleepy does not aid the listening effort – in class, on the job, or when the children are being tucked in for the night. In the same way, emotional fatigue or distress can hinder listening. When physical or emotional stresses make it difficult to listen, at least two choices are open: (1) You can try to "fight off" the problems for the time being, particularly on the job or in class. (2) You can try to postpone the conversation until you are better able to really listen. You might, for example, try not to talk about financial matters or child discipline when you are tired or "out of sorts." When a relationship is ongoing, we frequently can put the discussion off until the chances of good mutual listening are better. The point is that being emotionally and physically able to listen well can be important.

Third, *give your full attention to the other person.* A friend of mine has discovered what I think is a great concept: convention ballet – referring to professional gatherings where people are milling around a hotel lobby, for example. He has noticed that as people are speaking and listening they are looking past the other person, seeking another familiar face. When both individuals do this (and they frequently do), the result is a kind of perpetual turning and looking which could be set to music. What happens is that one or both are not giving full attention to the listening–talking process. Unfortunately, this also occurs away from conventions. People listen while doodling, watching TV, looking at passing cars, and so on. Good listening requires more complete attention to the other person. Otherwise, "listening to" becomes "listening at."

Better listening can be achieved, fourth, if you *do not fall behind in the conversation.* I suspect you have experienced times when you were "half-listening" and suddenly responded to something said earlier – something irrelevant to the present conversation. You may have apologized saying, "I guess I drifted off for a minute," or "I'm sorry, I just thought of . . ." However the situation is explained, the problem is the same. It is all too easy to fall behind in a conversation.

Fifth, it is important that you *do not race ahead in the conversation.* This may not be advice often given. Still, I think, it is among the most important of listening skills. Let me give you an example.

Professor	Ah, yes, did you want to see me?
Student	Yes, I had a problem with the assignment. . . .
Professor	You were here when I gave the assignment?
Student	Yes, what I don't understand . . .
Professor	Just take a contemporary advertisement in a magazine and apply the principles of persuasion. Evaluate the ad in terms of those principles.

Student	Yes, I don't have a problem with that. What I want to know is . . .
Professor	And then you make a judgment about whether or not the ad is well conceived, and why.
Student	What do you mean by "contemporary"?
Professor	Is that all? I just mean within the past year, or so. Does that do it?
Student	Yes. Thanks.
Professor	Always have time for my students!

If you think the example is exaggerated, begin observing how some of your friends listen. You may find them starting to answer a question before it is asked – and before they understand exactly what you mean. You may find them finishing sentences for you – maybe in ways different from how you intended it. They may nod a head and begin to say "Yes, yes" even before you are finished. Such behaviors are not vicious. The result, though, is that actual listening suffers. A longer term result may be that people who race ahead in every conversation find fewer and fewer people talking to them.

Sixth and finally, good listening can be better ensured if you *do not immediately evaluate what you are hearing.* People frequently begin disagreeing with an idea that has not even been completed by shaking a head. They may begin to interrupt or, at the very least, may begin to think of how they will respond. All of this is at the expense of really listening to the complete idea of the other person. And obviously, none of this aids the total listening process. You obviously have the right to disagree with another. The major idea is that your evaluation should be postponed at least until he or she has finished speaking.

The major problem with these listening strategies is that they are easier to learn than to put into practice. Time and again I have seen students correctly answer questions on a test related to these strategies. Then I have seen them fail to implement the strategies in classroom work. These strategies take more than memorization; they require constant attention and thought. In order to listen better, you need to listen to yourself and to observe what *you* do as you listen. Only by correcting yourself and putting into practice the strategies discussed will you increase your skill in listening *to* other people.

The strategies of "listening to" have involved what you can do to increase your listening efficiency and thereby avoid interpersonal problems based on poor listening habits. Listening to another person can be of help in class, on the job, and in your personal life. Still in those relationships that you want to deepen and broaden – in relationships whose goal is communion – other factors are involved.

Listening with   Most of the research into listening has involved how people listen to speeches. The strategies just discussed that can help you listen *to* the other person are mainly the result of that kind of research. When your interest is

167

in listening, the goal of comprehension is most important: Do you now know what the other person was trying to say? What I call "listening to" another person emphasizes *what* one person communicates with another. What I shall discuss here as "listening with" another person stresses not only *what*, but *how* two people communicate together. *In addition to* emphasizing the *content* of the communication—the *what*—"listening with" also emphasizes the *relationship* of the communication—the *who.*

The reason for my stress on the relationship is that in communing relationships the transmission of ideas may not be very important. Of more importance may be the feelings, love, or caring between two people. If that is the case, listening *to* the ideas of the other may not be so important as understanding feelings. Let me provide an example of two different conversations.

Harry   I am so tired. That math test I finished was really something. I get so frustrated I
        don't know what to do.
Alice   How do you think you did on the test?
Harry   I don't know. . . . Who can tell. I study and study, and it doesn't seem to help.
Alice   Did you go to class regularly?
Harry   Yeah. That's not the problem. It's just . . . Oh, I don't know.
Alice   Well, we could try to study together. Maybe that would help.
Harry   Yeah, well, maybe so.

Contrast what you have just read to the following:

Harry   I am so tired. That math test I finished was really something. I get so frustrated I
        don't know what to do.
Alice   You do look tired. And I know that you'd really studied for it.
Harry   Yeah, I study and study . . .
Alice   That's the frustrating part. You know how badly I do in theme writing. Who knows,
        though, you may have done better than you thought. You did on the last one.
Harry   I studied more for it this time, too.
Alice   Do you want to get a cup of coffee, and talk a little?
Harry   Yeah, let's do.

The two conversations begin exactly alike. Yet Alice uses a very different style of listening in the second example. Clearly, she was listening to Harry in the first conversation, but in the second she was doing more: She listened in a way that stressed the people and the relationship—not the math test itself. In this latter conversation Alice was listening *with* Harry. But what does that mean? How can the difference be described?[2]

Listening with another person, first, implies that you *listen with an*

---

[2] Notice that these strategies do not emphasize understanding messages as much as they do understanding the person speaking. Most studies of listening have focused on accuracy in comprehension. Our concern here is far more broad.

alertness to nonverbal cues. Harry was not simply talking about a math test. In addition, he was disclosing his feelings of frustration and disappointment. Maybe he was even revealing something of his general stress level when he talked of being tired. In the first example Alice ignored all these possibilities and concentrated on the math test. She was apparently listening well and understood what he was saying. However, she did not seem to understand how he was feeling. In the second example she noticed that he did look tired. From this alertness to nonverbal cues which probably accompanied his comments, she suggested a cup of coffee and a talk. She was concerned about Harry and how he felt.

Listening with another person means, second, that you *listen with empathy.*[3] In the latter example Alice listened and tried to put herself in Harry's place. She recognized something of the way he felt because she felt the same way about theme writing. Harry's problem was partly her problem, and she could begin to feel some of the frustration he felt. She began to understand and empathize with his feelings—regardless of how she felt about math tests. The specific idea of the math test was less important to her than Harry himself and their relationship.

Alice's empathy with Harry's problem allowed her, third, to *listen with sensitivity to the needs of the other person.* Alice assumed that Harry needed help with math. But his more immediate need was for a sympa-

---

[3] For an excellent discussion of empathic listening see Charles M. Kelly, "Empathic Listening," in *Small Group Communication: A Reader,* ed. Robert S. Cathcart and Larry Samovar (Dubuque, Ia.: Brown, 1970), pp. 251–259.

Yet there are times when the content is not as important as the people and the relationship. [*Gloria Karlson*]

thetic ear—someone to listen and to appreciate his frustration. And finally, Alice tried to *listen with the hope of helping meet those needs*. She *knew* he was tired, frustrated, and in need of a sympathetic ear. Perhaps she could not actually help him with the math score, but she could offer coffee, a chair, and the willingness to listen further. One person cannot always help meet the needs of the other. In this case it was possible for Alice to help Harry in an immediate and concrete way. Alice, however, had listened with alertness to nonverbal cues, with empathy, with a sensitivity to his needs, and with a willingness to help. The score of the test will not be affected. Alice's understanding of the math test was not improved in the second example, but one important difference did arise: Alice helped Harry. And in the process she herself may be helped and their relationship may become even deeper.

The communing relationship, then, can be helped by listening skills that are different from listening *to* the other person. Listening at times will be a matter simply of listening thoroughly for information and ideas. Yet there are times when the content is not as important as the people and the relationship. At such times, you will want to listen *with* the other person.

CHAPTER SUMMARY

The chapter was the first of 11 that describe certain "interludes," or potentially problematic situations or processes, in communication and human relationships.

Listening is a crucial part of interpersonal communication, and yet there are ways of "listening" that can actually harm relationships. "Listening at," as described in the chapter, is the act of pretending to listen. Whether done intentionally or accidentally, "listening at" can create antagonism and hurt interpersonal relationships.

"Listening to" another is much more preferable and the strategies that can improve your listening are explained. Still in interpersonal relationships, a different kind of listening is important: "listening with." "Listening with" another person means in general that you are emphasizing both the content of the ideas and your relationship with the other. Such listening can be an indispensable part of your effort to build deeper, closer relationships.

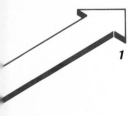

LEARNING
BY APPLYING

1   *It has become a joke in our culture that people often pretend to be listening when in fact they are not. The joke is often expressed in cartoons, monologues of comics, as well as in television programs. If you have any doubt*

about the prevalence of "listening at" behavior, concentrate on your con-versations over several days. When you think someone is "listening at" you, introduce an irrelevant idea, such as, "I sprained my ankle yesterday." The person may not respond to the idea—he or she was "listening at" you—or the person may suddenly begin "listening to" you.

2   *Collect cartoons, jokes, and stories about listening in general. Once you start being aware of the wealth of these, you may wish to separate them into categories. The characteristics of "listening at" can be used as possible cate-gories.*

3   *Whom do you know who is* your *best listener? What does she or he do that makes you so sure you're being "listened to"? Does this person listen better to you than to some others? Is there something special about your relation-ship that may account for this? Explain.*

4   *Keep track of your listening behavior during several days. Are there times during the day that you listen best? Does your listening improve in certain situations (e.g., in class, at work, in your apartment)? Do you listen best when you are in certain moods? Do you listen to people best when you are alone with a single person, in a small group, in a crowd—where? Now what does all this tell you about how you might wish to "prepare" when some-one says, "I really want to tell you something important!"?*

5   *"Listening to" someone is not the same thing as "listening with" someone. Are there special people in your life who seem to do more than just listen to the words you say? If so, how does that make you feel? Are there certain people with whom you have no particular empathy? Do you find yourself often just listening to the words? What effect might that have on the possi-bility of a deeper relationship?*

6   Try this one only with someone who is interested in your personal develop-ment. *When talking with a close friend, glance over his or her shoulder, doodle on a note pad, brush lint from your shirt, fail to look at the person, and/or periodically turn your body slightly away from the person. How does he or she react? How do you think people react when you do these things unconsciously? Carefully explain to your friend that this was an exer-cise, apologize for appearing not to listen, and see if each of you can learn from the activity.*

LEARNING BY DISCUSSING

1   *Describe the notion of "listening at." What interpersonal problems can that lead to?*

2   *Discuss the nature of "listening to." How can that help you to be a better communicator?*

3   *Discuss the concept of "listening with." How can an awareness of this approach help your relationships?*

LEARNING
BY READING FURTHER

Crable, Richard E., *Using Communication*. Boston: Allyn and Bacon, 1979, chap. 9.

Kelly, Charles M., "Empathic Listening" in *Small Group Communication: A Reader,* ed. Robert S. Cathcart and Larry A. Samovar, Dubuque, IA: Brown, 1960.

Nichols, Ralph G., "Do We Know How to Listen? Practical Helps in a Modern Age." *The Speech Teacher* 10 (1961):118–124.

15

QUARRELING, MANAGING CONFLICT, AND ARGUMENTATION

STUDY OF THIS CHAPTER WILL ENABLE YOU TO

- *understand the concept of "quarreling"*
- *understand the characteristics of quarreling*
- *understand the concept of "conflict"*
- *understand how conflict can be either positive or negative*
- *understand the importance of managing conflict*
- *understand strategies of managing conflict*
- *use strategies for managing conflict*
- *understand the concept of "argumentation"*
- *understand the basic features of argumentation*
- *use argumentation for making decisions in interpersonal situations*

May I help you, madam?

I certainly hope someone can. You see, this is the first time I've ever bought anything here, and I purchased a mixer that doesn't mix.

You are having trouble with this mixer, then?

Indeed, I am.

That's peculiar. . . . This is probably our best selling model.

Have you had many complaints about it?

We have had no complaints about it. . . . *(smiles)* . . . Until today.

Well, I assure you that it doesn't work. . . .

What makes you think that it doesn't work? . . .

What makes me think that it doesn't work is the fact that it doesn't work. Is that hard for you to understand?

Well, our policy of ensuring customer satisfaction has been very successful in the past. . . . I can assure you that . . .

I'm not satisfied. . . . What is your policy going to do now?

We shall certainly make every effort to satisfy you. One of our problems is that some people abuse the appliances they buy and then attempt to return them for a refund. . . .

Are you implying that I misused the mixer? . . .

"Abused" was the word I used, but all I am saying is that some people do abuse products. . . .

I don't.

You don't what?

Abuse products.

I didn't say that you did; I said . . .

Yes, you did. . . .

No, please forgive me, but I didn't say that you . . .

Yes, you did. I heard you.

I did no such thing. . . .

Did, too.
Did not.

Quarreling   "Quarreling" can be defined as *unproductive verbal disagreements between or among people.*[1] That seems to be a broad definition, but it is necessary. If you want to see a quarrel in progress, observe children playing "cops and robbers," "war," or some other shooting game. You may hear:

I got you.
No, you didn't. I got you first.
What? I got you—you know I did.
Got you.
Got you first.
and so on.

Quarreling does not just occur on playgrounds. In any election year you can hear:

You sure changed your stand on the issue. . . .
My worthy opponent seems to have forgotten that I adopted this viewpoint early and have retained it.
Since yesterday. . . .
I have remained consistent. . . .
You have not. . . .
Have, too. . . .
Have not. . . .

The example may be somewhat abbreviated and just a little exaggerated. Quarreling, though, is a familiar kind of human communication activity. A discussion may seem to be satisfying enough and, suddenly, it becomes something other than a "discussion." What changes? What are the characteristics of a "quarrel"?

First, *quarrels are composed primarily of "claims"*: statements meant to be believed, but which are either questioned or challenged in some way by the other person.[2] The most obvious example of claims in the opening case study was the final stage:

I didn't say you did. . . .
Yes, you did. . . .
. . . I didn't say that you . . .

---

[1] The definition is consistent with that in Richard E. Crable, *Argumentation as Communication: Reasoning with Receivers* (Columbus, O.: Merrill, 1976), pp. 11–13.
[2] The discussion of claims is based on the work of Professor Stephen Toulmin in *The Uses of Argument*, Report (Cambridge, England: Cambridge University Press, 1969). The explanation here is also related to that found in Crable, *Argumentation as Communication*, chap. 5.

"Quarreling" can be defined as unproductive verbal disagreements between or among people. [Southwick, Stock, Boston]

Yes, you did. . . .
I did no such thing. . . .
Did, too.
Did not.

Each of these statements was meant to be believed but was questioned or challenged by the other. So each was a claim. But notice also that there was almost nothing else mentioned *except* claims. *Why should anyone believe* that "We have had no complaints," or that "I don't abuse (products)," or that "Our policy of ensuring customer satisfaction has been very successful. . . ."? When the communication consists almost exclusively of claims — without any sort of support or reason to believe — a quarrel may well be in progress.

Second, *quarrels are characterized by the unwillingness of one person to examine the claims of the other person.* In the case, each person failed to provide any reason to believe the claim, and then the other person failed to *ask* for a reason to believe. The only exception in the opening example was when the salesperson asked, "What makes you think that it doesn't work? . . ." At that point the customer had an opportunity to provide a *reason* so that the salesperson would believe her claim that the mixer did not work. The customer, however, couldn't avoid the chance for sarcasm: "What makes me think it doesn't work is the fact that it doesn't work." In replying that way, she failed — perhaps understandably — to save the discussion from becoming even more quarrelsome. A quarrel, then, is communication where the claims of the other person are not taken seriously and examined for merit.

Third, *quarrels* may or may not *be prompted by strong emotion.*[3] Generally, I suspect, people think of quarreling as "heated" or "hotly contested." At the very least, a quarrel may be seen as having its share of anger, irritation, or hostility, all of which is possible. But emotion and quarreling do not necessarily occur together. I have a staunch Democratic friend who delights in the creation of quarrels, particularly with staunch Republicans. He does this calmly and deliberately since great displays of emotion are foreign to him. Quarrels are not merely the results of great emotional feeling. They can occur anytime when the communication focuses on claims and neither party seems to examine seriously the other person's claims.

Because of the emphasis on claims and no examination of the claims of others, fourth, *quarrels lack any sort of progress toward a mutually satisfying agreement.* Notice that when the children, the politicians, and the customer and salesperson were quarreling, the communication was not really "over." I stopped the dialogues because there was no place for them

---

[3] See also, Crable, *Argumentation as Communication*, pp. 12–13.

to go. "Got you/Got you first." "Have, too/Have not." and "Did, too/Did not." are fairly typical examples of when a discussion deteriorates into a quarrel. Only claims are exchanged; neither party is willing to examine and consider the other's claims; and so there is little hope of progress. The exchange of claims could continue or the exchange could stop and an icy silence could occur or ash trays and books could be exchanged where words failed. Whatever happens, quarrels provide little if any hope for productively resolving human problems. Progress is not a characteristic of quarreling.

Yet human problems that have to do with defective mixers, campaign strategies, and playground gunfights somehow have to be settled. Communication theorists and researchers have investigated techniques of "conflict management" as an alternative to quarreling.

Managing conflict By definition, quarreling can be viewed as an unproductive verbal exchange. Traditionally, "conflict" has been looked at in the same negative way. After all, *conflict means a disagreement or a lack of harmony.*[4] That has to be undesirable, doesn't it? The contemporary answer to the question is a firm "No."[5]

Obviously, conflict *may* be undesirable and negative. War is an example. So is the clash between parents and children that creates permanent alienation. But there are other equally clear examples of *constructive* conflict. Conflict that both strengthens bodies and entertains occurs on football fields and tennis courts. Industries that make the same sorts of products make conflicting efforts that we call "free enterprise." Legislators of various viewpoints clash over the merits of a proposed bill; the result is supposed to be better legislation. The point is simply that conflict may or may not be undesirable.

Similarly, *compatibility—agreement or harmony* that is the opposite of conflict—may either be constructive or destructive.[6] Harmonious relationships between wives and husbands would seem to be desirable. Good relationships between the governor and state legislature also would seem positive. Yet compatibility—or lack of conflict—can be a problem. A business where everyone agrees with the boss may soon be out of business. A nation where leaders never experience conflict with lower level officials may become a total dictatorship. Compatibility may be just as undesirable or productive as conflict.

Contemporary approaches to conflict stress—not always how to get rid of conflict, but how to manage it. Conflict, for instance, may make people

[4] For an excellent, brief treatment of conflict see Robert J. Doolittle, *Orientations to Communication and Conflict* (Chicago: Science Research, 1976).
[5] See Richard E. Crable, *Using Communication* (Boston: Allyn and Bacon, 1979), chap. 1.
[6] Ibid.

rethink their ideas or may help them think of new ones: How do we allow a healthy level of conflict to continue in a business, or a family? The acceptance of conflicting thoughts may make people feel freer and accepted generally: How do we encourage the acceptance of conflict? Conflict may bring a hint of fresh air into a friendly relationship that has become set and too stable: How can a constructive level of conflict be encouraged? Conflict can be healthy for the interpersonal relationship, but it needs to be managed. Several strategies may help you to manage conflict more productively.

First, *develop a positive attitude toward constructive conflict.* As discussed, conflict can be a healthy component of an interpersonal relationship. When there is disagreement between you and another, analyze the situation carefully. Is the conflict simply the natural result of two different people being together? Most times two or more people will not agree completely about everything. Even if the conflict seems more serious, be cautious. Conflict that is managed well can save a friendship or a marriage. The idea is to try to avoid quarreling and to approach conflict as a potentially good thing.

Second, *decide whether the conflict you experience is simply a misunderstanding.* Let me illustrate what I mean.

John	Let's go to the game.
Gloria	Naw, I have to study for this . . .
John	You can study anytime. The game will be over in a few hours.
Gloria	John, I don't need this. You know that grades are important to me and my folks.
John	I just meant . . .
Gloria	I know what you meant, but this test is important to me.
John	I just meant that we could study together later. I have a term paper to work on.
Gloria	Oh, you didn't mean . . . I see . . . Well, okay, let's go.

In the example, what Gloria saw as a conflict between her and John's priorities was basically a misunderstanding. John was willing to study, but he also wanted to see the game. Gloria wanted to study, and if she could do that, she was willing to go to the game. What seemed to be a conflict ended with what is probably a familiar comment to you: "Oh, I see what you mean now." A misunderstanding—if cleared up—does not have to become a conflict.

There are times, of course, when two people will experience a real conflict. If you think that is the situation you are facing, you should, third, *decide what sort of conflict you are experiencing.* Some researchers, for example, have divided "conflict" into three major types: conflict over content (issues or ideas), over procedures, and over personalities.[7] The opening case study in this chapter can be used to describe each sort of conflict. The

[7] For a discussion see D. Johnson and F. Johnson, *Joining Together: Group Therapy and Group Skills* (Englewood Cliffs, N.J.: Prentice-Hall, 1975), p. 171.

179

customer originally disagreed with the salesperson over a matter of *content:* Did the mixer, in fact, work? That should have remained the major focus of the discussion. Yet a conflict over *procedure* occurred in the discussion of the store's policy of customer satisfaction: If the policy was satisfaction (and it had been effective in the past), then why wasn't the customer satisfied? Finally, the quarrel began to center on the *personality* of the customer: Was the customer the kind of person who would abuse a mixer and then demand a refund? From the comments in the case it is not clear that the salesperson actually intended a personal attack. Yet there was enough indication of a possible insult that the customer felt justified in getting angry. "The conflict" here that degenerated into a quarrel was really at least three different kinds of conflict: conflict over content, procedure, and personality.

In trying to manage conflict, you should, fourth, *try not to get distracted from the major point of conflict.* In the opening situation, for instance, the working – or nonworking – condition of the mixer should have been the main focus for the discussion. But the conversation veered off into a defense and attack on store *policy,* and in the end it became a possible *personality* clash. Both people allowed themselves to be distracted away from the main issue.

Decide what your main goal is in the situation as a fifth strategy for managing conflict. What is it that is most important to you in the situation? Different things may be important at different times, or for different people. These various goals or purposes should influence how you try to manage conflict. Let me illustrate.

Your parents (let's assume) are getting ready to retire. They are becoming more and more dependent on you for advice and information. At the same time, they resent their growing dependence on you. You discover one day that they are planning to buy a smaller house in a neighborhood that you view as "lower class." You tell them that you disagree with their choice but they say they are satisfied with their decision. What do you do?

Several things might be helpful. As noted earlier (1) make the assumption that this conflict – like so many others – can be productive. (2) Decide on what sort of conflict it is. (3) Do not be distracted into other conflicts. This situation, for example, seems to center on an issue or decision – a matter of content. Yet it would be easy to be distracted into discussion about *how* their decision was made without consulting you (procedure) or whether they were getting too old to make such decisions without you (perhaps personality). Once you have employed these strategies, then you can determine what your goals are – what is important to you. Are you interested in playing the role of "child to the rescue"? In saving your parents from a potentially bad investment? In proving to your parents that you "were right, after all"? In avoiding an attack on your parents' dignity – an attack that might come when you "rescue" them? Are you interested in them keeping the larger house as a better investment for their heirs — among them, you?

What happens when you ask yourself such questions is that you begin to balance factors in the situation. *Is* it important that they remain more independent of you, and is that more important than the decision? *Are* you more interested in the wisdom of the decision than in their feelings? The same sort of goal balancing can be done even in the attempted refund of the mixer. The customer should decide whether her ego, the store's view of her complaint, the condition of the mixer, or the feelings of the salesperson might be of little (maybe very little) concern. In each situation of conflict you should decide what is important — what your goals are — in the situation.

Sixth, in a conflict situation you should *employ a win-win gaming strategy whenever possible.* "Gaming strategy" is nothing more than *a concise way of talking about how you will relate with another person in a conflict situation.* Conflict situations can be perceived as either *win-lose, lose-lose,* or *win-win* "games."[8] If the conflict is perceived as a "win-lose" game, one person or both assume that when one accomplishes his or her goal, the other person cannot accomplish his or her goal. In a "lose-lose" game each person (or one of them) assumes that *both* must lose since neither will allow the other to win. Finally, in a "win-win" game the assumption is that both can gain roughly what they want. Let me illustrate the differences among these three perceptions of conflict.

Jack was polishing his car when his young brother asked him to help clean the rust off his bicycle. Jack had a date for the evening, so he did not want to take time to help James. Jack wanted to help but was also irritated when James pestered him about the bicycle. Jack was also angry that he started so late on the car and would probably not get the job finished in time to shower and prepare for his date. James was angry that his brother seemed to show no interest in *ever* helping with the bicycle. James laughed when Jack asked for his help.

If their potential conflict is looked at as a lose-lose game, the result is obvious: James does not get the bicycle cleaned and Jack will still be late for his date. If the conflict is viewed as a win-lose game, one of two things could happen: either James would get the help and Jack would be even later, so James would win; or James could help, but his bike would remain rusty, so Jack would win. There is another obvious possibility if a win-win approach is used: James could help Jack with the car *now* in exchange for Jack's help with the bicycle *later,* so they would both win.

Each of the young men had decided what they wanted from the situation. Their problem at that point was to employ a strategy that might allow

---

[8] Another explanation of these concepts appears in Crable, *Using Communication,* chap. 13.

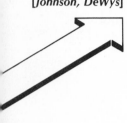

In a "win-win" game the assumption is that both can gain roughly what they want. [Johnson, DeWys]

each of them to have their goal met. Some interpersonal situations are not so simple. The important point, however, is that in most situations you can employ different approaches to resolving the conflict. By taking a lose-lose or win-lose gaming strategy, you run the risk of antagonizing the other person. In addition, you risk not accomplishing your own goal. Your concentration on a win-win strategy may well be the most valuable facet in your management of a conflict situation.

To employ this win-win strategy, three ideas are most important.[9]

1   Adopt a "we versus task" attitude instead of a "me versus the other" attitude. Instead of immediately focusing on how *you* can win, think of how both you and the other person can each win. The "enemy" is the conflict — not each other.

2   Take into consideration the views of each person: What does each of you want? What is the goal of each? What does each person need in order to feel that he or she has "won"?

3   Attempt sincerely to establish open and honest communication. Each of you must make an effort to state clearly what you feel and want. Neither person probably will accomplish a goal if the goal or need is secret. Opening up lines of communication can best assure that you and the other person can work as a team toward a win-win solution.

[9] The ideas here are related to those in Allan C. Filley, *Interpersonal Conflict Resolution* (Glenview, Ill.: Scott, Foresman, 1975), pp. 25–30.

In summary, managing conflict is not magic. Conflict can be kept from becoming a quarrel if certain approaches are taken. You can help an interpersonal conflict by developing a positive attitude toward constructive conflict; by trying to see if the "conflict" is simply a misunderstanding; by deciding the type of conflict — if there is one; by not getting distracted from the focus of the conflict; by deciding what your goal is in the conflict; and then, by adopting a win-win strategy. Most interpersonal conflict, in fact, can be managed.

As an illustration of conflict management, let's rerun the case at the beginning of the chapter. This time the salesperson will demonstrate greater insight in how to settle the problem with the mixer.

May I help you, madam?

I certainly hope someone can. You see, this is the first time I've ever bought anything here, and I purchased a mixer that doesn't mix.

In what way are you having trouble? Does it run at all, or what exactly is the problem?

Well, it runs, but too slowly. . . . It doesn't mix anything.

I see.

Have you had many complaints about this mixer, then?

We have had no complaints about it. . . . But every once in a while something is bound to happen, I guess — despite all the quality controls.

What are you going to do about it?

Well, our policy is customer satisfaction. . . . The only factor would be customer abuse. . . .

I can assure you . . .

No, no . . . I mean that's no problem here. . . . The mixer doesn't look like it's had a hard life. . . .

Oh.

What do you want done?

Pardon me?

What would you like us to do? You may have a full refund — or a different mixer — or another one of this same type. . . . What would you like?

Well, I guess . . . I figured you would put up a fight about this.

Oh, no. We get business from repeat customers — not from the sale of a single item. If you are satisfied that you can trust us, I suspect you will be back. . . .

I was all set for a battle. . . .

Sorry — no battle today.

I'm not sorry. Let me see that other mixer model — the one that costs a little more. . . .

The situation described is by no means exaggerated, based on my teaching and consulting experience. A few simple strategies by the salesperson kept the discussion from becoming a quarrel, even though the customer was prepared for a "battle." The salesperson adopted a positive attitude toward the conflict; the discussion was kept on track—the mixer and the customer's satisfaction were always the focus; and each one appeared to win: The customer lost a mixer that didn't work and the store was about to sell an even more expensive model. If the salesperson had allowed the discussion to become a quarrel, the chances are good that the mixer would still have been returned; the customer, on the other hand, might not have returned. Conflict management seems clearly superior to quarreling in the interpersonal situation.

Conflict management, then, is a set of techniques aimed at helping you keep a conflict from becoming more serious, or worse, from becoming simply a quarrel. In relationships that develop over a period of years, however, you may want to use "conflict" to help make better decisions. You may wish to *create* constructive conflict.

Decisioning by argument

"Arguing" is what many people call what I have termed "quarreling." To me, *argumentation is a process of presenting and examining the reasons for claims.*[10] That definition makes argumentation a potentially constructive tool for interpersonal relationships. More important, this notion of argumentation makes it indispensable for the communing relationship: As a relationship grows and deepens, each person can help the other make better, more acceptable decisions. Let me give you an example.

Husband You know, I've been thinking, maybe we ought to finally take a vacation south. The kids are old enough to really enjoy waves and sandy beaches. . . .

Wife What brought all this on?

Husband February. I'm so tired of snow, I can hardly stand it. We could pack up and really get away from it all for a while. What do you think?

Wife It sounds great, but I don't think anyone's whole world changes with a vacation. We both have a lot of things to do.

Husband We could put a lot of that stuff off till we get back and then . . .

Wife And then it would still be here when we got back.

Husband Yeah, . . . It was just a thought. . . . I've got it. How 'bout if we go late in the summer. If we had a goal to shoot for, maybe I could get interested in some of this writing. . . . Yeah, then we could really enjoy it. What do you think?

Without waiting to hear what the wife thinks, let me interrupt here. What has been happening is that the husband and wife are engaging in argumentation—an effective way of *creating* conflict in order to make a good decision. The discussion might have become a quarrel if one or both of them had stressed only the statement of claims. But the discussion did not become a quarrel: The wife was interested in examining the worth of the claim, "we ought to take a vacation," and also wanted to know his reasons

[10] See Crable, *Argumentation as Communication*, p. 8 ff.

for wanting to go. She did not seem anxious to go if they were just escaping, for two weeks, from work that would remain. Just as important, the husband was willing to examine his own reasons for going. As I interrupted the case study, they seemed to be becoming more enthused about the prospect of going. Even if they did not know (technically) that they were employing argumentation, they used it to help them reach a decision.

You can gain insight into what they were doing by learning some of the basic features of argumentation.[11] First, argumentation involves *claims*, which (as we saw earlier) are *statements we wish to have accepted, but which are questioned or challenged.* The husband stated, "We ought to go south," and the wife questioned his statement: "What brought all this on?" — meaning, "Why *should* we do that?"

Second, argumentation involves *qualifiers: statements explaining how sure we are of the claim.* The husband did not actually say, "We ought to go"; he said, "*Maybe* we ought to go." The husband was not sure that his idea was a good one but was "sending up a trial balloon" or testing his idea. Qualifiers include such phrases as "sometimes," "perhaps," "often," "never," "all the time," and so forth.

Third, argumentation involves evidence: *anything given as a reason for a claim.* Why did the husband bring up the idea? He seemed to feel they should go on vacation because of snow, because of February, and because he (and they) needed to "get away from it all." Evidence is sometimes viewed as just statistics or fingerprints or eyewitness accounts. But evidence in the interpersonal situation is anything presented as a reason that the other person should accept the claim.

Finally, argumentation has to do with *reservations: statements that relate when the person might not want to continue making the claim.* The wife, for example, seemed to want to go on vacation *unless* the vacation was pure escape. The husband seemed to be more excited about going *if* some work could be done beforehand. In both cases there were certain factors that affected the claim and certain situations that influenced whether the claim about going south was one they could accept.

Of course, in this argument neither person seemed aware that he or she was using the tools of constructive argumentation. But they were doing the sorts of things that can make argumentation a useful interpersonal process: The husband made a *qualified* claim, which he wanted to see examined. The wife, who could merely have said, "That's stupid, Lazy!" instead asked for his reasons. Then, she pointed out her *reservations* in making the trip an escape. The result was that a potential conflict was created just so that a good decision could be made. This couple did accidentally what you can do on purpose. They used argumentation as a way, not of

[11] The basic terms used here are based upon Toulmin, *Uses of Argument,* and on Crable, *Argumentation as Communication,* chap. 5.

managing conflict, but of creating conflict responsibly in a relaxed, secure, and communing relationship.

In short, people can respond to conflict in different ways. They can engage in quarreling behavior that seems clearly unconstructive or they can assume that conflict can be either positive or negative and seek to manage the conflict in constructive ways. Conflict can be seen as a positive step toward better decisions. Strategies of argumentation can be used to examine claims and the reasons for them and to improve the chances for interpersonal communion.

CHAPTER SUMMARY

Any ongoing relationship will involve questions, disagreements, and problems to be solved. There are various ways of approaching these situations which can either harm or help improve relationships.

Quarreling, for example, can be used to approach problems. On the whole, though, quarreling seems usually to be unproductive in problem solution and counterproductive for the relationship. "Managing conflict" is a general strategy of approaching human disagreements and problems. The chapter details attitudes and behaviors that can aid your attempt at "managing" the conflicts in your life.

Still there are times when conflict is not apparent, but when decisions have to be made jointly. These are times when even a basic knowledge of argumentation can help you and another solve problem situations constructively and without harming the relationship. Indeed, the result of appropriate argumentation can be a sense of oneness in the solution of human problems.

LEARNING BY APPLYING

1 Observe one or several prime time "situation" comedies on television. During some part of most of these shows at least two people will become engaged in what they might call "an argument." Given your reading of the text, you probably will recognize it as what I call a "quarrel." Describe the situation and explain what makes it a quarrel.

2 Use newspapers, television news, or direct observation of how a local or national "issue" is dealt with by different parties. In a political year such a situation is not difficult to find, but even in "off years" issues of trash-hauling rates, union strikes, bond issues, and so on will occur. In what sense—and how well—is "conflict" being handled by the major interested parties? Do some of the discussions simply deteriorate into quarrels? Explain.

3 Recall recent "disagreements" you have had with someone or several peo-

ple in a group. Was the attitude with which the conflict was approached win-lose, lose-lose, or win-win? Was there some way that a win-win approach could have been suggested (if it was not already considered)? Would that have taken more time and thought? Would it have been worth it?

4   What do you (or did you) consider to be "evidence"? Have you noticed that different people will think that different things can function as evidence? The next time someone makes a statement with which you disagree or have a question, ask politely for "evidence" for what he or she has said. You will hear a variety of things, all of which may function as evidence.

5   The approach to argumentation discussed in the chapter takes some time and effort to learn. The terms themselves are not nearly so important as the overall use of them. When you and another begin some sort of decision-making process, take the time to approach the problem by using argumentation. Practice in asking for evidence, for qualifiers, and for reservations can help avoid simple quarreling. It can help you make decisions more thoughtfully.

LEARNING BY DISCUSSING

1   Describe the activity of quarreling.
2   What do you think the differences are between quarreling and experiencing conflict?
3   Explain ways, and give examples, in which conflict can be either positive or negative.
4   Discuss the importance of managing conflict. How good a "conflict manager" are you?
5   Discuss the important aspects of argumentation.
6   Describe how argumentation can help you manage conflicts, or create conflict, as a way of helping to build strong relationships.
7   How can skill in argumentation help in building relationships in general?

LEARNING BY READING FURTHER

Crable, Richard E., *Argumentation as Communication: Reasoning with Receivers.* Columbus, OH: Merrill, 1976.

———, *Using Communication.* Boston: Allyn and Bacon, 1979, chap. 7.

Doolittle, Robert J., *Orientations to Communication and Conflict.* Chicago: Science Research, 1976.

Filley, Alan C., *Interpersonal Conflict Resolution.* Glenview, IL: Scott, Foresman, 1975.

Jandt, Fred E., ed., *Conflict Resolution Through Communication.* New York: Harper & Row, 1973.

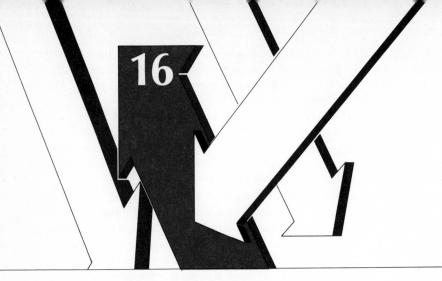

EMOTING, THINKING SYSTEMATICALLY, AND BEING RATIONAL

STUDY OF THIS CHAPTER WILL ENABLE YOU TO

- *understand the concept of "emoting"*
- *understand the characteristics of emoting*
- *better avoid emoting in interpersonal situations*
- *understand the nature of systematic thinking*
- *understand strategies of systematic thinking*
- *use strategies of systematic thinking in interpersonal situations*
- *understand the concept of "rationality"*
- *adopt an attitude of rationality better in interpersonal situations*

The first of the month is once again on them. Gregg and Nancy do not exactly look forward to the time when "the bills" begin to arrive in the mail. Regardless of how hard they try, the bills are always more than they anticipated. They attempted to limit their spending to a prearranged budget that falls within their income. Still every month there seem to be unplanned, but essential, expenses: a physician bill, a new muffler for the car, or a set of braces for one of the children. Then, of course, there is insurance, taxes, or some other nonmonthly expense.

Gregg and Nancy are well aware of how upsetting such times can be, so they plan accordingly. They wait until most of the bills have arrived, choose an evening that is free from distractions, then after the kids go to bed, pour themselves a glass of wine, and begin dissecting their paychecks.

Nancy	Here's the Sears bill—wow, I thought we were getting caught up!
Gregg	We were until winter coat time, dear.
Nancy	Oh, yes. . . . Here's the gas bill—do you think we ought to switch to electricity? . . . I guess we talked about that last month, huh?
Gregg	Yes. Here's the Penney's bill—and the insurance came due. . . .
Nancy	Oh, no! I thought that was last month . . . no, that was property tax month, wasn't it?
Gregg	Yes, dear. You know, I've been thinking about this whole business of insurance. You know, we have more money tied up in insurance than we do in the house. We have car insurance, house insurance, personal accident insurance, life insurance, disability insurance, theft insurance . . .
Nancy	Theft insurance is part of the house insurance. . . .
Gregg	Oh, good! There for a minute, I thought we were going broke on insurance . . .
Nancy	Humor, huh? You forgot little league insurance and antilaw suit insurance. . . .
Gregg	Do we have insurance in case we can't afford our insurance payments? Probably not, we can't afford it with all the insurance bills.
Nancy	This is no time to be childish.

189

Gregg	Childish? No child in his right mind would pay for all this insurance. . . .
Nancy	But we need the protection. . . .
Gregg	Yeah, did you know that General Custer had insurance? Unfortunately, his horse was not the beneficiary.
Nancy	But don't you feel that he was a lot more relaxed knowing he was insured?
Gregg	The horse?
Nancy	No, Custer.
Gregg	Frankly, if he hadn't been so relaxed, he might have fought a smarter battle.
Nancy	I think you're off the subject. . . . What do you think would happen if we didn't pay all these premiums?
Gregg	I think I'd have a lot more money. . . .
Nancy	But what about me and the kids . . . or you and the kids if something happened to me? We'd feel terrible.
Gregg	We feel terrible now.
Nancy	Which do you want? Financial security or peace of mind?
Gregg	Do I have to choose? I'd like to have both, and I'm not sure I have either.
Nancy	This is just like you. We try to approach these things logically, and you want to play games. We've gotten good out of those policies. . . .
Gregg	Yeah, our car was dented by a fireplug and it cost $150. . . .
Nancy	See!
Gregg	But we had to pay the first hundred dollars as a deductible . . . after paying that company . . . let's see: 11 years, at hum . . . Yeah, we paid them something over $2750 dollars over the years and they kick back $50—hope they could spare it.
Nancy	I've had it. You go in and watch TV. I'll figure the bills, and I'll tell you about it to-morrow . . . when you're more stable. . . . I hate it when you get this way.
Gregg	Fine with me. I'd rather *see* what the oil companies are doing to us than to *experience* what the insurance companies are doing to us. . . .

Emoting Clearly, there is nothing particularly evil about emotions. Anger, fear, love, dejection—these and all the other feelings classified as emotions seem to be a part of human existence. In addition, I have difficulty thinking that emotions are somehow the opposite of intellect—or logic. Highly intelligent people are frequently also highly emotional. The great controversies, argued logically, have invariably been highly emotional. Emotions (whatever they actually are) are not necessarily destructive in interpersonal relationships. They seem to be a completely acceptable part of being human.

In this section I discuss—not emotions—but *"emoting": the overly dramatic display of emotion that hinders clear thinking*. In drama an actor or actress is said to be "emoting" when he or she is simply overacting. The characteristics of interpersonal emoting are not unlike overacting. Let me explain.

First, I think it is important to point out that *emoting can be prompted by the natural desire to respond with strong feeling*. In the case study

Gregg responded with intense emotion. And that seemed appropriate. In the face of continued budget problems you probably would have been surprised to hear him say, "Oh, yes, we are broke again this month." In troublesome situations people somehow expect others to respond intensely. The wife who does not cry at a husband's funeral might be perceived as not caring about the loss. The child who has been injured expects at least some obvious show of sympathy from a parent, and perhaps a "kiss to make it well." The person fired from a job is not expected to take the loss calmly. Certainly, there are people who do not respond easily, and we have clichés for them: "He is really a cold fish!" "He has ice water in his veins!" "Why, she has no feelings at all." These people may be admired for their "composure." They also may be distrusted for it. Can you trust someone who does not respond the way people are supposed to? In essence, the showing of an emotional response seems a perfectly natural human tendency.

Second, *emoting can be characterized by the overly dramatic display of emotions.* It was not enough for Gregg to say he was concerned that too much money was being spent on insurance. He was extremely sarcastic in talking about insurance against not being able to pay insurance premiums, Custer's (and his own) peace of mind, car insurance deductibles, and so on. He was not just trying to be humorous, and had already made his point. What he was doing was responding to the urge to be melodramatic, and he wanted to give voice to his emotions, and more: He wanted to wallow in them, to roll them around behind his clenched teeth, and, of course, he wanted everyone else to breathe the air of his anger and frustration. Gregg was not just expressing his emotions but wanted to act out a play about them.

Finally, *emoting can create an aimless and haphazard approach to problems and situations.* Nancy was entirely accurate when she accused Gregg of getting pretty far from the main point. Gregg's melodramatic display led him in several directions at once, making the situation worse. Instead of discussing the current bills, planning objectives and goals and current finances, he wanted to discuss the general issue of insurance. He cited all the doubts he had had about insurance probably for years and specific instances of how it had not paid off. In general, Gregg simply was avoiding the major specific issue that faced them: How to handle the month's financial pressures. He may well have given vent to some powerful (if overly dramatic) emotions, but he did not help with the immediate problem. In the end, even Nancy became dismayed. She began emoting herself. And that was even "better" for Gregg. At that point he had a new, and more immediate, focus for his hostility.

Again, I am not arguing that emotions themselves are evil or destructive. Instead, the object here is to indicate that "emoting" is not a constructive approach to interpersonal problems or problem solution. Fortunately,

191

there are ways of handling such situations that avoid the mistakes of emoting—there are ways of responding to problems even in emotion-filled situations.

*Thinking
systematically*
The concern for problem solving and decision making has resulted in the creation of all sorts of methods for helping those processes. One of the easiest to learn and most popular of these is also perhaps one of the oldest. Developed by John Dewey and refined over the last 50 or so years, it is called "Steps in Reflective Thinking."[1] I prefer calling it a "systematic approach to decision making and problem solving." Dewey's approach does not depend on the "steps" being taken in any particular order—with some exceptions. Moreover, the approach is good for decision making and problem solving, not just thinking (as that term is usually used). Finally, the emphasis on "systematic" is important. Being systematic means that a person is careful and accurate in what is being done; that the person is thorough and complete; and that the person can express strong emotion without engag-

[1] See, John Dewey, *How We Think* (Lexington, Mass.: Heath, 1933).

Being systematic means that a person is careful and accurate in what is being done. [Forsyth, Monkmeyer]

ing in emoting behavior. With this as an introduction, let's turn to the points of Dewey's approach.[2]

First, the people involved must *be aware of the problem.* Usually, this is easy. Normally, no one plunges into a problem-solving or decision-making process without being aware of a troublesome situation. Occasionally, however, people only accidentally become aware of the problem, or they become aware of it late. Gregg and Nancy, for instance, seemed to be unaware that the problem they faced was not related to *that* month. It was related to their finances and attitudes in general. Only in the midst of Gregg's outburst did the central problem emerge. Whenever it occurs, though, awareness is an important step in the process.

Second, people using a systematic approach should *define the problem.* This seems almost too obvious to mention. Yet this was one of the basic mistakes made by Gregg and Nancy. At first the problem seemed to be *how* to handle the month's finances. Then, the problem seemed to be whether they were what is called "insurance poor": broke, but rich in insurance. Which problem were they confronting? As it turned out, they faced both – and neither. As the discussion progressed, it became clear that they were struggling with problems about the month's finances *and* about insurance. Their major problem, however, seemed to be, "How do we balance our current needs with our need for insurance protection?" But neither of them could state the problem definition clearly. The definition is not always difficult to formulate, but it is important. Without it, the two people – as Gregg and Nancy – probably will try to create solutions for things that are not the major problem.

Once the problem or situation has been realized and defined, the people involved should *analyze the problem.* This third point prompts answers to questions such as, "Who is most affected by the situation?" "How are they affected?" "What are the most important factors in the situation?" "Why does it seem to be a problem to us?" Questions such as this help those involved to understand clearly the problem they are trying to solve.

Note so far, no mention has been made of solutions. The effort has been to see the situation in all its aspects before thinking about solutions. One of the most common temptations in solving problems or making decisions is to begin immediately searching for answers – answers to questions that are not understood. The systematic approach discussed here is meant to guide people in understanding the problem – only then should the discussion of solutions begin.

The fourth point, then, is to *create standards or criteria for a solution to the problem.* Standards or criteria can be considered the "yardsticks" by

[2] Over the years these steps have acquired various names and slightly different interpretations. The terms used here and their descriptions are what I consider to be their clearest expression.

which solutions will be evaluated. A clearer way of thinking about yard-sticks may be to consider them as adjectives that would describe a "good" solution. In the case of Gregg and Nancy a good solution to their problem—balancing needs and protection would be affordable, financially safe, financially protective for the children, and so on. These factors of affordability, safety, and protection could be used as standards for an eventual solution. They might help tell Gregg and Nancy what a "good" solution would be like. Armed with a knowledge of what they expect from a solution, they are prepared to look for their own solutions.

Fifth, the people involved can *search for all possible solutions.* The idea is to get as many ideas about solutions as possible. Any idea—no matter how strange—should be voiced. Even a strange suggestion might lead to an idea about a better one. Solutions can be evaluated later, but now is the time simply to hear them all, and perhaps write them down. Specifically, the process is called "brain storming."[3] Two ideas are important: (1) list solutions until the ideas "run out"—quantity will lead to quality and (2) make no evaluation of any solution.

Only at this point should the process of evaluation of the solutions begin. In this sixth step the people involved should *match all the solutions with each of the standards or criteria.* Gregg and Nancy may have listed a number of possible solutions: end all insurance, get a second job for one of them, declare bankruptcy, "weed out" the "unessential" insurance, look for less expensive insurance policies, get a second mortgage on the house, and so forth. Now they are prepared to match each one with their criteria. Figure 16-1 illustrates an easy approach to keeping the process clear. The matching of solutions to criteria may not always yield one superior solution. But it can help people decide between the clearly better and clearly unacceptable solutions.

The final step in the approach occurs when the people involved *select the solution or alternative and act on it.* This is really simply the result of matching the solutions with the criteria. And yet it is important. Problems can be discussed literally forever. Solutions can be selected but never implemented. For the situation to be resolved, this final step is crucial.

Again, these steps can sometimes be taken in various sequences. The criteria can be stated after possible solutions are suggested. This, however, involves the danger of suggesting only those criteria that match a favored solution. Sometimes people are involved in analyzing a problem (as Gregg and Nancy were doing) before they become aware of the actual problem. There is no magic in Dewey's steps. The advantage is that by following the

---

[3] Though brainstorming has various interpretations, the treatment here is based on the discussion in Alex F. Osborn, *Applied Imagination: Principles and Procedures of Creative Problem-Solving*, 3d ed. (New York: Scribner's, 1963), chap. 13.

Figure 16-1
Matching criteria
with solutions

POSSIBLE SOLUTIONS	AFFORDABLE ?	FINANCIALLY SAFE ?	FINANCIALLY PROTECTIVE ?	ETC.
BANKRUPTCY	YES	?	?	
WEED OUT UNNECESSARY INSURANCE	YES	YES	?	
LESS EXPENSIVE POLICIES	YES	YES	?	
SECOND MORTGAGE	YES	NO/?	NO	
ETC.				

suggestions, you can be reasonably sure of approaching the problem systematically. Emotional responses can still be strong. People can still become very "involved" with what they are doing. Still this approach helps avoid the problems associated with emoting.

But "reflective thinking" is still a technique – even with all its advantages. The systematic approach is helpful – and yet not all human problems can be solved systematically. In relationships aiming toward a communing level even more attention needs to be paid to the individuals involved and to how the relationship and situation can change. Such relationships do not depend so much on being systematic as they do on being rational.

Being rational   There are all sorts of ways to define "rationality." Words such as "reasonable," "logical," and "unemotional" come to mind. Professor Stephen Toulmin of the University of Chicago, however, approaches rationality in what I think is a very helpful way. *"Rationality,"* he suggests, *is appropriate and modifiable behavior.*[4] He uses the concepts of rational and irrational fears – not logic – as a way to understand the term.

Let's say that I have never seen a doorbell. I approach one, ring it, and am frightened when it makes a sound. Given my inexperience, I have a rational fear. The fear is *appropriate* and reasonable since I have never seen one. Now suppose that you explain to me what a doorbell is and that it is completely harmless. I say that I understand and believe you. Yet I still

[4] For a discussion see Richard E. Crable, *Argumentation as Communication: Reasoning with Receivers* (Columbus, O.: Merrill, 1976), pp. 204–209.

The good relationship will grow better with the ability of the people to accept change and to modify behavior and decisions. [Kroll, Taurus]

avoid doorbells. At this point my fear has become irrational: I know my behavior is *inappropriate* (I do believe doorbells are harmless), but I *cannot (or will not) modify* or change my behavior. Once I learned the truth about doorbells, I should have been able to *modify* my behavior into something *appropriate*. Being rational means doing what is appropriate, but being prepared to change if you have good reasons.

Let's return to Gregg and Nancy. Once they decided on an approach to their clearly defined problem, they had created what was to them the "appropriate" course of action. It was not necessarily the "right" solution. Nor was it the "only" solution, or the "correct" one.[5] It was simply the solution that seemed the best at that time. To this extent, they were being rational.

But suppose that their solution had been to end their "major medical insurance" as a way of retaining more money. That would be no particular problem. Not expecting any major illnesses or hospital visits, they might have seen this solution as an appropriate way of "weeding out" unnecessary expenses. But let's also suppose that Nancy adds one element to the discussion. The morning after the decision, she says to Gregg:

"Honey, I know you'll be pleased. I'm pregnant again." Now that may or may not be welcome news. That depends on Nancy and Gregg.

What such a change in situation means for them—regardless of their view of pregnancy at that time—is the need for reevaluating the problem. A new arrival to the family would mean additional expenses, the loss of Nancy's paycheck for a time at least, and the desirability of continuing the major medical coverage. To be rational, the couple must reevaluate—this time, with an additional factor. They must realize that their earlier solution was not "logical," "right," or "correct." It simply was what seemed at that time most appropriate to them. But now something else might be more appropriate. Nancy and Gregg will demonstrate their rationality, not by being upset, but by being willing to modify their decision if it seems desirable.

Clearly, the announcement of a new pregnancy is a fairly dramatic way of illustrating a changing situation. But interpersonal situations and relationships are always changing. The good relationship will not survive because there are no new problems. It will survive—and deepen—because the people involved act and make decisions appropriately. The good relationship will grow better with the ability of the people to accept change and to modify behavior and decisions. In sum, rationality is based on appropriateness and modifiability, both of which are important in building toward interpersonal communion.

---

[5] The contrast between this approach and logic is great. The quest in logical analysis has traditionally been for the right or correct conclusion—a conclusion that was seen as "obviously" acceptable to the people involved. The approach here emphasizes the actual acceptability—the strength—of the conclusion instead of the once-and-for-all correctness of the conclusion.

CHAPTER SUMMARY

It is no accident that this and the previous chapter are presented so closely together. This chapter examined other factors and approaches in problems that human beings encounter. Here the emphasis was on different ways of approaching the same, preexistent problem.

"Emoting" is a general attitude toward problems that tends to be an overly dramatic display of emotion that hinders clear thinking. The emoter

may indeed wish to express strong feelings, but the characteristics of emoting make it a normally unacceptable and unproductive behavior.

Far more helpful is an approach—borrowed from John Dewey—that was explained in the chapter as a series of "steps" that can aid clear and systematic thinking.

Still any two people, even those using systematic thinking, can benefit from being "rational." Rationality as used in the chapter means that both appropriate decisions are made and the people involved are prepared to alter their views and decisions as events unfold. Communing relationships by definition are ongoing and long term; such relationships can benefit by both individuals being rational as well as systematic.

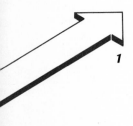

LEARNING BY APPLYING

1   *One of the best ongoing examples of people who "emote" far more than anything else is the cast of characters in the comic strip "Blondie." If a local newspaper "runs" that strip, observe it for a week or so to get a good idea of how not to solve problems. Dagwood's boss characteristically rants, raves, and screams when the (whatever) account is not completed; Dagwood's neighbor Herb flies into a fury at overdue borrowed lawnmowers, misunderstandings with Dagwood, and so forth: and Dagwood himself rages at door-to-door salespeople, disturbances of his bath, and teenagers who monopolize the telephone. From this strip, try to find anyone who does much else besides emoting!*

2   *Do you know someone who seems to have a "quick," "hot," or "nasty" temper? Think about—or observe—the person. Is it possible that the emoting is a substitute for actually trying to solve problems and to confront situations? Give examples or explain.*

3   *Take a decision that you are now facing. It can be something as critical as what kind of career to pursue or something as seemingly trivial as what to do on Friday night. Use the approach to systematic thinking discussed in the text. You may find that one of the more difficult things is to define the problem—a step often overlooked because "everyone" knows the actual problem. By forcing yourself to be methodical, you may uncover some important aspects to the problem. Analyze the problem and then create criteria: You may be surprised at what you really want from a solution. Work through the whole process. Practice makes the process become very easy, and not very time-consuming. The actual choice of a solution or decision may still be difficult, but the chances are good that you will make a better one.*

4   *Apply the principles of systematic thinking to the following:*

You and your best friend share an apartment. You both want to redecorate, but the friend is "into" contemporary stylings and you want something more "antiquish." Your budget is limited. What do you do?

5   *Rationality is crucial in interpersonal relationships. After you have worked through exercise 4, add this to your thinking: Your friend will only share the apartment for another six months. A marriage means that you will have to get another roommate. Now how do you react to the new information?*

6   *Sometimes being modifiable is the hardest part of being rational. Do you, or does someone you know, have trouble adjusting, changing, or adapting to new information or events? Does that affect any of your or his or her relationships? If so, how?*

LEARNING BY DISCUSSING

1   *Discuss the nature of "emoting." Do you, or do people you know, ever indulge in such activity?*

2   *Explain the differences between emoting and thinking systematically when confronted with a problem in an interpersonal situation.*

3   *Discuss the concept of rationality as explained in the text. Does that differ from how you would have defined it before reading the chapter? Do you see the concept as explained in the text helpful? How?*

4   *How can a concern for rationality help you with the goal of building better relationships?*

LEARNING BY READING FURTHER

Crable, Richard E., *Argumentation as Communication: Reasoning With Receivers.* Columbus, OH: Merrill, 1976.

Dewey, John, *How We Think.* Lexington, MA: Heath, 1933.

Gordon, William J. J., *Synectics: The Development of Creative Capacity.* New York: Collier, 1961.

Osborn, Alex F., *Applied Imagination: Principles and Procedures of Creative Problem-Solving,* 3d ed. New York: Scribner's 1963.

REAL REASONS, GOOD REASONS, AND REASON ENOUGH

STUDY OF THIS CHAPTER WILL ENABLE YOU TO

- *understand the human preoccupation with reasons*
- *understand that what something is depends a lot on why we think it occurred*
- *understand the meaning of "real" reasons*
- *understand the characteristics of the search for real reasons*
- *avoid the problems of searching for real reasons*
- *understand the nature of "good" reasons*
- *understand the characteristics of good reasons*
- *deal with interpersonal situations on the basis of "good," not "real" reasons*
- *understand the significance of the phrase "reason enough"*
- *understand strategies for deciding what is reason enough*
- *use strategies to help decide what is "reason enough"*

Well, Craig, what do you think of the applicants?

To tell the truth, Paul, all of them began to look alike.

I know what you mean. I kept looking for that "something extra" — you know, that spark of creativity, or enthusiasm. Everybody's college grades are so high nowadays that a grade average doesn't mean a whole lot. . . .

Well, Paul, none of this helps us. . . . The screening process has to be done, and we're the ones who have to do it. When you came to work here in personnel, I told you that some of this would be hard.

Yeah, I guess you were right.

Paul, I respect your opinion. Do you favor any of the applicants? . . .

Of all of them, I find myself leaning toward O'Brien. . . .

I do too, Paul, but I won't tell your wife if you don't tell mine. . . .

What do you mean? . . .

Nothing. . . . Just a joke. Why O'Brien?

Well, Craig, her credentials were excellent. . . .

I noticed.

Her grade average was high, and she had been involved in a lot of campus activities. . . .

I bet.

Craig, are you trying to tell me something?

Listen, Paul, when you've been here as long as I have, you make decisions for all kinds of reasons. I don't think there's a whole lot of difference among any of them. . . . And in that case we might as well make the decision based on who can best perk up the office. . . . Joyce O'Brien really ought to perk this place up.

Well, she was attractive — and outgoing, but that didn't affect my judgment of her or the others.

Mine, either. On the other hand, I do kinda like auburn hair. Nobody around here . . .

201

Wait a minute. We aren't hiring a social companion. Why are we even talking about things like this, Craig?

Don't get all excited, Paul. I'm personnel director, and I want to see the best possible people hired for the plant. I depend on you for input, and if you like this girl . . .

It's not a matter of liking. . . . I just think . . .

Paul, I didn't mean "liking" in any sense but professional. Now I don't think she ought to be overlooked just because of how she looks. . . . She really is attractive. . . . But that is not a factor for you—I understand, and it certainly isn't a factor for me. "Hire the best"—that's how we do things here. Now if she just happens to be a pretty, young, desirable woman. . . . Well, we just have to ignore that. I think she has just the qualities we're looking for. Right, Paul?

. . . Well, . . . There was Mike Johnson—the guy from Indiana University. . . .

Paul, he was . . . We have other people with his qualifications. I don't think we need to be wishy-washy about this. We've made up our minds . . . and I think we ought to stick with it.

Well, okay.

Good. Then it's settled.

Later, at the drinking foundatin, Walter—also in personnel—meets Paul.

Paul, did you guys make a decision about the opening?

Yeah, I guess we did. I'm afraid that Craig wanted one of the women because of her appearance. . . .

Later, Walter meets Craig at the cafeteria.

Craig, I hear you guys found someone for the opening.

Yes, but I'm afraid that Paul was against hiring one of the women. . . . I think he thought he might be tempted.

Real reasons One factor that seems to differentiate humans from lower animals is our fascination with the question, "Why?" As far as we know, nonhuman animals do not spend time wondering or explaining *why* they did something. That may seem obvious, but the point is crucial in understanding humans. Beavers, for example, are known to slap their tails on the water at the appearance of some movement or sound. Three questions are important:

Do beavers *choose* to behave in this way?
Do they realize that they had *other options* for behavior?
Are they asked to *explain why* they acted as they did?

The answers to all three questions seem to be "No."

Beavers and other animals, first, seem to respond simply to instinct, training, or loyalty to a human companion. Even Lassie—if there had ever been such a marvelous, talented beast—was a product of instinct and loyalty (and camera illusion). Only a well-stretched imagination can envision Lassie weighing the merits of going for help or running from a fire. As the word is commonly understood, nonhuman animals do not *choose* to act.

In terms of the second question we have only scanty evidence to suggest that animals actually are aware that they have made judgments about alternatives.[1] Even if we think they choose, the ability to understand the choice and alternatives to it seems far beyond the ability of nonhuman animals. And finally, no animal except a human is ever asked to justify or explain behavior. If a person were to step on your foot, you might ask why that happened. If a cow did the same thing, I don't suppose you would ask it for an explanation. If a human is responsible for taking another human's life, he or she always has the right to explain—accidental homicide, manslaughter, justifiable homicide, and so on. If a horse tramples and kills a human, no explanation is demanded—even though "being put to sleep" may be the punishment.

In essence, nonhumans do not seem to be the focus for questions about "why" things were done. Unaware of alternatives, they act by instinct, training, or loyalty, but are never asked to explain their behavior. The question "why?", however, is much more important in the realm of human relationships.

In the opening case study both Craig and his subordinate, Paul, were humans who were involved in a decision-making process. They made the decision to report favorably on Ms. O'Brien. Craig seemed to endorse the applicant enthusiastically, while Paul was much more reluctant. We can pose the same questions about these actions as we did about the beaver's warnings:

Did these men *choose* to behave in the way they did?
Did they realize that they had *other options* for behavior?
Are they asked to *explain why* they acted as they did?

Here the answer to all three questions is "Yes"—but to varying degrees.

To begin with, each was aware that other decisions could be made—there were other applicants. Toward the end of the discussion, Paul even began suggesting another applicant as an alternative. So they both chose to behave as they did while being aware of other options. What about the third question? Were they asked to explain why they acted as they did? Whether they actually and explicitly realized it, they were asked to explain—and knew they would be. As soon as Walter had asked *whether* they had made a decision, Paul explained *why* he thought the decision had been made and Craig explained *why* he thought Paul was reluctant about the decision. Walter had not asked any "Why?" questions. But humans, being what we are, almost automatically seem to *describe* actions by telling *why* the action was done.

---

[1] Even the recent "teaching" of apelike animals to "communicate with symbols" does not illustrate definitely that other animals are aware of their alternatives.

Did you go to the learning center?
No, I was too tired.

Or

Did you go to the learning center?
Yes, I figured I needed the extra study time.

What a human action is, is very much related to *why* the action took place. Consider the following event being labeled in various ways depending on *why* the event occurred.

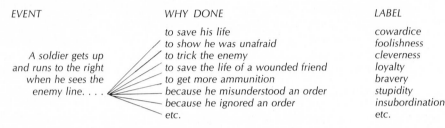

EVENT	WHY DONE	LABEL
	to save his life	cowardice
	to show he was unafraid	foolishness
A soldier gets up	to trick the enemy	cleverness
and runs to the right	to save the life of a wounded friend	loyalty
when he sees the	to get more ammunition	bravery
enemy line. . . .	because he misunderstood an order	stupidity
	because he ignored an order	insubordination
	etc.	etc.

I use "etc." to finish the sequence because surely there are other reasons for the same action—and thus other descriptions or labels for the "same" action. The point, though, is that the actions are not all the same: They vary depending on *why* the action occurred.

Since humans tend to be preoccupied with reasons, Walter's exchange with Craig and Paul should come as no surprise. Paul and Craig each had explanations—why's—for their behavior as well as for each other's actions. The problem with the human focus on reasons is that people are prone to discuss the "why's" of an action in terms of "real reasons." Paul told Walter that he was afraid Craig was "really" more interested in Ms. O'Brien's physical qualities than in her professional skills. Craig, on the other hand, explained that he felt the "real reason" Paul was reluctant was that he saw Ms. O'Brien as a temptation to physical encounter. These explanations might be shared by you as you read the study. But there are several ways in which the search for "real reasons" is misleading. To explain these difficulties with "real reasons," let me contrast two events:

1 You turn around.
2 You vote in a November election.

"Why?" What were the "real reasons" that prompted these hypothetical actions?

First, *the search for real reasons assumes that an explanation is true.*[2] Was that *really* why you did something? Why did you turn around?

[2] I argue against such a view in Crable, *Argumentation as Communication: Reasoning with Receivers* (Columbus, O.: Merrill, 1976), pp. 179–183.

The reason might be explained easily: You turned because someone called your name. You would be confused if someone asked, "No, why did you *really* turn around?" You would be confused because you assume that the person would automatically believe you. This is what you believe is true and assume that others will as well. But what about your voting behavior? Why —really—did you vote? You might answer, "Because I wanted to be patriotic," or "Because I wanted to see Jones rather than Smith win." Yet here, even more than with turning around, a person might say, "Hey, I want the real reason." Again, you might be confused. My point is that a concern for a "real" reason implies that there is a true explanation for behavior. My problem with this is that there is no way to *prove the truth* of why you did something. Consider the following example.

I saw you go into the candy store.
Yes, I wanted a stick of gum.
Why did you really go there?
Huh?
Why did you really go there?
I told you. . . .
Yeah, I know that you told me . . . but I want the truth.
Look, see the gum?
You did that to trick me. . . . Why did you really go in there?
Why would I lie about a piece of gum?
That's *my* point. Why would you—and why did you really go in there? . . .

I suspect no one will ever confront you as you emerge from a candy store. Yet there is no way to prove why a human action was done—either the purchase of a stick of gum or the hiring of a new employee.

Second, *the search for real reasons involves the belief that there is* one and only one *true explanation.* Reasonably enough, if there is a real reason, there must be reasons that are unreal, wrong, or false. *One* reason is sought that truly explains the act. Why did Richard Nixon fail to reveal all he knew about the Watergate break-in and cover-up? Ego? the desire for continued power? loyalty to his subordinates? embarrassment? concern for his family? concern for the future of the presidency? a concern for his image in history? a desire to get on with the business of international and domestic affairs? The search for real reasons means that one of these, but not more, can be "picked." A more rational approach, however, is to assume that people do things for all sorts of (possibly simultaneously strong) reasons.[3] The search for real reasons implies an all too simple way of explaining the complex actions of complex beings.

[3] This idea is basic to much of the writing by literary theorist and critic, Kenneth Burke. I am indebted to conversations with him for more complete understanding on this point.

Third, *the search for real reasons means that reasons are true now and will always be true.* "Logically," if a reason were true and real when the action was done, the reason will always be true and real. And yet I suspect that you have done things—and explained the "real" reasons. Later, you have "realized" that you actually did it for another "real" reason.

March 1979
Larry, why did you run into that other car?
The streets were wet, and my vision was impaired.

April 1979
Larry, why did you run into that other car?
Well, I wasn't paying as much attention as I should have been. . . .

May 1979
Larry, why did you run into that other car?
Well, the streets were wet, and I guess I wasn't paying as much attention as I should
      have been. . . . And well, Joan was kind of nestled close and . . . I guess, I just
      gave her a little kiss, and . . .

I don't believe anyone would keep repeating the identical question, but I also think that "changes" in explanations occur regularly. Has Larry finally arrived at the "real reason"? Only time will tell. As he rethinks the situation, there may be other factors—other reasons—that become the "real" reason. And yet these, too, may suddenly not be the real reason. The search for real reasons focuses on a lasting and unchanging explanation. In human action there may be no such thing.

Finally, *the search for real reasons implies that people actually can know exactly why they did something.* There is a cliché that expresses the desire "to get inside someone's head." There is another that says, "I wish I knew what makes him (or her) tick." Obviously, no one can do that. In the absence of being able to know why someone does what he or she does, we speculate about it. In the case study both Craig and Paul felt they knew what prompted the other's behavior. Craig (Paul felt) acted because he was attracted to the candidate. Paul (Craig felt) was reluctant to hire a tempting young woman. Both explanations may be terribly chauvinistic but that doesn't make them any less believable to the people involved. The problem is that each of these explanations was a judgment, a speculation, a guess, based on comments, past experience, "knowledge of human beings," and nonverbal cues. Each man was making a guess about the other's behavior. That can be a problem, but I think there is more of a problem here.

An even greater misconception is that each man is the only one who understands why—truthfully, singly, and once and for all—why he acted as he did. Human experience—including yours and mine—is filled with times when we have changed our perceptions of why we or someone acted. Even the person him- or herself does not seem to be capable of expressing real reasons that are true and unchanging. Certainly, our interpretations of why someone else acted are at best educated guesses. But our own explanations for why we acted are not much better. The evidence provided by experience is strong: People themselves cannot know the "real" reasons for their behavior.

This discussion may sound a bit pessimistic. In one swing of the typewriter I argue that humans always use reasons to explain behavior. In other sections I argue that we should not be fooled into thinking that these reasons are real, and that certain others are unreal or false. There is an answer to the problem, however, that has to do with a concern for "good" reasons.

Good reasons   The search for "real" reasons is an effort to narrow down explanations for why something was done. Ultimately, only one reason is selected as *the* reason. In contrast, a concern for "good" reasons means that there may be several and possibly many potential explanations for something. A *"good" reason* is simply *a factor to which someone has attached a positive significance and importance.*[4] This definition should sound familiar because it is almost identical to how "interpretation" has been defined in the text. The similarity is no accident. When any stimulus is interpreted, there is some meaning or significance or importance attached to it. Here when a human action is interpreted, some possible reason is explained as important or significant to the action. A concern for the real and ultimate reason is irrelevant. Consider a modification of an earlier example:

I saw you go into the candy store.
Yes, I wanted a stick of gum.
Why did you really go there?
Huh?
Why did you really go there?
Gum. I go there whenever I want gum.
Ah, but the real reason?
Look, I don't know what you mean. I wanted gum. I went there to buy gum. Buying
    gum is a good reason to go into a store. I don't know why you go into
    there. . . . Who are you anyway?

The person who was explaining the behavior felt she had a good reason for going into the store. There are, of course, other reasons for going into a candy store—candy, for example. The explainer allowed the other person the right to other reasons: "I don't know why you go in there. . . ." Yet buying

---

[4] For the idea, I am indebted to Professor Stephen Toulmin for conversations on the matter. See either his *Reason in Ethics* (Cambridge, Eng.: Cambridge University Press, 1968), pp. 70–71 or Crable, *Argumentation as Communication*, pp. 190–199.

candy was, for the explainer, a significant and important reason for going into the store. There are some characteristics of good reasons that may be helpful in understanding how people explain behavior.

To begin with, *good reasons are human creations.*[5] Factors themselves, such as a lust for gum, are not necessarily man-made (if we ignore advertising). But the *use of factors as reasons* is based on human decisions. I may be hot and perspiring, and so I walk to a grocery for a soft drink. Being hot and perspiring are good reasons for walking the distance to the grocery. In contrast, you may be hot and perspiring, but you decide not to walk to the grocery. "Good reasons" are not simply factors that decide or control what you will do. They are factors that you may decide *help to justify your action.* Semanticists—people who study various aspects of language use—have argued for years that no one, for example, can *make* you angry. Deceitful behavior or insults may seem a good reason to you to hit the person. Someone else may experience the same things and react quite calmly. Was the behavior a "good" reason for either response? That depended on the person experiencing the behavior. In the first case it was considered a reason for violence; in the second it was not considered a reason. Which one was right? They both were. Reasons are not born: They are created when humans attach importance and significance to them.

Relatedly, *good reasons differ only from "bad" reasons because of human judgment.*[6] Consider this:

Why did you cheat on the test?
I *had* to do well on the simple thing.
I needed the grade too, but not enough to cheat on the test.

The exchange may sound a bit pious, but it illustrates the point. Almost anything can be a good reason for some people. That same factor, however, may not be a good reason for someone else. The basic difference between good reasons and bad reasons is different interpretations—different attachments of significance and importance. What is a bad reason for doing something (to your way of thinking) may seem perfectly natural to someone else. The comment, "I don't understand why she did that" may mean more accurately, "I don't think I agree that that was a good reason." The difference between the two comments is important in interpersonal terms. The first may lead to frustration, hostility, and anger. The second allows disagreements to be discussed, evaluated, and perhaps even "understood": "I see why you did it, but I don't think that was a very good reason."

In order that all this does not make a "good reason" sound like a term for anything that people want to do, I hasten to add a third characteristic of

[5] This is to contrast them with such things as "instincts" and "physiological needs" which do not seem basically to be human creations.
[6] What I call "bad" reasons are often also known as errors, miscalculations, or (in logic) "fallacies."

good reasons. *Good reasons are guided by individual, social, and field-related factors.*[7] Obviously, a reason is judged to be good partly because of individual factors. Everyone has certain desires, needs, and biases that help separate what he or she thinks are the good reasons from the bad. A desire for a soft drink may be a good reason for going to the grocery. Without that individual need the trip to the grocery might have no good reason. A dislike of liberal politics might be a good reason for voting for a conservative candidate. The need for companionship might be a good reason for dating someone. These are *individual* factors. And yet many of what we call good reasons are based on "social factors," a general term for religious views, political group affiliation, level of education, socioeconomic status, and so forth. For years, for instance, I was convinced I would never vote for a Democratic candidate. Why? As a child, a friend in my hometown had told me that "You never saw a Republican who was a Communist." Being against Communists, of course, I also was against Democrats. That seemed, at the time, to be a perfectly good reason for future voting. In much the same way a lack of education or awareness can influence the creation of good reasons. Some people I know are convinced that man never landed on the moon—it

---

[7] Again, I am indebted to discussions with Stephen Toulmin. What must be avoided is to assume that the "goodness" of reasons is a purely subjective, individual sort of thing.

was, they say, a simulation on television. Others are convinced it actually happened—they saw it on television. In both cases a certain lack of sophistication allows television to be a good reason for having conflicting beliefs about moon landings. In sum, social groups and affiliations are frequently major factors in determining whether something will be a good reason.

Less obviously, a reason can be judged "good" or "bad" depending on the "field" of discussion.[8] By "field" I mean the occupation, subject matter, or situation that is the context for the action. Sports, for example, provide rules and guidelines that help people know how to create good reasons. In baseball's American League where pitchers do not bat, they are never taken out of the lineup just because a hit is needed. Only the effectiveness or health of the pitcher is reason enough for a change. In the National League where pitchers are required to bat, the need for a hit may be a very good reason for changing pitchers in the next inning, and for putting in a pinch hitter immediately. The rules help determine what is a good reason, although managers are free to make their individual decisions.

Similarly, occupational groups provide their own set of ways that help decide between good and bad reasons. Success with a procedure in medicine may be a good reason not to make changes. Yet manufacturing corporations continually change procedures, knowing that they must experiment with new products in order to retain customers. In law, a precedent—something done in the past—is one of the best reasons for approaching a case in a particular way. In advertising, much more emphasis is placed on the new, the dramatic, and the unusual. One of the most important factors in getting accustomed to a new job is finding out how people make decisions. Good reasons, to you as a student, may be rejected by people in your chosen profession. The field for discussion can have an important effect on what is and is not a good reason—as can individual and social factors.

Finally, *a focus on good reasons allows people to use certain other terms more accurately.* I refer to terms such as "main reason," "better reason," "best reason," and "deciding reason"—each of which is clarified by the concern for good reasons. Once someone accepts the idea that the reasons for doing something are human creations, discussing reasons becomes easier and clearer.

Well, I did it for several reasons, but *mainly* because . . .
Well, I guess that was a good reason, but I think there was a *better* reason for *not* doing it. You see . . .
Well, I'm sure she did it for the very *best* of reasons . . .
Well, there were a number of factors, but the *deciding* reason—the thing that tipped the scales was . . .

[8] The work of Toulmin in "fields" of judgment is important here. See Crable, *Argumentation as Communication*, chap. 7.

Notice that in all these no attempt is made to isolate the real, true, unchanging reason that something was done. The people involved recognize that things can be done for all sorts of reasons. Some are good (they judge), some are bad (they judge), some are better than others (they judge), but others are best (they judge); some are trivial, while others are the main ones (they judge), and some simply tip the scales and are the deciding factors (they judge). My repetition of "they judge" is crucial. All these discussions of reasons are judgments. But once we avoid the search for real reasons, we can begin to discuss reasons with more clarity.

What I have attemped here is to defend the idea that interpersonal relationships are helped more by discussions of good reasons than by a search for the real reasons. In an earlier example Walter was asking Paul about the hiring of the new applicant. Observe how that conversation might have gone:

Did you guys make a decision about the opening?

Yeah, I guess we did. I'm afraid that Craig wanted one of the women because of her appearance. . . .

What makes you think so, Paul?

Well, we were reviewing credentials—he just seemed to make everything suggestive.

Then you didn't think she was qualified? . . .

Oh, that wasn't it, Walt. I just . . . Well, you should have seen the look on his face.

Was there anyone else more qualified?

211

Not really. I thought she was the best of the lot.

Paul, you don't mean you picked her because of her body?!?

Don't get funny. . . .

I just mean that I don't know why you're so upset. . . . If she was qualified—none
    better—why *not* hire her?

Well, Craig was . . . Well, I guess he also felt she was the best, professionally, I
    mean . . . Maybe her looks just tipped the scales toward her. . . .

And for you, her appearance tipped them the other way?

That doesn't seem all that smart, does it?

All I can say, Paul, is that it wouldn't have affected me either way. . . . On the other
    hand, what *does* she look like? . . .

In this expanded case study the problem between Paul and Craig may not have been solved. But, then, Paul was better able to express how he was feeling—and why (he thought) Craig did what he did. And the understanding of reasons for behavior is crucial to interpersonal communication.

Still in relationships that aim toward a communing level, the discussion of reasons is not complete. In such relationships there should be a concern for what is "reason enough."

Reason enough   The discussion of *real* reasons focused on a search for the true, ultimate reason—the reason that simply existed. The discussion of *good* reasons emphasized the human creation of reasons and how individuals make those decisions. Here, though, the discussion concerns people who make decisions and judgments about reasons in the context of a relationship. How do people judge reasons in terms of their love or friendship with another? What makes a reason, not just good, but good enough to be constructive in a relationship? Two factors, I think, are important.

First, *good reasons—to be good enough—ought to be analyzed in terms of the relationship and whether the other will also accept them as being good.* I might, for example, receive a job offer from another university. For me the offer might be a good reason for changing jobs, houses, neighborhoods, and states. But those factors that I find attractive may or may not be equally acceptable to my wife. And that would be important to me. After a discussion of all the positive and negative factors, we both might judge the offer as very good. In that case the offer might be "good enough," interpersonally, to accept. If my wife, in contrast, had reservations about the university, the new city, or something else, she might not consider the offer a good reason for a move. In this particular case I probably would still consider the offer a good reason, but not a *good enough* reason, to move.

In interpersonal communication, generally, the point is the same. When a relationship is meant to become deeper and more intimate, the other person's judgment of the reasons for action are important. The relationship can be helped by the mutual acceptance of reasons. That point, however, can be taken too far.

Second, *good reasons for one of the two people may have to take precedence.* The healthy relationship probably cannot always be governed by a democratic vote – with 2 to 0 always the score. What each must realize is that in some matters one person's extremely strong acceptance of a reason may have to be more important than their mutual agreement. For instance, I may be negotiating a contract for a new book. The advance money and the opportunity to write the book might seem to be good reasons for accepting the contract. My wife might say I have enough to do, that I may suffer from overwork, or that I might miss opportunities to work on other, shorter writing and research projects. Even in this state of disagreement, I probably would sign the contract. The question of writing the text – unlike the change in university – has more to do with me, and less to do with "us." Since these objections concerned factors about me, I would reserve the right to be the primary decision maker in this case. I certainly would consider her thoughts, feelings, and reservations – but having reason enough does not always mean a vote by the two people. The communing relationship, then, avoids the temptation to search for real reasons. It goes even beyond the concern for individually judged good reasons, but still allows consideration of the individuals within the relationship. However, one person's judgment, made in regard to a relationship, might be reason enough. The result can be open discussion between two honest, responsible, but disagreeing individuals. The ability to cope with that situation is a sign of the communion that is developing between two interpersonally mature individuals.

CHAPTER SUMMARY

People, unlike lower animals, always seem to be concerned with "why" something happened or was done. In fact, we tend to identify what *something was in large part by* why *it occurred. In this search to explain why it is easy to assume that there is an absolutely true, once-and-for-all description of why something took place: a real reason. What seems to be the case, however, is that people do things for a variety of reasons. They can tell us "why" they did what they did, but their description may change over the years or as events change. Humans are complex, and "why"— really—we do what we do seems destined always to be uncertain.*

The chapter suggested a better, more constructive approach to dealing with the "why" of human beings. An emphasis on "good" reasons provides a key to more constructive thinking about such matters. The concept "reason enough" was added as a way of indicating that even a "good" reason to do something may not be "reason enough" to do it; the good reason

213

may not take into consideration the other person and the relationship. In communing relationships, people do things because there was "reason enough."

LEARNING BY APPLYING

1   Ask a friend to explain what happened in a social setting, a committee meeting, or a family quarrel. Notice how often the *what* is explained in terms of *why* the thing occurred. Try to find others who participated in the same situation. See if their description of what happened is the same or different. If it is somewhat different, were there different *why's* explained?

2   Try this exercise with yourself. Develop a statement that proves *why* you did or are doing something—something even as common as enrolling in a certain class. Think of all the ways someone could explain your action in different ways. Can you ever prove the real reasons for one of your actions? What does this tell you about people who insist on the real reasons in an explanation?

3   Make a list of all the "good" reasons for your choice to attend a particular school or to work at a particular kind of job. Do you think these will all be good reasons to everyone? If you think they will be, present them to the class or a group of other people. See how often that what you consider a good reason will not seem good to someone else.

4   Take the list you made in exercise 3. Assume that you are married (if you are not), or assume that you are single (if you are not). The reversal of the situation might change some of your "reasoning." Do all of the "good" reasons (in this new situation) give you "reason enough" still to think that your school or career choice was justified? What other factors come into play? How do strategies for deciding what is reason enough help you? Are there other factors you wish to add?

LEARNING BY DISCUSSING

1   Explain how statements of *what* something *is* seem generally involved with *why* the thing is said to have happened. Do you see how important "reasons" are to humans?

2   What is the nature of, and problems with, the search for "real reasons"?

3   Explain the nature of "good reasons."

4   What does the phrase "reason enough" mean to you now?

5   Explain why a concern for "reason enough" can help you build and maintain better relationships—one to another.

LEARNING
BY READING FURTHER

Crable, Richard E., *Argumentation as Communication: Reasoning With Receivers.* Columbus, OH: Merrill, 1976, chap. 7.

Toulmin, Stephen E., *Reason in Ethics.* Cambridge, England: Cambridge University Press, 1968.

————, "Reasons and Causes," in *Explanation in the Social Sciences,* eds. M. Berger and F. Cioffi. Cambridge, England: Cambridge University Press, 1970.

Wallace, Karl, "The Substance of Rhetoric: Good Reasons," in *The Rhetoric of Our Time,* ed. J. Jeffrey Auer. New York: Appleton, 1969.

18

VAMPIRING, SEEKING COUNSEL, AND MUTUALLY SUPPORTING

STUDY OF THIS CHAPTER WILL ENABLE YOU TO

- *understand the nature of interpersonal "vampiring"*
- *understand the characteristics of vampiring*
- *avoid interpersonal vampiring better*
- *understand the concept of "seeking counsel"*
- *understand the characteristics of seeking counsel*
- *seek counsel more effectively in the interpersonal situation*
- *understand the concept of "mutual support"*
- *understand strategies of mutual support*
- *engage in mutual support better in the interpersonal situation*

R-r-r-i-n-n-g!
She comes from the shower, wrapping a towel around her to catch some of the
    water.
R-r-r-i-n-n-g!
She trips on the cord of the hair curler.
Achh. My toe!
R-r-r-i-n-n-g!
Hello.
Hello, Janie! This is Mike. Hope I didn't catch you at a bad time.
Hi, Mike. I was in the shower.
Well, this will only take a minute.
Okay, *she shivers,* What's up?
Janie, you know that girl I've been dating?
Polly?
Yeah, well, we had a fight last night.
You didn't really drag me out of the shower to tell me you had a fight with a girl
    friend, now did you?
I guess I did. Janie, I really like her. . . . She is something special. And well, you
    know, I always come to the big sister for advice.
I know.
But that wasn't the only reason I called. I know you and Sam had been . . . well, you
    seemed uncomfortable together the last time I saw you . . . and . . .
And what, Mike?
Well, I thought we might be able to help each other.
Do you know how wet and cold I am standing here?
Why are you wet?
I was in the shower. . . . Remember, I told you that.
Oh, yeah. I just got up, but I bet a good shower would feel good. . . .
Mike, it *felt* very good . . .

I don't know what to do, Janie. . . .

About what?

About Polly. Do you have some time this morning. Maybe I could come over for a cup of coffee.

Mike, I've really got a ton of things to do today. . . .

Well, I thought you might want to talk about you and Sam, too. Sorta two birds with one cup of coffee — get it?

I get it, Mike. Sam and I are okay. . . . He was just a little tense. . . .

But he seems like that every time I see him. . . .

That's one explanation. . . .

What?

Oh, nothing. Look, this morning is not a very good time. Can it wait until . . . tomorrow?

Look, I don't know where Polly will be tomorrow. We had a fight last night about . . .

But, Mike, you are always fighting with girl friends. . . .

Yes, but this is different. . . . Polly's different.

You always say that.

But this time, it really is different. How 'bout lunch?

I have a luncheon to go to . . . then . . .

Well, I'm sorry if I bothered you. . . .

Don't pout, Mike. . . .

I'm not going to pout. I just thought we could talk — no problem, sis. . . .

Okay, okay. You can come over. . . .

Can I come over right now?

I need to finish my shower — and get warm.

Oh, were you in the shower?

Yes. . . . I guess I forgot to tell you.

Well, good. We can talk about Sam and Polly and get the whole thing straightened out. . . .

Mike, there is nothing to straighten out between Sam and me. . . .

Look, Janie, I'm your brother. You don't have to play games with me. I understand . . . See you in a few minutes. . . .

Vampiring   Vampire legends — some involving Count Dracula, and others not — seem to be part of the culture in numerous countries. They seem to gain popularity in cycles. For a time the legends may seem buried under a blanket of social sophistication — only to be unearthed again. The late 1970s gave rise to the fresh appearances of vampires on television, movies, and the Broadway stage. Vampire legends, indeed, seem to be almost in our blood.

But Count Dracula himself and his male and female counterparts are not my primary concern. Not every vampire literally lives on blood, and not every victim becomes another vampire. Still vampires are about us. *By vampires,* I mean *the people who "live off" other human beings and seem*

By vampires, *I mean the people who "live off" other human beings and seem to sap their strength, their wisdom, and their energy. Thomas Hopker, 1978, Woodfin Camp]*

to sap their strength, their wisdom, and their energy. I speak of interpersonal vampiring, and Mike provides the example of the behavior. To understand interpersonal vampiring better, let's explore its various characteristics.

First, *"vampiring" seems characterized by the genuine* personal *desire for aid and comfort.* This in itself is a perfectly natural and understandable desire. All of us need other people—people who will touch us and allow us to reach out for them. But second, *vampiring is often masked as an attempt at* mutual *aid, or simply aid for the other.* Mike called his older sister about his relationship with Polly. Consciously or subconsciously, this seemed the major motivation. Yet he tried to show concern for the problems he felt Janie and Sam were experiencing. This may have been partly a genuine concern for their marriage or simply a way for Mike to justify the help he was hoping Janie could provide or perhaps a way for Mike to convince himself that he and Janie could help one another. Regardless of the "real reason"—which no one will ever know—the primary impulse of the call seemed to be self-help. Mike had noticed earlier that Sam seemed tense, but he waited until he himself had a problem. Then, he called. The evidence is strong that Mike sought personal help but tried to conceal it as an effort at mutual help.

Third, *vampiring involves the belief that the other person is somehow the vampire's lifeblood.* The vampire not only wants these things, but needs them from the other person. The traditional vampire script shows the major character flitting about, biting necks here and there. A more recent television show presented Dracula as keeping his own blood supply. His victims were bound, fed well, and continually drained intravenously. The makeshift blood bank not only saved a lot of nightstalking, but it made the script more bloodcurdling. The ready reserve of strength, wisdom, and energy is the reason that interpersonal vampires need ongoing human relationships so much. "What would I do without you?" is the plea of both Mike and the Count.

Finally, interpersonal *vampiring seems often to involve little or no actual concern for the other person.* The television vampire just described showed some degree of concern for his guests. But then, he had a stake in whether they were healthy, full-blooded people. In the same way, Mike showed some superficial concern for Janie. He said he was concerned, for example, about Janie's marriage. At the same time, he never quite realized his interruption of her shower or the problem with having to rearrange her schedule to meet his desires. Janie seemed to be important to Mike—not because of her own welfare—but because he needed her to be able to help him.

What I have called vampiring, then, stems from the natural human desire for aid and comfort. The difficulty arises when it becomes obvious that the desire for comfort and help overshadows everything else in the relationship. There is, however, a more positive approach to responding to the need for others. We call it "seeking counsel."

Seeking counsel Contemporary people—the stereotype goes—could not exist without counseling. There are psychologists, psychiatrists, marriage counselors, social workers, financial counselors, legal counselors, research consultants, and yes, even communication consultants. These labels identify people who specialize in various types of counseling, but their function is much the same. As a dictionary might read, a counselor provides help or advice. A counselor is one who may be known as a "comforter," "a shoulder to cry on," "a listener," or simply an expert. All of us seek aid and comfort from others. That is even true of the vampire. But "seeking counsel" in its most positive interpersonal sense is much different from vampiring. Let me explain.

Seeking counsel wisely means, first, *that the person realizes the need for help*. Without pretending that the goal is mutual help or help for the other, the person simply requests aid. That is easier to do when the "counselor" is a professional of some sort. In those situations it is easier to admit the need for personal help. Most of us, however, need advice and comfort more often than we can go to a professional. Even when the aid and advice are sought from a nonprofessional, the realization of the need for personal help is crucial. Professional counselors have long recognized that the first step in solving problems is to admit that there is a need to confront and cope with the problem. That is true of anyone who seriously seeks advice. Seeking counsel wisely, then, means that first the need for help is admitted.

Seeking counsel wisely means, second, *that the person realizes the importance of self-help*. Most counselors do not pretend to have all the answers nor to have magical cures for every human problem. What they will do is listen, try to understand, and make observations. At times they may give direct advice and make evaluations. What counselors most want to do is to help others to help themselves. Ultimately, the person seeking counsel will have to make certain evaluations and decisions, which in most instances can be made by the individual him- or herself. Counselors provide additional information, "objective" evaluations, and other points of view or alternatives. What the person does with these is normally a personal decision. Self-help—in acting on the advice—is important in seeking counsel wisely.

Finally, *in the interpersonal situation, seeking counsel means that the person is considerate of the counselor*. The informal counselor should not have to be "drained," "sapped," or made to feel "burned out" by the other. In direct contrast to vampiring, the person seeking counsel has a concern for the other person. The relationship is not simply a free supply of advice, wisdom, and attention. The informal, interpersonal counselor does not simply supply the raw material on which the other survives. The person seeking counsel wisely accepts the fact that there are limits on being a burden to others. Counseling that becomes habitual is the sign of a one-sided, undeveloping relationship. Counseling, though, can be sought for serious reasons when legitimate problems arise. When the seeker is sensitive to the time and energy of the other, the process can be a positive force in a relationship. Consider the following example:

Teddy	Have you got a minute? Actually, a few minutes?
Carie	Well, I guess. What can I do for you?
Teddy	Good question.
Carie	What do you mean?
Teddy	I mean I hope you can do something for me. I have an important interview tomorrow. I know I have to go through with it by myself, but I wanted to ask you a question or two.
Carie	Sure, I've got some time now.
Teddy	It's okay if you don't. I could phone you later.
Carie	No problem. How do you think I can help?
Teddy	Well, you've already gone through a lot of these things. What do you think I ought to do if they ask . . .

In this case Teddy is straightforward about seeking help and advice. Still he seems to be aware that Carie may have more to do than counsel him at that time. The contrasts between Teddy and Mike (from the other case) underscore the differences between vampiring and seeking counsel.

And still vampiring and seeking counsel are "one-way" processes. In the serious and ongoing relationship, times will arise when each person may need to counsel the other. Those times call for people who can be concerned both about themselves and each other. That simultaneous concern may not be easy, but the ability to help one another simultaneously is one of the ways of aiming toward interpersonal communion.

Mutually supporting Interpersonal relationships that are deep and important to two people often require what I shall call "mutual support." By that I do not mean that the two people simply take turns seeking and giving help. *"Mutually supporting" means that two people act on the interrelationship between giving and seeking aid and comfort.* This can be explained by focusing on three major strategies of mutual support.

First, to be mutually supportive, *each person must know that helping him- or herself may be a way of helping the other.* In serious relationships a "personal" problem really is an "interpersonal" problem because both people will be involved. Problem drinking or feelings of jealousy do not affect only one person in the relationship. They affect both. So one of the ways of helping the other person is to seek counsel that promotes self-help. The advice and comfort you receive from another can help you and, consequently, help that person as well. But then, second, the reverse is also true.

Each person must know that helping the other may be a way of helping the self. The advice and attention you give to the other person may help you sort out some of your own problems. Talking to the other person about insecurity and self-confidence, for example, may help you with your own shortcomings. But remember, you are involved in a relationship. You are affected by how the other thinks and feels and by what the other does. Any aid and comfort you provide him or her may be of help. When that person is better able to cope with feelings and situations, your relationship may become easier. For very practical reasons, then, you should know that self-help can be mutually advantageous: that by helping the other person, each of you can help yourself; by helping yourselves, you can actually help the other.

Third, *each person can concentrate on both each individual* and *their relationship.* Good mutual support does not mean forgetting the people involved and only helping the relationship. But in the same way, mutual support does not mean focusing on the individuals and ignoring the relation-

. . . each person can concentrate on both each individual and *their relationship.* [*Diakopoulous, Stock, Boston*]

223

ship. The advice and comfort exchanged between people in a relationship can focus on *both* the individuals and the relationship. Not all aid and comfort is comfortable. Sometimes mutual counsel may be painful to one or both people—the mutual counsel may point toward a change in the relationship. But in the best of situations, mutual support means better, stronger people and a better, stronger relationship. The result can be something that helps the development of communion.

Mutual support, then, is far more than simply taking turns in seeking counsel. It deals with providing the kind of aid and comfort that will help both the people and the relationship. Consider the following exchange:

Taylor	The last thing I want to do in the world is go to the company picnic.
Rita	I know what you mean. You remember what a terrible time we had the last time? Why do they have these things, anyway?
Taylor	To boost morale.
Rita	So far it's doing a great job—and we're just at the dreading stage.
Taylor	What can I tell you?
Rita	You can start by telling me if the many-handed Rick is going to be there. Last year he patted me so often I felt like a lump of dough.
Taylor	It's his way of being friendly.
Rita	I bet.
Taylor	Well, I don't think . . . I think you can avoid him.
Rita	Yes, that bit of sage advice always makes the fox feel safer around the hounds.
Taylor	Forget him.
Rita	Easy for you to say. He didn't paw you all afternoon.
Taylor	Okay, okay. Let's not let this thing get out of hand. We can just not go if you think you can't handle it.
Rita	Well, . . . I know we really ought to go.
Taylor	Then, we'll go.
Rita	But I would feel a lot better if you hung around me more. Rick may have busy hands, but he's careful.
Taylor	Okay, I won't play volleyball. That'll allow me to guard your body all afternoon.
Rita	I don't need sarcasm. I just don't want to have to run from Rick all afternoon.
Taylor	Okay. Sorry. I am just dreading another time like last year. We fought all the way home about something.
Rita	You know what it was?
Taylor	Let me guess. Rick?
Rita	Jackpot.
Taylor	Oh, okay. I'll stay with you. Maybe we can get through the situation—just you, me . . . . and Rick.
Rita	Funny.

In ongoing and serious relationships the need for seeking and giving support will arise. Those times call for sensitivity on the part of both people. An awareness of the relationship between helping the other and self-help

can allow both people to make the best of situations. An awareness that both individuals and the relationship are important can smooth the way for mutual support. And mutual support can help with the development of interpersonal communion.

CHAPTER SUMMARY

One of the common situations—or interludes—in interpersonal communication is when one person needs help or advice from another. If sharing is so important in building better relationships, then surely this need for help should be a positive part of the relationship. And yet certain kinds of behaviors can actually keep relationships from improving.

"Vampiring" is what I call the act of one person in "sucking dry" the time, the effort, advice, and help of another person. Though vampiring may be prompted by a genuine desire for help, the chapter explained the more negative parts of vampiring.

In contrast to vampiring, people who wish help and advice can engage in what the chapter described as "seeking counsel." The attitudes that can help you seek counsel wisely—and without hurting the relationship—were discussed and illustrated.

But what is even more important in the serious relationship is a sense of mutual support—not just one-way help. By adapting an attitude of mutual support, two people can help themselves build toward a communing relationship.

LEARNING BY APPLYING

1   Think about several people with whom you are good friends. I suspect that you will find that some of them exhilarate and enliven you: just being with them can "perk" you up. On the other hand, conversations with some may mostly tire you—drain you of energy. Most, I suspect, are capable of doing either to you, depending on the circumstances. Do you, then, have some vampires around you? Are you at times something of a vampire yourself to those who "perk" you up? You may find that the notion of vampiring is more common than you thought.

2   There is no basic harm in seeking counsel and advice from others. What do people do that make you *most willing* to give advice and counsel? What does that tell you about how you can best seek counsel?

3   Observe one of the ongoing situation comedies in prime time television. Do you see people mutually supporting one another—or is one character basically the "giver" of wise advice? If you are old enough to remember—or if you can see rerun, syndicated presentations—"Father Knows Best," "The

Big Valley," and "Bonanza" offer prime examples of one-way advice and counsel . . .

4 Is there a special relationship in your life that is mutually supportive—or was there once such a relationship? In what ways does or did the mutual support occur? Why is or was it important? How does mutual support enhance that feeling of oneness?

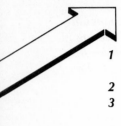

LEARNING BY DISCUSSING

1 Give your own description of the interpersonal vampire. Why is vampiring a potential interpersonal problem?
2 Explain what is meant by "seeking counsel."
3 Explain the meaning of "mutual support." Why is that not simply a situation in which two emotionally unhealthy people lean on one another?
4 How can mutual support be a constructive approach to having better relationships?

LEARNING BY READING FURTHER

Buber, Martin, *Between Man and Man*. Trans. Ronald Gregor Smith. New York: Macmillan Paperbacks, 1965.

Fromm, Eric, *The Sane Society*. New York: Holt, Rinehart and Winston, 1958.

Giffin, Kim and Barnes, Richard E., *Trusting Me, Trusting You*. Columbus, OH: Merrill, 1976.

O'Banion, Terry and O'Connell, April, *The Shared Journey: An Introduction to Encounter*. Englewood Cliffs, NJ: Prentice-Hall, 1970.

Reik, T., *Listening with the Third Ear*. New York: Farrar, Straus, 1948.

Rogers, Carl, *On Becoming A Person*. Boston: Houghton Mifflin, 1961.

AUTONOMY, SELF-ASSERTION, AND ENLIGHTENED INDEPENDENCE

STUDY OF THIS CHAPTER WILL ENABLE YOU TO

- *understand the concept of "autonomy"*
- *understand the characteristics of autonomy*
- *understand the concept of "self-assertion"*
- *understand the characteristics of self-assertion*
- *understand the concept of "enlightened independence"*
- *understand the characteristics of enlightened independence*
- *respond with enlightened independence in the interpersonal situation*

Where are you going?

Out.

Out where?

Just out . . . with the guys.

How long will you be gone, do you think?

I don't know. . . . It depends on what we get into.

What do you mean, "What you get into"?

Look, mom, I'm 17 years old. I'm not a baby anymore.

You are still living at home, you know.

Yeah, but I won't be in three months. Will you call me at the university in September to ask me where I'm going?

That's not the point, is it?

I don't know. What *is* the point?

The point is that you've just graduated. You are still our responsibility. And we have a right to know where you are going and what you plan to do.

Okay, okay. I'm just going out with some of the guys. I don't know what we'll decide to do, so I don't know when we'll be back.

You're not going to that bar that serves beer to minors, are you?

What do you mean?

I think you know exactly what I mean.

'fraid I don't.

You know, everyone says that some day that bar will be raided.

Raided? Is Elliott Ness in town? . . . Just kidding.

I wish I knew for sure.

Knew what?

Do you know how irritating it is when you act so naïve?

What do you mean? . . . Strike that. . . . Listen, I'm old enough to stay out of trouble. Believe me. I got to run; here comes Ed in his Dad's car. Bye.

(In the car) Hey, Ed, let's get there early. I want to get a seat near the juke box.

Autonomy   In dictionary terms, autonomy means a sort of "self-governance" or some kind of self-motivated action. Clearly, one of the goals of nearly everyone at some time is to be in control of his or her own life. The case presented a 17-year-old trying to exercise some measure of autonomy. But the desire to be free to do one's "own thing" occurs in every other kind of human relationship. It is ironic but natural, then, that a book on *interpersonal* relationships should deal with the *personal* desire to be free of others.

There are several ways in which people see themselves "free from others," but the first one is what I call *"autonomy": a complete freedom of one person from the restrictions of others.* Autonomy, as I shall use the word, has several characteristics.

First, autonomy is characterized by *self-awareness.* As far as we know, for example, babies assume that they are "a part of" mommy and daddy. Even older children often have difficulty understanding that they themselves are people—and not just an extension of their parent or parents. Similarly, husbands and wives can come to think of themselves as simply one-half of a pair of people: they are a part of a marital partnership. In the same way, friends can become so dependent on one another (or one on the other) that their individual selves seem to disappear.

At one time or another, however, these feelings of being an inseparable part of someone else begins to fade. What emerges is a new (or renewed) awareness that everyone is an individual person and has him- or herself to look out for and develop. Suddenly or gradually, the person becomes aware of his or her responsibility to that self. Self-awareness is born—or reborn. And so we see husbands and wives who want to develop themselves—not as a partner, but a self. We see friends finding a relationship "smothering" their development. And as in the case, we see an adolescent wanting desperately to exert a long-neglected self.

But autonomy is more than self-awareness. Second, self-awareness is frequently accompanied by a (real or imagined) *self-confidence.* "If I am a person"—perhaps the thinking goes—"then I can take care of myself." I mentioned *real or imagined* self-confidence because there is no requirement that the person actually believes what he or she says about the situation. The 17-year-old may or may not have believed he could take care of himself, though I suspect he felt he could. There is no guarantee that the husband or wife can actually "make it all right" without the other. The point is that regardless of the ability to care for one's self, the feeling of self-confidence may be expressed.

Third, autonomy is characterized by a *self-centeredness.* "Logically," if I am self-aware and self-confident, then I am probably going to "try and look out for 'number one.' " In the case the son seemed fairly unconcerned about his mother or anyone else. The situation, as seen by him, was that he was old enough to have a good time and he intended to have it. If someone had asked whether he still cared for his family, he most likely would have been insulted by the question. Clearly, there was little in the discussion to suggest any hostility or hatred between the parent and teenager. Self-centeredness, then, does not necessarily mean a dislike of others. It means simply that everyone has priorities, and the self becomes the focus of attention.

Finally and most importantly, autonomy seems to imply *self-celebration*. When I was approximately the age of the son I became very impressed with the idea that I was a full-fledged person. I became intoxicated with the notion that I was old enough to make my own decisions (even if they were bad ones) and reveled in who I was and what I could do. I was no longer Mr. and Mrs. Crable's son: I was me! All that, I know, sounds a bit silly, but it is how I felt. I "had new wings" and was determined to see how well they worked. This feeling of power and ability—this celebration of self—is part of autonomy.

This discussion probably leaves the impression that autonomy is not necessarily the best way to "win friends and influence people." That is probably an accurate impression. But the impulse to *be a person* is a very real human force. What contemporary writers have done is to notice that too many people find autonomy distasteful. But is there a more constructive approach to being a person?—an approach that more constructively helps people? The answer, it seems to me, is a qualified "yes," and it is called "self-assertion."

Self-assertion   Autonomy focuses on feelings a person has—feelings that may lead to either irresponsible acts or frustration. Self-assertion, or "assertiveness" training, focuses on actions rather than on feelings.[1] *Self-assertion is an act of* responsibly *functioning as a full human being with certain rights.* Some of the writing on self-assertion teaches people how to generate the "nerve" to send a charcoalized steak back to the restaurant kitchen. Some of it focuses on how one gets even with a sand-throwing bully at the beach. More seriously, though, the general effort is aimed at helping people "get what they deserve," "stand up for their human rights," or "fairly influence someone else." Approaches to assertiveness training have been criticized because they make bullies out of people who used to be meek—or because they make a once easy-going person into a demanding ogre. It seems obvious that there have been abuses in training for self-assertion. And yet there is good reason to help people be confident enough to function as a whole person. Being obnoxious is not a requirement for self-assertion.

Self-assertion can be characterized by a number of factors or viewpoints. First, *a healthy respect for one's self is important.* I do not mean that you have to be completely self-centered; I do not mean that you have to

[1] I am speaking here of no one particular book but, rather, the whole "genre" of books and courses on assertiveness training. Books on the topic are generally available wherever popular press books are sold and in public libraries.

be in love with the idea that you are a distinct person. I simply mean that you should be aware that you are a person with a positive self-image. You are a full-fledged person just as everyone else is. So you have certain needs that you can admit. You have certain wishes that can and should be expressed and certain rights that should be honored—simply because you are a human being. In essence, everyone needs a healthy respect for him- or herself.

Self-assertion, however, also is characterized by the idea that not everyone you meet will have as much respect for you as you do for yourself. Self-assertion implies a certain (but not exaggerated) amount of what I shall call *"me-themism."* Not everything that someone else wants or needs will be something you can provide. For example, a parent may want very much for a child to "take piano—like I always wanted to do." Or a friend of the opposite sex may want you to do something you really do not wish to do. In such situations attention to self-assertion can be helpful. You must realize that you *are* separate from the other person. Assertiveness training prepares people to be strong enough to say, "This may be what *you* want, but it is not necessarily what is best for me—do you see? You and I are separate people." I *do not* mean that assertiveness should lead you to feel "alone against the world." I *do* mean that it is possible for people to see themselves as distinct individuals.

Third, with self-assertion comes an awareness of *self-power.* Americans have always prided themselves on "self-reliance;" on "pulling themselves up with their own bootstraps." Some of that — especially in the extreme — is pure myth. Some of it, however, is entirely accurate. The self-asserting person knows that he or she can change things. Personal action can, in fact, cause a steak to be reprepared as it was supposed to be. A single person can make a neighborhood — or a relationship — more like he or she wants it to be. People can even make themselves more like they would like to be. Even the person with little money and no education can learn to take action that helps the personal situation.

Finally and unfortunately, self-assertion may also be characterized by *self-defensiveness.* There seems to be a very fine line between being self-assertive and completely paranoid that someone will violate a right. The worst of self-assertiveness training seems to be the temptation for people to become so impressed with their ability to demand their rights that they *look* for violations of their rights. So . . . steaks must be done, not adequately, but perfectly; friends must not only show respect, but they must perform flawlessly; "off-hand" comments come to be viewed as insults requiring an apology. In sum, self-assertiveness as an alternative to thoughtless autonomy *can* become nearly as negative as autonomy itself.

Let's take our young friend — we'll call him "Jack" — and hear him reenact the discussion with his mother.

Where are you going?
Out.
Out where?
Just out . . . with the guys.
How long will you be gone, do you think?
I don't know. . . . It depends on what we get into.
What do you mean, "What you get into."
I'm not a baby anymore. I know enough not to get myself into trouble — if that's what
    you're afraid of.
I just want what's best for you.
Don't you think I know that? The problem is that I think I'm the one who knows
    what's best for me. . . .
You are still living in this house. . . .
I know, but in a few months, I won't be. I have to be responsible for myself. . . . And
    I have to learn sometime. . . .
Oh, Jack . . .
Look, I'm not going to get into anything. I just don't know where we're going yet.
    . . . That's all — nothing evil.

You're not going to that bar that serves minors, are you? They say that that place is going to be raided one of these days.

Do "they" say that because I'm going out, I will automatically get into trouble?

No, but I think you know what I mean.

I know what you mean, but I'm hoping you know what I mean. I won't always be under your care. I have to grow up sometime. I have enough respect for myself not to *want* to get into trouble with the law. . . . Nobody wants an ex-con on the football team, huh?

Jack, be serious.

I am. I want what's best for me—same as you. But I'm not a baby. Here comes Ed in his Dad's car. Bye.

(In the car) Hey, Jack—where do you want to go?

Let's not go to the bar—I heard it may be raided. That's all I need. Let's get a twelve-pack and go to the ol' drinkin' spot.

In the reenactment, Jack handled himself and his problems differently. He was still attempting to do as he pleased, but he at least balanced it with more consideration about who he was and what was less risky for him. He was trying to be self-assertive, without being blindly autonomous. Still I suspect the conversation was unsettling to his mother. In essence, there seems to be little doubt that assertiveness education can be helpful to people who traditionally act as doormats for the world. Yet it is also true that self-assertion may become a hindrance, not a help, in an interpersonal sense. In relationships meant to last over a period of years and problems, something besides self-assertion may be more desirable. An alternative might be what I shall call "enlightened independence."

Enlightened In dictionary terms, independence might sound the same as autonomy.
independence After all, when a nation becomes "independent," it has broken free of some other country or controlling force. Yet every country that has ever won or been given its independence soon finds that complete autonomy is not possible. Other nations are needed for mutual defense. Other countries become the source of needed natural resources, as markets for products or resources—or both. The "independent" nation soon learns that it still must rely on other nations. There is a difference, however: now the reliance is probably more selective, more a matter of choice, and more mutually beneficial. *The ability to* choose how *the country wishes to be* dependent *is what I mean by* enlightened independence.

In the same way, people are never really independent or completely autonomous—regardless of what they think. There will always be other people who are important, either because of what they can do for you or to you. In interpersonal terms, then *enlightened independence means that people are wise enough about themselves and their surroundings to choose how they will be dependent.* Enlightened independence, then, does not mean

233

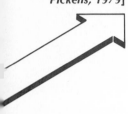

. . . enlightened independence means that people are wise enough about themselves and their surroundings to choose how they will be dependent. [© Marjorie Pickens, 1979]

that an adolescent has to break ties with parents, that wives and husbands must separate in order to become "who they are—really," or that friends are suddenly unimportant. The enlightened, independent person simply knows that he or she can help choose what the relationship is to be.

Enlightened independence is characterized by a number of characteristics. Each one allows the individual to be an individual, but each ensures that healthy interpersonal relationships can be formed and deepened better. In that sense, enlightened independence is a tremendous asset in the communing relationship.

First, what allows enlightened independence in the communing relationship is *a respect for the other person.* This respect for the other person is a balance for the self-respect so basic to assertiveness training. Just as you are a person worthy of honor and respect, so is this other person. Just as you have wants and needs and wishes, so does this other. Just as you have a right to expect consideration and understanding, so does the friend, the parent, or the lover. Among other things, this is a reason that men should not treat women as "sex objects"—or any other kind of object. This attitude of respect for the other is why women should not treat men as "babies" or "macho" men. Enlightened independence depends in part on other people being treated as humans—with all the respect that they deserve.

Second, enlightened independence means *an awareness of the results of individual actions.* Self-assertion stresses self-power as a human characteristic. In the communing relationship people learn that their exercise of self-power must be balanced by an awareness of effects. Certainly, you *can* humiliate a friend who has betrayed a secret, but is that what you really want? You *can* go to a bar specializing in underaged drinking—as the son did in the opening case—but what might be the effect on parents or younger brothers or sisters? You *can* engage in extramarital affairs, but what might be the impact on a whole family? The point is—as a relative of mine often says—"for every action, there is a reaction." You can exercise a numberless range of powers. Enlightened independence that helps the communing relationship means that people look carefully at the results of their actions on important other people. The exercise of personal, individual power begins to be viewed as a *choice*—frequently, a very important one.

With respect for the other person and an awareness of the results of action, enlightened independence, third, means *the assumption of interpersonal responsibility.* Persons in a communing relationship begin to "take on" or assume a very heavy burden: the knowledge that they still have responsibility to other people. There is no such thing as full autonomy. Other people are still important. They have feelings, desires, and needs. Enlightened independence means that you have chosen to accept some role in whether those feelings are hurt; whether their desires and needs can be partially met by you. Just as the newly independent country discovers that it needs—and wants—friends, enlightened independence means you will discover the same thing.

Relatedly and finally, enlightened independence is characterized by *the choice to help others.* In the communing relationship people do not help and interact with the other because they *have* to; they do it because they *wish* to. As a part of what seems like autonomy, they have decided *not* to be autonomous. They begin exercising their right to choose relationships and to help deepen them. They do not have to appear hostile and aggressive in order to show that they are full human beings. Enlightened independence means that the relationship has reached a new and higher level: a spouse is suddenly seen as a friend; a parent is seen as a friend; and a friend is seen as a person freely chosen for a deeper relationship. Part of the right to be an individual is the right to enter into meaningful, more intimate, and communing relationships.

In order to contrast enlightened independence with autonomy and self-assertion, let's enact yet a third time the scene between Jack and his mother. They are to the point where Jack's mother says,

What do you mean, "What you get into"?
Bad choice of words. . . . I just meant that I really don't know where we'll go, so I
   don't know when we'll get back.

I heard that some of the people your age are going to that bar that serves minors —
    they say that that place is going to get raided.
Is that what's bothering you?
Well, . . .
You know in a town this size no one can do anything without everyone knowing
    about it.
I just don't want you to do something we'll all regret. You are going to be leaving for
    college soon. I can't baby you all your life. I just want what's best for you.
Is this really that important to you?
You know it is. Your father and I have worked to give you a better start than we had.
    I guess we're a little overprotective.
You really are thinking of me, aren't you?
I'm not trying to be noble. . . .
If it will make you feel better, I promise not to go to the bar. Neither you nor Dad
    needs an arrested son, do you?
That's not the main point. . . .
Oh, I know. Look, here comes Ed in his dad's car. Bye.
(In the car) Jack, C'mon the beer awaits!
Hi, Ed. Hey, I don't think I want to go tonight.
Whatsa matter? Won't mommy let you?
That's not the point. When you get older, you'll understand. . . .
What??
Oh, nothing. Hey, have you seen that new flick at Cinema II? . . .

In this final interaction Jack's conversation with both his mother and
his friend is different. Some of the same things are said, and some of the
same issues arise. But Jack handles them differently. In this last scene Jack
made a different kind of decision from those he made in the other two. Of
course, there is no guarantee that he would have chosen to avoid the illegal
drinking. Still it was obvious that however he chose to act, he would, in fact,
be *choosing.* He would have taken into consideration his respect for his
mother and the potential effects of his action. A sense of enlightened independence gave him the ability to choose to accept responsibility — and to
choose to act in ways meant to help or consider others. These things were
not forced on him. He acted as an independent person, someone who was
free to choose his obligations and concerns for others.

    This last enactment is not meant to be a fairy-tale answer to difficult
decisions but to illustrate how people — concerned about developing a communal relationship with another — can choose to help deepen an ongoing relationship. The person adopting an attitude of enlightened independence
has the burden of balancing self-interests with the concerns for the other.
Certain kinds of choices — such as Jack made here at last — use communication as a way of stepping toward a sense of communion.

CHAPTER SUMMARY

*Interpersonal communication means communication between two people
. . . two separate people. In certain sorts of relationships a common situation
is for one person to wish to "break away" from the other. The parent–
child relationship probably comes to mind first, but just as relevant may be
such relationships as those between employer and employee.*

*The chapter began by illustrating one approach to this desire: the
approach of "autonomy." Characterized by such things as self-awareness,
self-confidence (real or imagined), self-centeredness, and self-celebration,
the person claiming autonomy fails to consider anyone but him- or herself.*

*"Self-assertion" is an approach discussed in books, essays, and self-
help sessions. Here the emphasis is on functioning responsibly as a full
human being with certain rights. The chapter discussed this and also introduced the phrase, "enlightened independence." Enlightened independence is based on the realization that everyone's life is bound up with
others. There is no real sense in which anyone is completely independent—
but we can be wise enough to have something to say about how we wish
to be dependent. An awareness of how our actions affect others is basic to
understanding enlightened independence . . . and the sense of communion
that can be furthered by it.*

LEARNING
BY APPLYING

1 *Many people have characterized the 1970s as the "Me-generation," meaning that almost everyone is more interested in him- or herself than anyone
else. People jog, diet, and stop smoking for their health; people read books
on how to "become what they are," how to "become more self-asserting,"
and how to "be a success in whatever they do"; and people buy expensive
products because, after all, "I'm worth it." Do you agree with these accusations? Explain your feelings about the importance of "me."*

2 *In the 1960s some observers were concerned that with the civil rights movement, the Vietnam War protests, and student unrest generally on campuses
that the United States was headed for "anarchy." What—to you—is
anarchy? How do you think that might be related to the human effort to be
"free"—to be autonomous? Has there been a time in your life when you
have been highly concerned about autonomy? Explain.*

3 *Now that you've read how I define "enlightened independence," how do
you define it? Does that seem to be a valuable perspective, an overly
"moral" perspective, the rantings of an over-30-year-old, or what? Explain
your reaction—specifically as it relates to your present interest in establishing and improving interpersonal relationships.*

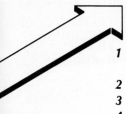

LEARNING
BY DISCUSSING

1 Discuss the nature of "autonomy"—and why that can cause interpersonal conflicts that are not desirable.
2 Explain the idea of "self-assertion."
3 Discuss the meaning of "enlightened independence."
4 How can an attitude of enlightened independence help two people improve their relationship?

LEARNING
BY READING FURTHER

Coles, Robert, *Helping Relationships*. Boston: Allyn and Bacon, 1972.

Goodman, Paul, *Growing Up Absurd*. New York: Vantage, 1960.

Jacobson, Wally, *Power and Interpersonal Relationships*. Belmont, CA: Wadsworth, 1972.

Langer, Ellen and Dweck, Carol, *Personal Politics*. Englewood Cliffs, NJ: Prentice-Hall, 1973.

Potter, Stephen, *The Complete Upsmanship*. New York: Holt, Rinehart and Winston, 1970.

Wheeler, Ladd, *Interpersonal Influence*. Boston: Allyn and Bacon, 1972.

20

YOKES, COMMITMENTS, AND ALLIANCES

STUDY OF THIS CHAPTER WILL ENABLE YOU TO

- *understand the concept of "yoke"*
- *understand the characteristics of yokes*
- *understand the concept of "commitments"*
- *understand the differences between yokes and commitments*
- *use communication to help establish commitments*
- *understand the concept of "alliances"*
- *understand the characteristics of alliances*
- *use communication to help establish alliances*

He looks nervously around the room, seeing relatives he doesn't even remember. He smiles, and thinks, "This is the happiest day of my life." Then he hears across the room.

Hey, where's the new groom? Well, John, how does it feel to bite the dust? She's a fine girl—you'll love being married. Hey, there's your uncle Ted. . . . Ted, come over here.

I'm coming. You don't think I'd forget to say farewell to the last bachelor in the family, do you, Milt? John, this is the happiest day of your life. Getting hitched was the best thing that ever happened to me. Oops, I see your aunt is into the bubbly too far. . . . Coming, dear.

(Milt watches him go.) John, there goes a happy man. I always say that a man is not a whole man until he ties up with some filly. Say, where is the new ball and chain?

I beg your pardon?

Your new bride? Where's the 'ol yokemate?

Oh, Jill. She's over there talking with Uncle Ted. . . . ooh . . .

What's the matter?

Nothing, nothing really.

Well, I hope not. Remember, this is the happiest day of your life.

Yeah.

John looks across the room at a young woman who is looking nervously around the room. She has just finished smiling politely at John's Uncle Ted.

No, I won't forget, this is the happiest day of my life. . . . Oh, Marcia, I hadn't seen you.

Hello, Jill. I am so happy for you I can hardly keep from crying. You two make such a great pair.

Marcia, this is John's Uncle Ted. Mr. O'Brien, this is Marcia Williams, a good friend of mine.

Hello, Marcia.

240

Hello, Mr. O'Brien.

Jill, I have to run. . . . I know you and John will be so happy. Getting the knot tied is
the best thing in the world.

Good-bye, Uncle Ted. . . . Well, what do you think, Marcia — How do I look?

Not bad for someone out of circulation. You may even like settling down and getting
out of the action. I'm only kidding. You look great. . . . John is fantastic, and this
is the happiest day in your life. Wow, I have to go, too.

Bye.

*Jill turns and sees John looking at her. They approach one another, slowly . . . even
cautiously.*

(Someone says,) Look at them. This is the happiest day of their lives.

Yokes In some respects, I suppose, John and Jill *are* involved in what is popularly
known as the "happiest day" of their lives. This is a day that members of
our culture may equate with love, hope, joy, and the promise of the future.
As the newlyweds approach one another during the reception, they probably feel the cultural demand to feel that this is, in fact, the happiest day of
their lives.

Yet that happiness is not the only thing connected popularly with marriage. John and Jill are not only getting married, John is also perceived as
"getting hitched," and gaining a "yokemate." For her part, Jill is now perceived as being part of a "team," of experiencing the "tying of the knot," of
"settling down," and of being "out of circulation." The wedding day seems
to be ambiguously viewed as a day of *unbounded* happiness felt by people
who have suddenly become *bound* together. Not everyone in a wedding
reception might choose exactly these words and phrases, but one thing is
certain: Quite often, wedding rings are seen as large enough to form a yoke
that ties two people together.

Yokes, however, are more appropriate for oxen. Marriage is generally a
state chosen by people who *want* some ties between them and another person. But marriage is not the same thing as self-inflicted bondage. To put it
another way, marriage is a relationship between two people who are, however, still alive.

In that respect, marriage is in part simply a human relationship that
has been formalized more than, say, friendship or the parent–child situation. Let us look at yokes, as both a problem in marriage and a hazard in interpersonal relationships generally.

To begin with, *yokes* are seen as things that *bind people legally, mor-
ally, or both.* There is nothing essentially evil about that. On the other hand,
a danger exists that the legal or moral yoke becomes the clear focus of the
relationship: a wife is faithful to her husband because of the marriage vow,
instead of because she wants to be faithful; a parent rears a child because,
after all, he is a parent; a friend chooses to honor a confidence because

241

telling a certain tale violates a friendship. In all these cases good things may be the result. Still I would argue that each act would be qualitatively better and more satisfying because the person *chose* to act in a particular way—not because of a binding obligation.[1] Oxen move in a set manner because they are tied together; humans should act in a particular way because they *choose* to do so.

Second, *yokes impede progress* because each "yoked-up" individual can move only as quickly as the slower partner. Regardless of how quickly or slowly one or the other partner wishes to move, the yoke prevents anything but joint—and thus dependent movement. One partner may wish to move more quickly; one may wish to go more slowly. The result may be mutual dissatisfaction, disharmony, and a lack of potential progress. Marriages suffer from this phenomenon when the energy and enthusiasm of one partner is far superior to the other's. Friendships exhibit the same condition when one partner seems always to slow the development of the other person. The parent–child relationship suffers when an ambitious parent fails to appreciate a child's handicaps or lack of ability. In essence, a relationship that focuses on the yoke may impede the progress of each individual.

Third, *yokes of obligation dictate that both partners move in an identical or similar direction.* One of the chief reasons for tying two individuals—whether oxen or people—together is to guarantee that neither has much freedom of movement. Where one goes, the other follows; where one wants to go, the other is committed to follow—or risks breaking the yoke. All this makes practical good sense for oxen, horses, or other dumb animals—but little sense for people. Most children at some point seek to move in an independent direction. There is generally a time when even the closest friends act on unshared wishes. And clearly, the current divorce rate indicates that marital partners are increasingly seeing a need to pursue directions that differ from their partners'. People do not always tend to move in identical or similar directions.

Finally, *yokes that continually chafe and are fought against must be lifted if the yokemates are to survive.* One friend "outgrows" another and moves to a new circle of friends. A child eventually leaves home and "cuts the apron strings." A married person finds the yoke of marriage too binding and decides between the survival of the relationship and his or her own survival: "balls and chains" can be accepted or removed; "marital knots"—even those tied in heaven—can be untied.

Relationships between parents and children, friends, and husband and wife are not cemented by visible, physical yokes. Still the obligations between pairs of people can become the *focus* of the relationship. When peo-

---

[1] Kenneth Burke, *Permanence & Change*, 2d ed. (Los Altos, Calif.: Hermes, 1954), 284–285.

ple begin doing things because "they ought to," "they have to," or "they must," and not because of love or feeling for the other, then their progress and direction are being impeded. They may begin to feel the full weight of an overly heavy obligation and may decide that they need the psychological, moral, or legal yoke lifted from a very tired neck.

Human relationships, however, do not have to be guaranteed with any kind of yoke. Effective interpersonal communication can be a key in establishing, not a yoke, but a sensible human commitment.

Commitments   Again, to explain this particular concept of "commitment" I want to focus on the marital relationship—and then to generalize to other relationships. Let me start with a personal anecdote.

When I was getting married, the wedding ceremony was only the second one I had witnessed. I was not, let's say, very familiar with the exact wording of the vows. During the wedding rehearsal the minister explained carefully where everyone was to stand and how and when they should move. He simply alluded to what he would ask us and how we should respond. He "abbreviated" the ceremony to save time. No problem ... maybe.

During the ceremony—in which I was perhaps a bit nervous—the minister had us repeat the appropriate vows. The problem, however, was that I was not expecting to have to repeat quite as much as was required. The result was that, at one point, I had to ask *him* to repeat the vow before *I* could repeat it. Never at a loss for words, I said something clever such as, "Could you repeat that?" That was the high point of the whole ceremony for my father who thought it hilarious that a "communication major"—I was only a sophomore—had failed to listen.

I relate this story, not to reembarrass myself, but to make a point: I was prepared to marry this wonderful woman, even though I did not *exactly* know what the wedding vows were. I was prepared to make commitments —whatever they were.

In the 1960s and into the 1970s, people seemed to become more sensitive to the need for making the marital vows a special agreement between husband and wife. So they frequently began writing their own marriage vows. I interpret this wish to create special vows in at least two ways: (1) Some couples simply wanted to do what was becoming popular—just as people in years past had taken the traditional vows because "everyone did" so modern couples had written their own vows because it was "the thing to do." (2) Some couples, I suppose, were honestly saying, "Hey, we don't want our relationship sealed with a static and traditional set of vague ideas. We want to create a dynamic and living set of agreements."

This second explanation is what I mean by the difference between static agreements about what the relationship *should be;* commitments can be thought of as ongoing and dynamic agreements about how the relationship *will work*. Yokes focus on the *obligation* of the relationship; commitments focus on the *dynamics of the people* involved. Let me illustrate:

Yoke   I will love, honor, and obey . . . until death . . .

Commitment   I will always try to be warm, loving, and responsive; I will respect the physical, emotional, intellectual, and spiritual characteristics that make you who you are; I will do all I can as a person to understand you and to act whenever I can in ways that help you as a person and "us" as a relationship. I promise to do these things as long as there exists the hope of a constructive relationship between us.

The most basic difference between these interpretations is that the yoke focuses on *an obligation for the relationship*; the commitment is *an outgrowth of the relationship*.

    I have no particular interest or special knowledge as to how well these specifically tailored vows affect marriage. But I *am* interested in the idea that these special vows are a product — not of tradition — but of communication between the partners in the relationship. And that seems important! Honest communication between two people can lead to clearer explanations of what is expected in the relationship and can provide certain valuable statements about commitments — in marriages and other relationships.

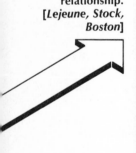

. . . the yoke focuses on an obligation for the relationship; the commitment is an outgrowth of the relationship. [*Lejeune, Stock, Boston*]

First, *communication can help establish the desired commitment for an ongoing relationship.* In the marital relationship, communication before the ceremony can be used to explore the extent to which each partner *wants* to be committed to the other. It is not enough to say, "Let's get married." What is needed is clear and honest discussion about the meaning of such an obligation. The *desire for the obligation* and not the obligation itself (yoke) becomes the focus. In a word, communication helps establish the interpersonal *commitment* that the two people wish to make. The focus is on the people and their desires and not the obligation itself. In less formalized relationships such as the parent–child and friendship situations, communication can be just as valuable. Instead of merely *assuming* the obligation that each person has for the other, the desire for the relationship (the commitment) can be made explicit: I say to my children, "I am so glad to be your father;" I say to a friend, "I really enjoy our relationship; I want it to continue." Such communication focuses on the people involved in relationships; it shifts the focus away from emphasis on obligation.

Second, *communication can help establish the minimum requirements of the commitment.* Note that one of the differences between the "love, honor, and obey" vow and the reinterpretation of it as a commitment is that the commitment is much more specific. The commitment spells out more specifically what is meant by love, honor, and obey. Obeying, for example, was not intended to mean: I will do whatever you say. Instead, it meant: I will try as a person to act positively to your wishes whenever I can. Even the "until death"—in the context of very high divorce rates—was interpreted to mean that the relationship could die even if the people were still alive. I do not mean to suggest that you should *agree* with these interpretations which have been molded into a commitment. I simply wish to demonstrate the advantages of agreeing on the conditions—the minimum requirements—of the commitment to the relationship.

And finally, *communication can help establish the consequences of problems in the commitment.* What happens when there are problems in the relationship? Well, two people involved in the relationship can assume that there will be no problems. That would be a bit naïve, however, if we can believe national marital surveys and interview investigations. The wiser assumption is that there will be difficulties in the relationship—whether between spouses, parents and children, or friends. Communication can help determine what is to be done when these problems arise. Two people may decide to dissolve their relationship or to attempt to modify the problems as long as there is something left in the relationship. Note again the reinterpretation of the "love, honor, and obey" vow: "I promise to do these things as long as there exists the hope of a constructive relationship between us." This does not mean that divorce is out of the question, but simply that divorce is not the most immediate answer to the problem. Counseling, therapy, financial advice, prayer, ongoing communication—these and other alternatives may be tried. The interpreted vow is that only when none of these processes work is the relationship (not the people) deemed to be dead. Divorce, at that point, might be a constructive alternative *based upon the vow previously mentioned.*

The discussion on how communication can aid the development and maintenance of a commitment has focused so far on the marital relationship. Our perspective, however, can be wider. Parents and children or friends can use communication as a method of developing an understanding about commitments. In 1979, for example—"The Year of the Child"—various groups publicized a list of societal obligations toward children. Consider the following:[2]

MANKIND OWES THE CHILD THE BEST IT HAS TO GIVE

- *The right to affection, love and understanding.*
- *The right to adequate nutrition and medical care.*
- *The right to full opportunity for play and recreation.*
- *The right to a name and nationality.*
- *The right to special care if handicapped.*
- *The right to be among the first to receive relief in times of disaster.*
- *The right to learn to be a useful member of society and to develop individual abilities.*
- *The right to be brought up in a spirit of peace and brotherhood.*
- *The right to enjoy these rights, regardless of race, color, sex, religion, national or social origin.*

Note that these are responsibilities—commitments—that both adults and children at appropriate ages ought to understand. A similar list about commitments of children to society or parents could be devised—and should be interesting. These basic lists could be modified, added to, and molded by parents and children to fit their particular situation and needs. The same sort of "list," but one that might seem more awkward, could be developed explicitly or implicitly for friends. What is this commitment that exists between you and me as friends? Such a process is usually done informally. Friends have to "get things straight" with one another. But that usually happens when problems arise. How much better it might be if clear and honest communication could help establish the commitment between friends before a crisis in the relationship. My major point, then, can be restated simply: Communication can be used to establish the nature of the ongoing commitment between any two people. People can trade in a yoke of obligations as parents, children, friends, or marital partners for a set of dynamic areas of commitment.

[2] From material distributed by The United Stand for Children, January 1979.

Alliances Communication, however, can be used even more constructively in human relationships. In moving toward the goal of interpersonal *communion*, two people can form what I shall call "alliances." Alliances, at first glance, might seem the same as commitments; however, there is a crucial difference. Alliance, as I use the word, implies a particular kind of commitment: *a commitment to progress and growth.* Let me explain with an illustration.

Years ago, the United States and certain other countries of the Western Hemisphere created an Alliance for Progress. Now this was not intended to be simply a defense or security treaty. It was not supposed to be a way of keeping things the same; it was meant to be a way of coping with change and even bringing about change. In fairness, the Alliance has been criticized as a way that the United States tried to control the hemisphere. I am not interested in defending or criticizing the Alliance, but only wish to show that the principle of a commitment to progress is very helpful.

Two people can agree to certain commitments that help each other grow. Instead of focusing on the question, "How can we keep this relationship the same?" they can focus on the question, "How can both of us be better because of this relationship?" The shift in focus moves from a concern strictly for the relationship to a concern for the people in the relationship. This has several meanings.

First, *interpersonal alliances mean that the people in the relationship are encouraged to grow.* No attempt is made to keep the people just as they are when the relationship is formed. Friends are allowed to change, to make other friends, and to develop as people. Parents are people, too, allowed to change, to grow, and to readapt to children who are getting older. Children are allowed to develop as people: "He may still be *your baby*, but he may be some *woman's man.*" Wives and husbands are allowed to develop parts of their world not necessarily related to the office, the job, or the home. Second, *an alliance allows this growth to proceed for each person in different directions and at different rates.* Friends do not always have to share everything to remain friends. Children can develop their own "selves" and their own social world. Parents do not have to center their entire lives on their children until after "the children are grown," but can be themselves as well. Finally, wives and husbands need not let spouses be their entire world. In addition and equally important, this growth does not have to be at the same rate: a friend should not be forced to develop other friends nor a child pushed to create his or her own social world nor a wife encouraged to earn a separate income nor a husband forced to develop a social group of "the boys." The point is that an alliance encourages growth — but *allows* for different directions and different rates of growth.

Third, *alliances imply mutual support.* The marriage can become viewed, not as a yoked-in relationship, but as an ongoing commitment to in-

247

dividual growth. Growth and change are not forced by the other person, but they are allowed and supported by the other. The marriage is not a relationship between two half-people. It can be a relationship between two whole and still developing people. Friendships and the parent–child relationship can be viewed as sources of warmth and support — characteristics that can help the individual growth process.

Fourth, *alliances mean continual assessment and evaluation.* Some years ago certain individuals began to popularize the idea of "marriage contracts." These contracts would specify what each person was to gain by the relationship. Every few years the contract would "come up for review." The couple would evaluate what had occurred in terms of the contract and then decide if it was to be renewed for another specified period of years. I am not arguing that marital contracts are necessarily good or bad, but the idea is interesting. An alliance between any two people can include a periodic — or better, an ongoing — evaluation of what is happening. In what ways has growth occurred? What have been the problems perceived by each? How has each aided — or hindered — the growth of the other? These questions get discussed every day, but usually only when a married couple, friends, or parents and children are experiencing severe problems. The advantage of a periodic or ongoing evaluation is that such communication might well prevent problems from getting too severe. It is commonplace knowledge that when relationships are broken — whatever type they are — "old" problems and continuing difficulties are brought to the surface: I may not end our friendship because of what you did today; but I may end it for what you "always do," what you "did in '71," or because "I have always hated it when you . . . ." The periodic or ongoing evaluation allows members of the alliance to treat problems as they occur, while they are "smaller."

And finally, *the alliance*—because of its evaluation—*allows continually higher goals to be set for the growth of the partners.* The key, here again, is *progress.* When two people in a relationship can see what progress thay have made (or failed to make), they can reset goals. They know what things need more effort, see how they can begin to grow beyond their present status. They can begin to see the relationship, not as a yoke, but as a means of continually growing as people. Friendship, the parent–child relationship, even marriage, can be viewed as a positive factor in personal growth.

The interpersonal alliance, then, is a crucial factor in a relationship whose goal is communion. The relationship gets better as the people are allowed and encouraged to grow. As they grow, the relationship can be more and more satisfying and rewarding. Sharing becomes not a matter of "things" shared, but a matter of shared growth and progress, which seems to be a vital part of the communing relationship. Communication is not the end product; however, it can be a key to the goal of communion.

CHAPTER SUMMARY

One of the reviewers who read this chapter before publication said that it should be required reading for every prospective bride and groom. I hope that it is seen as helpful by these people, but the ideas here can be translated into other relationships as well. This chapter was concerned with the quality of relationships.

"Yokes," for instance, were viewed as relationships that hindered growth, that strained relationships, that lowered the possibility of communion. In contrast, commitments were viewed as more positive arrangements based on agreements and desired obligations. Communication—good interpersonal communication—can help make commitments more appealing and more beneficial.

Still the term "alliance" was introduced as being a way of describing a relationship whose primary aim was to promote the mutual growth of each person and the relationship as a whole. The alliance quality of a relationship indicates what I have said before: The communing relationship is not a thing created by two "half-people" getting together as one. Instead, it is a dynamic arrangement where two people and the relationship are more "whole," more satisfying than either two people could experience in other ways. The creation of an interpersonal alliance for progress is a giant step toward communion.

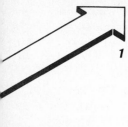

LEARNING
BY APPLYING

1   Think about the marriages with which you are most familiar, whether they are in your family or among friends. Without identifying the people involved, can you comment on any of them that seem similar to the "yoke" relationship discussed in the chapter? Use the characteristics of "yokes" to explain.

2   Consider family relationships with which you are familiar (excluding marriages). Do these sibling, parent–child, and so on relationships seem cemented by yokes, commitments, or alliances? Use the characteristics of each to explain your answer.

3   In terms of marriage, think about your situation:

a.   If you are now married, consider the state of the marriage. You may not wish to share this with others, but it may be valuable to analyze it from the standpoint of the chapter. Remember that the state of the marriage can become something different from what is is now!

b.   If you are not now married, but someday wish to be, what kind of marriage do you want? Remember that a marriage of alliance takes time to build—and takes the willingness of both parties.

c.   If you never want to marry, does the material on yokes and commitments relate to your reasons? Do you see any possibility of there ever being an alliance between you and a spouse?

4   Consider several close relationships you have with other people. Would you consider them more to be yokes, commitments, or alliances? How does the material in the chapter provide insight into ways to make all of these more like alliances?

LEARNING
BY DISCUSSING

1   Discuss the nature of "yokes," using both the text and your own experience. Why are these often problems in interpersonal relationships?

2   Explain the nature of a "commitment" and how it may be different from a yoke.

3   Explain the text's conception of an "alliance."

4   In what ways do alliances seem better suited to relationships that are meant to endure over time?

LEARNING
BY READING FURTHER

Ardrey, Robert, The Social Contract. New York: Atheneum, 1970.
Bracken, Peg, I Try to Behave Myself. Greenwich, CN: Fawcett, 1963.
Murray, Davis, Intimate Relations. New York: Free Press, 1973.

21

MARTYRING, ACCEPTING RESPONSIBILITY, AND BEING MUTUALLY ACCOUNTABLE

STUDY OF THIS CHAPTER WILL ENABLE YOU TO

- *understand the nature of interpersonal "martyring"*
- *understand the characteristics of martyring*
- *help avoid martyring behavior in the interpersonal situation*
- *understand the concept of "accepting responsibility"*
- *understand strategies for accepting responsibility*
- *accept responsibility better in the interpersonal situation*
- *understand the nature of "being mutually accountable"*
- *understand strategies that enhance mutual accountability*
- *use mutual accountability as a helpful interpersonal approach*

R-r-r-i-n-n-g-g!

Hello?

Hello, . . . Martha? Martha, this is Gladys.

Oh, yes, Gladys. How are you?

I'm fine. How's yourself?

Fine.

Martha, I called to see if you were going to attend the company picnic on Saturday.

Oh, gosh, I don't think I'll be able to.

That's too bad.

Well, Gladys, I would like to, but I think Lenny wants to go golfing with his friends. You know he gets out so seldom. It's good for him, you know.

Yes, I know. Everyone has to get out occasionally — including you, Martha.

Oh, Gladys, you know I'm perfectly happy to stay here on weekends and get caught up a bit. Poor Lenny has enough to do working all week. If I can help out a little by watching the kids . . .

Why don't you just bring them along? There will be lots of kids there . . .

Oh, no, Gladys, I couldn't really. Joanie has a big test I told her I'd help her with. Doug has Boy Scouts Sunday afternoon. We're a busy group. A mother's work is never done, as they say.

Well, Martha. I guess I'll see you at work tomorrow.

Oh, yes. I have a bit of a cold, but — you know me — always there when the work needs to be done.

Yes, well, I have to run. . . .

I guess I haven't missed work since last August. That was when Aunt Dolores died and someone had to cook for all the relatives. It always seems like there's one member of the family who has to be dependable.

Yes, that's the truth. Well, Martha . . .

I would certainly like to come. . . .

Come where?

To the picnic, like you wanted me to. . . .

Oh, yes, well, I really . . .

Yes, I would like to come. But I really don't mind. After all, Lenny needs to get out
of the house a little. . . .

I bet he does.

What do you mean?

Well, nothing . . . er, . . . I was just agreeing with you.

And I do like to do little things for the kids. They're only young once, you know.

Yes, well, I really . . .

Someone has to help them. Now I don't mean that Lenny doesn't try. But you know
how men are.

What do you mean?

Men work from sun to sun, but a mother's never finished . . . something like that.

Yes, well, I really . . .

Not that I mind being a mother—don't get me wrong. I love being a working mother.
That's why I don't mind not getting to go to the picnic. . . .

Martha, I really need . . . oops! The doorbell rang. I have to go now.

I didn't hear it.

Well, . . . you can't sometimes through the phone. . . . I've noticed that . . .

Oh, I see.

Have to run, now. Good-bye, Martha.

Good-bye, and call again real soon, Gladys.

Martyring The dictionary would define a "martyr" as a person who sacrifices him- or herself for a cause. I suppose the most common associations with martyrs have to do with political and religious situations. People can become martyrs by giving up their lives instead of changing their beliefs. They are people who suffered pain or death—and usually both—as a testimony to their strong beliefs. Such acts of self-sacrifice seldom go unnoticed. Religious groups, social movements, and nations look with pride on "their" martyrs. Surely, these groups reason, if these people sacrificed so much, should not others sacrifice a little of their time, effort, and resources?

The martyring that I want to discuss is a distorted version of the real martyrs of history. Interpersonal "martyring" *is the self-centered and willing acceptance of self-sacrifice.* Let me explain what I mean and at the same time differentiate legitimate martyring from interpersonal martyring games.

All martyring—legitimate and gamelike—seems to *arise from the impulse to sacrifice for "causes" or for other people.* This characteristic of martyring is entirely positive. No matter how evil and bad the world may sometimes look, it would be worse without people helping other people. In the example of interpersonal martyring, Martha was willing to miss the company picnic. Although she really wanted to attend, she was willing to

253

sacrifice, putting Lenny, Doug, and Joanie's interests and desires above her own.

Interpersonal martyring, however, is characterized by some much less positive factors. Second, this kind of gamelike martyring is characterized by *some degree of announcement about the sacrifice being made.* Martha was determined to have Gladys realize the extent of her sacrifice. She was a working mother—just as Lenny was a working father. Still she said—and said, and said—that she did not mind sacrificing. One is tempted to modify her statement: "I don't really mind, as long as the world (starting with Gladys) knows about it!" I have the feeling that Lenny, Doug, and Joanie will all know the exact nature of the sacrifice that Martha is making. After all, interpersonal martyring is no fun unless people are aware of it. Historical martyrs have suffered in silence. The interpersonal martyr suffers with trumpets blaring.

Third, interpersonal martyring is characterized by *the martyrs' belief that their martyring is caused by events out of their control.* Martha *had* to miss the picnic because Lenny *needed* a day off, because Joanie *had* to have help, and because Doug *had* to be prepared for his scouting. Why did *she* have to help? Well, after all, she *was* a mother. So Martha presented the situation as one in which she had no control. She was a victim of events. She was not choosing to miss the picnic; she had to miss it!

While the interpersonal martyr may seem forced to sacrifice, martyring seems to be characterized, fourth, by *a thinly disguised willingness— even eagerness—to sacrifice.* The martyrs of the past seem not to have been eager to die. There is no evidence, as far as I know, that Martin Luther King, Jr. or Joan of Arc ever really wanted to become martyrs. Even though the death of Jesus is basic to the Christian belief of God's plan, the Bible reports his wish to avoid "the cup" if God were willing. Such is not the case with the interpersonal martyr. These people may actually seek out ways to suffer. They may search for ways in which they can (noisily) suffer in silence. The explanation seems almost too simplistic. The true martyrs were group oriented and were willing to die if that would aid some plan or group effort. On the other hand, the interpersonal martyr seems to be self-oriented. Anything that will demonstrate a willingness to suffer is eagerly grabbed: self-sacrifice is a way of showing others the martyr's selflessness. Self-sacrifice becomes a good way of self-elevation.

Finally, in interpersonal martyring—as in all games—there is *the "payoff."* The martyr expects sympathy, understanding, and special consideration because of the sacrifices made. Martha expected Gladys to understand and appreciate her self-sacrifice. Martha probably expected Gladys to inform everyone at the picnic why she was not present. The payoff? "Poor Martha. Always doing something for others." And Martha probably will go to work on Monday, asking everyone how the picnic was. This will provide a way of reexplaining her selflessness to anyone that Gladys failed to inform.

"I'm so sorry you couldn't be there, but I understand" will be sweet music to Martha's ears.

The discussion of martyring may seem a bit unkind. I suspect that all of us martyr from time to time. In addition, I suppose that when we do engage in such activity, we are not conscious of it. If you assume—as I do—that martyring stems from the desire to help others, then the martyr should be understood instead of condemned. And fortunately, there are more constructive ways of answering the impulse to help others. In the next section I shall discuss the accepting of responsibility.

Accepting responsibility

"Responsibility" is an interesting word whose generally accepted meaning varies with its use. Accepting responsibility is an approach aimed at helping you help others—without engaging in martyring behavior. To understand better how to accept responsibility, the following strategies can be helpful.

First, be sure you *decide what sort of responsibility you have.* The dictionary might define "responsibility" as a task one has to perform or an obligation one has assumed. Actually, responsibility as a task and responsibility as an obligation may be somewhat different. Responsibility may be the actual physical act or thing that must be performed: The running of a

255

particular college level course might be my responsibility. But philosophers know that responsibility may refer to something more abstract: an obligation. I may have made an agreement so that I am responsible for running the course. That obligation is now part of my responsibility. The difference may seem subtle—even "picky"—but it may be important. In the interpersonal situation you may need to separate the focus on the task from the focus on the obligation to complete the task. For example, I may take on myself the responsibility for doing a *task*—even though I have no *obligation* to do so. By doing this, I have taken on responsibility (task) although I had no responsibility (obligation) to do so.

In interpersonal situations you should decide whether what you call "your responsibility" is the result of an obligation or whether you have simply chosen to do the task or act. In the opening case study Martha assumed that she had an obligation to help others even if it was not her wish. After all, she was the mother. Martha would have benefited from seeing that her reasons for not going to the picnic were not actually matters of obligation. She had chosen to help Joanie on that particular day, to allow Lenny to escape any obligation to the children or her, and to help Doug get ready for the meeting. These were not necessarily things she had to do on *that* particular Saturday. She decided to do those things; they were not actually part of her special responsibilities (obligations) as a loving mother. As it turned out, she chose to be responsible for them, which helped her play martyr. She could just as easily have chosen not to assume those responsibilities *for that particular day*, which would have been a step toward accepting responsibility in a positive and intelligent way.

Another step toward the acceptance of responsibility involves (again) a matter of definition. There is a great difference between being *responsible for* and being *responsible to.* Second, accepting responsibility means that you *decide* for what *and* to whom *you are responsible.* Martha had no trouble deciding the tasks for which she was responsible: letting Lenny have a day off; helping Joanie study; and getting Doug ready for the meeting. However, she failed to consider *to whom* she was responsible. She knew by instinct that she had obligations to Lenny, Doug, and Joanie. If she failed to help them they might be upset, angry, or frustrated. But she failed to take herself into consideration. What was her responsibility to herself? How was she making herself feel by always putting everyone else first? Well, to begin with, she probably felt martyred—and maybe that was satisfying to her. But she probably also felt put-on, taken advantage of, and resentful. She had a responsibility *to herself* which she did not handle in a positive way.

Would concern for herself have been selfish? I don't think so. Envision how Martha probably would have acted toward her family—assuming she martyred with them as she did with Gladys: Everyone would have felt good that the things were done, sorry for mother, and probably guilty—'way down deep. Wasn't there a way for Martha's desires to be worked into the rest of the family's wishes? We cannot say from the opening case study, since Martha failed to take into consideration the responsibility to herself. In accepting responsibility, you must decide for what and to whom you are responsible.

In the interpersonal situation, then, you can decide whether the responsibility is an obligation or something you simply do. You can decide to whom and for what you are responsible. These decisions allow you to use a third strategy: you can *decide whether you actually wish to accept particular responsibilities*. The key word in the process of "accepting responsibility" is *accepting*. Things that are accepted are not forced on you – you are not coerced to do them. In occupational settings some responsibilities are said to be forced on people: They must be the United Way chairperson or they must be active in civic groups. Yet even in those settings a choice is present – even if it isn't attractive. People quit jobs frequently because they cannot conscientiously use particular sales techniques or do not like certain business procedures. In nonoccupational situations the choices are usually even more obvious. Martha needed to realize that the "reasons" she could not go to the picnic were products of her ability to choose. She could have taken the kids along, arranged for a baby-sitter, or asked Lenny to play later in the day. She could have helped Joanie and Doug at different times – at least given the information in the case. She considered these tasks as obligations which prevented her from going to the picnic. And yet they were her choices. Martha needed to realize this and either accept her assumed responsibilities or refuse them and make other arrangements. *Deciding whether* to accept responsibilities is an obvious – but frequently overlooked – strategy for "accepting responsibility."

Finally, accepting responsibility means that you *learn to live with the consequences of your decisions*. These decisions are matters of choice – not force. So if you decide to accept the responsibility, you need to live with the results. Martha failed to do this. She wallowed in her suffering, in her self-sacrifice. They were things she "had" to do for others and became a way of making her seem self-less. Martyring makes little sense when faced with the consequences of your own decisions. No one would have admired Joan of Arc if she had arranged her own execution. Learning to live with the consequences of your actions is a major step in accepting responsibility in a positive and constructive fashion.

Let's "replay" the telephone conversation between Martha and Gladys. This time, however, let's assume that Martha knew how accepting responsibility can help interpersonal situations.

R-r-r-i-n-n-g-g!
Hello?
Hello, . . . Martha? Martha, this is Gladys.
Oh, yes, Gladys. How are you?

I'm fine. How's yourself?

Fine.

Martha, I called to see if you were going to attend the company picnic on Saturday.

Oh, gosh, I don't think I'll be able to.

That's too bad.

Well, Gladys, I would like to, but I think Lenny wants to go golfing with his friends. I forgot all about the picnic. I didn't put it on the calendar . . . and well, I've made other plans now.

Yes, well . . .

I told Lenny to go ahead and go. I promised to stay with the kids, so . . .

You could bring them along. There will be lots of kids there—and Lenny could go on and play golf.

Well, I told Joanie that I'd help with a test she's studying for and Doug needs some sewing done on his Scout uniform. I wish I had helped with those earlier. Gosh, I'm sorry I forgot about the picnic.

Well, Martha, they say a woman's work is never done. . . .

I guess the point is that I should have planned ahead. Lenny already has plans made, so . . . I guess I'd better not plan to come. You have a good time. Have a hot dog for me. . . .

Okay, see you at work tomorrow. . . .

Oh, yes (laughing) I have remembered that.

Martha may still not be happy that she is going to miss the picnic. On the other hand, she is not playing the martyr game. She has analyzed her commitments and is now prepared to accept the responsibility for her earlier decisions.

This discussion of accepting responsibility is meant to provide a sound alternative to martyring. The acceptance of responsibility answers the need to help others, and still avoids martyring. Yet in relationships aiming toward communal levels, there are even more helpful attitudes and strategies that can be adopted. These have to do with two people being "accountable" to one another. Mutual accountability is an important ingredient in interpersonal communion.

Being mutually accountable   "Accountability" is a word receiving a great deal of attention. Politicians are supposed to be accountable to their constituencies. Industry is supposed to be accountable for what it does to the environment. Teachers and schools are considered accountable for the education they say they provide. But just what does "accountability" mean?

Accountability, as I use the term, refers to *the constant liability to explain, justify, or answer for what someone has done.*[1] The word liability

---

[1] For a more complete discussion, see Richard E. Crable, "Ethical Codes, Accountability, and Argumentation," *Quarterly Journal of Speech* 64 (February 1978): 23–32.

. . . mutual accountability . . . means that you are prepared to help the other person become more accountable. [Forsyth, Monkmeyer]

259

is crucial — and is a source of misunderstanding about accountability. To say that politicians, industry, and schools are accountable is not the same thing as saying that they have to explain or justify everything they do. To account for — explain or defend — everything would be impossible. "Liability" means that there is always the threat or possibility of someone having to explain or defend him- or herself and what is done. Even if a company is never forced to explain or justify what it has done, the liability is still there. On any occasion, company officials may be forced to answer for what they've done. That is accountability: the constant capacity or ability to be called to account.

Mutual accountability can be an important ingredient when individuals seek a communing relationship. Mutual accountability means, first, that *each of two people feels an ongoing responsibility* to *the other and* for *the relationship.* Virtually anything that one person does can affect the other person and the relationship. At any time one can question what the other has done. Being mutually accountable means that each makes decisions and then is willing to defend them if the need arises. In the communing relationship there undoubtedly will be specific responsibilities that one or the other assumes. But in addition, there will be this continual sense of responsibility to the other and for the relationship.

Being mutually accountable, second, implies *an ongoing responsibility to one's self.* Healthy relationships are not typically formed from two unhealthy people. Being accountable means a commitment to the other and to the relationship — but also self-commitment. What one person does that hurts him- or herself also hurts the relationship. So the liability of defending one's behavior also involves self-treatment. As we saw in Chapter 3, interpersonal communication cannot be considered separately from intrapersonal communication. Doing things that help yourself is one of the best ways of proving your feelings of obligation to the other person.

These first two characteristics may seem to be aimed at describing a continually responsible person. And so they do. But mutual accountability, third, means that *you are prepared to help the other person become more accountable.* In the first case study Martha was not prepared to help Doug, Joanie, or Lenny become more accountable for themselves. She wanted to do things for them, to help them; in short, she wanted to be accountable for them. The "things" may get done, of course, but Doug, Joanie, and the husband hardly become more accountable for their own behavior or problems. By doing all these "kindnesses" for them, Martha successfully kept each of them from becoming more personally accountable. She could have helped more by providing support for their own sense of responsibility. That would have been hard for Martha in the first case study: Her own self-concept was so involved in playing the martyr. In such cases helping people is easy, but helping them assume their own responsibility is much more difficult. In the second case study Martha did accept her own responsibility, but now there were a few traces of a desire for mutual accountability.

But people can change their communication and their behavior in ways that help the development of mutual accountability. Let's listen to a call that Martha made to Gladys after the second case study—and after a talk with Lenny:

R-r-r-i-n-n-g-g!
Holmes residence.
Gladys, this is Martha.
Oh, Martha. *(laughs)* I thought we just talked.
Well, we did, but Lenny came home and I talked with him. He thought I was being a little too protective of his leisure time—and a little silly for not going to the picnic. . . . I guess he was right. . . . Anyway, we have things figured out.
What do you mean?
Well, his foursome is going to play early, so they'll be back by noon or so. He'll— Lenny, I mean, will help Joanie with the test. She said she doesn't mind at all. I may be at the picnic a bit late, but I can still go. I'll do the sewing for Doug when I get back. It sounds sort of complicated, but I guess it will work.
Well, good.
I thought I would bring my potato salad—you know, that one that everyone said was so "unusual." . . . Well?
Well, what?
The potato salad. . . . Everyone had something to say about it. . . .
Uh, what we really need is a big bag of potato chips. Your potato salad was certainly . . . "unusual," but . . .

Without waiting for the explanation, let's return to the more general concern for being mutually accountable. In this phone call Martha was doing something other than accepting responsibility. She and Lenny had been able to work out the details of a plan that helped both her and Lenny. The children did not suffer, the golf game was scheduled a bit earlier, and the picnic was attended. In this last call Martha was doing no martyring and had gone beyond accepting responsibility. If only her potato salad were not so . . . unusual. . . .

CHAPTER SUMMARY

The issue of responsibility is a common problem in interpersonal situations. There are, however, different ways of approaching the issue.

The chapter began by discussing "martyring" as the self-centered and willing acceptance of self-sacrifice. In many situations someone has to be blamed—or assume the burden. Yet there are people who do this as a way of life, as a way of feeling needed and important. The chapter discussed this sort of behavior.

"Accepting responsibility" is a more thoughtful, helpful approach to the same need for someone to assume responsibility. In accepting responsibility, however, people need to consider the things for which they are reasonably responsible, the people to whom they are responsible, and so forth. This can be a productive approach to relationships.

Finally, however, it is important that both members of a relationship assume some sort of "accountability"—to the other person and for the relationship. The characteristics of being mutually accountable that are discussed in the chapter can provide a great deal of insight in how to build toward a communing relationship.

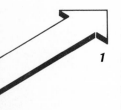

LEARNING BY APPLYING

1. I have yet to see a family of any size that does not have an uncle, a grandmother, a sister, a nephew who does not martyr. Maybe your family is an exception. Is it? If it is not the exception, might that person gain some insight from some of the material in the text? Or can you use the material to understand and deal with the person better? Explain.

2. Accepting responsibility is easier if the process began early in life. Do you know people who, as children, were not encouraged to be responsible for themselves or certain tasks? If you were that person, does accepting responsibility present a problem to you? If the person is someone besides you, how might earlier efforts have helped the person? How might he or she be helped now? Use the material in the chapter.

3. Consider certain relationships you have with other people. Do some of these people assume all the responsibility, instead of allowing you to be mutually accountable? Do some interact with you in mutually accountable ways? I suspect these last are members of the more satisfying relationships. If so, explain your feelings. If not, explain.

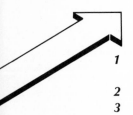

LEARNING BY DISCUSSING

1. Explain the concept of the interpersonal "martyr." Why might such martyrdom hurt interpersonal relationships?
2. What is meant by "accepting responsibility"?
3. Explain what is meant by "being mutually accountable"?
4. Why is mutual accountability a healthy attitude for two people interested in deepening and widening their relationship?

LEARNING
BY READING FURTHER

Berne, Eric, *Games People Play*. New York: Grove Press, 1964.
Blau, Peter, *Exchange and Power in Social Life*. New York: Wiley, 1964.
Gaylin, Willard, ed., *The Meaning of Despair*. New York: Science House, 1968.
Murray, Davis, *Intimate Relations*. New York: Free Press, 1973.

CARING FOR, CARING ABOUT, AND CARING

Nurse Adams	And how are we today?
	She opens the curtains, then shuffles over to fluff Ryan's pillow.
Ryan	I don't know how "we" are, but I'm feeling better.
Nurse	Good, good. Doctor will be in to see you soon. She makes her morning rounds bright and early. Doctor will be pleased to see you better.
Ryan	Great. I will enjoy Doctor's visit.
Nurse	If there's anything we can get for you, please ring the nurse's station.
Ryan	I would like a little quiet.
Nurse	Do we feel surly this morning? I thought we were better.
Ryan	Did it occur to you that I am an adult?
Nurse	Well, whether you are an adult or a child, you are still my patient. I will take good care of you.
Ryan	I feel so comforted.
Nurse	Did we take our medicine?
Ryan	I don't know whether you did, but I did.
Nurse	Doctor will be so pleased.
Ryan	I bet it makes her day.
Nurse	*(Leaving room)* Remember, we just press the button when we need help.
Ryan	*(Alone)* I'm going to have to be desperate to press that button and call her back here.
	At the nurse's station, Nurse Adams talks to her supervisor.
Nurse	There are some people who won't let you be nice to them.
Supervisor	Mr. Ryan, again?
Nurse	Yes, who else? I have treated him so well, and he doesn't seem to appreciate it. Do they have trouble with him on the night shift?
Supervisor	No, actually, they all seem to like him.
Nurse	Hmmm. He must feel better nights.
Supervisor	Yes, something like that.
	During visiting hours, Ryan talks with his brother.
Brother	How've they been treating you? Good service?

265

Ryan   Yes and no. The night nurse, Nell, is great. Nurse Adams is left over from a Disney movie. I don't know where they got her, but . . .

Caring for   People are urged to "learn to take care of themselves." "Take care," we sometimes say as we part from another person. "Show me you care" is a phrase heard in all sorts of interpersonal situations. Caring, in all its aspects, is an important human concern. Yet there are different levels of caring. In this section the focus is on "caring for" another person.

"Caring for" can be described as the almost mechanical response to the needs and wants of another person. Everyone at one time or another needs help or comfort of some sort. Caring for another person would seem to be a positive human impulse. Caring for another person, though, has certain other characteristics that make it a special case of human "caring."

First, *"caring for" is characterized by action, by doing things for another person.* This seems entirely positive. Nurse Adams was extremely careful about medicines being taken, pillows being fluffed, and the availability of other help any time Ryan needed it. What seemed to account mainly for Ryan's reaction to her caring, though, was that the help seemed so well rehearsed—so mechanical. This *apparently automatic, mechanical role-playing* is a second characteristic of "caring for." *She* was the nurse, *he* was her patient, *they* were a team (and so the "we"), and *Doctor* was in charge of both of them. Everyone had an established role and each was expected to act the role.

Relatedly and third, *"caring for" means that "duty" is a key factor.* Playing the role of nurse, Nurse Adams does what she does because it is her duty to do so. The role is accompanied by a certain set of responsibilities and obligations. Certainly she opens curtains, fluffs pillows, and sees about medicine—but why?—because they are what she is supposed to do. Anything less than that would be irresponsible, and Nurse Adams will never be accused of being irresponsible.

Finally, *"caring for" another person does not necessarily mean anything about personal feelings.* Nurse Adams "cared for" her patients and asked all the right questions. "How are we?" "Did we take our medicine?" "Can I get you anything else?" All these questions *might* express a genuine concern for the person asked. Language, however, has no meaning in itself. What the patients—Ryan, at least—heard was a well-rehearsed, mechanical list of the right questions. What about the answers to the questions? Ryan felt that the answers were fairly unimportant. She would have some other mechanical response to them: "Doctor will be so pleased." The point is that someone can "do things for" another person without any genuine human involvement. "Caring for" another does not necessarily mean that the relationship is anything other than role enactment and the fulfillment of duty.

"Caring for" another person is related not only to obvious fields such as

... "caring for" another person does not necessarily mean anything about personal feelings. [Sapieha, Stock, Boston]

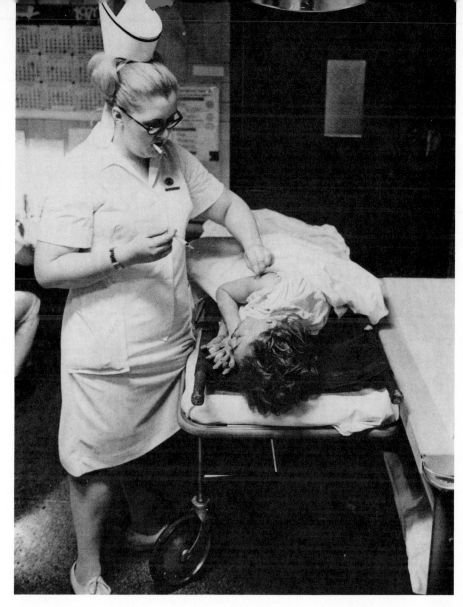

nursing. Parents can *do things* for their children because of the *duty* imposed on them by the *role* of parent; genuine love or concern is not a necessary condition, although "caring for" is often confused with love:

Child   Can you pitch me a few balls?

Parent   Good grief. I slave at the office to give you a good home. You have good food, toys, a television—anything a kid could want. What do you want from me? You have everything a child could demand of a parent.

267

The same scene could be changed to illustrate relationships between husbands and wives, lovers, or friends. "Caring for" another person is often not difficult. You do not have to like or love other people in order to take care of them. All you need is the ability to do what needs to be done.

Yet obviously, "caring for" is not the ultimate phase in human relationships. "Caring about" another person presents a whole different set of interpersonal factors.

Caring about   In the opening case study Ryan was very impressed with the night nurse. Let's see the difference between "Nurse Adams" and "Nell"—besides the first name.

Nell   Hey, Mr. Ryan, how are you this evening?
Ryan   Not bad. In fact, I'm much better.
Nell   Great. Let me look at that dressing. . . . Oh, yes, that looks a lot better. Want this curtain closed?
Ryan   Not just yet. I like to see the stars come out.
Nell   No problem. I can close them after you go to sleep.
Ryan   Thanks.
Nell   Say, you do look better.
Ryan   Could you help me sit up a bit? . . . Thanks.
Nell   Your medicine. This doesn't taste very good, but you have my guarantee you'll feel better. Just a pain killer. Don't let that thing dissolve in your mouth.
Ryan   Can you put this button a little closer—in case I need it later?
Nell   Sure. Ring if you want anything else.
Ryan   Thanks, again.

What we have just experienced provides an explanation about why Ryan favored Nell over Nurse Adams. Nurse Adams cared for Ryan; Nell cared about him. The difference is very important.

"Caring about" someone means that there is genuine feeling, concern, and/or love for the other person. There was no indication here that Nell was asking automatic and mechanical questions. Certainly, she will see just as many patients each day as Nurse Adams did. And yet for her, Ryan was a special individual with unique qualities and problems. Each of her patients demanded a personal approach. Nell responded to her patients with warmth, understanding, and genuine concern. Nurse Adams inquired about the *patient's* recovery—and said that *Doctor* would be pleased. Nell asked about *Ryan's* health—and told him *she* was pleased. Part of the difference may have stemmed from the idea that, second, *"caring about" does not necessarily involve any special roles or duties.* I have the impression that Nell is simply a warm, responsive human being. That does not mean that she plays the sensuous nurse so often portrayed on television and in the movies. It does mean that, as a person, she cares about other people. If she were not in the role of nurse, she would still want to help him. If she had no

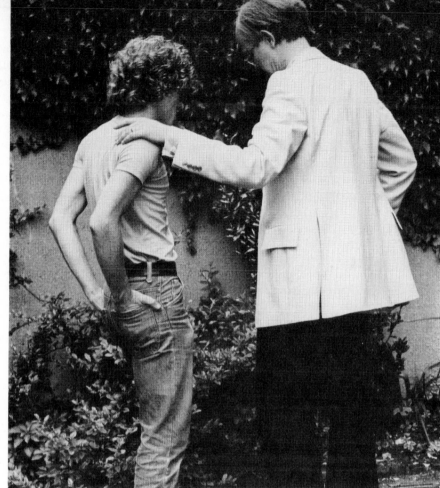

duty whatsoever to her patient, she would still be concerned about him. Caring about someone has nothing necessarily to do with roles or duties.

Finally, *"caring about" does not necessarily have to do with doing things for—caring for—the other person.* In some respects Nurse Adams was a better nurse than Nell. Nurse Adams saw for herself that the patient's position needed tending. She saw to it that the patient could reach the button that would summon help from the nurse's station. Technically, then, she did more to help Ryan than her more popular counterpart. Nell, of course, was helpful. The point is simply that it is possible to care about people—but not constantly be doing things for them.

"Caring about" another person can be expanded far beyond the hospital setting. It is possible for a child to care a great deal about an aging parent— and still do little to help the parent. It is possible to care about a friend or family member without trying to help that person directly. We can "care

269

about" the starving children in the world without offering help. The list is practically endless. Caring about is not the same thing as caring for someone. In Ryan's case, he was much more concerned with being cared about — whether or not he expressed it in those words. He was ready to favor the warm, concerned Nell over the efficient, but mechanical Nurse Adams.

In the illustrations we found a person who cared for but did not seem to care about another person. We found another who obviously cared about but was not so skilled in caring for another person. Are these extremes necessary? The answer is "no." Interpersonal relationships that aim toward communing levels involve "caring" in a more general sense.

Caring   In interpersonal relationships aiming toward deeper levels "caring" is more important than either caring for or caring about. As I use the term, *"caring" refers to the helpful, genuinely felt, but mature concern of people for each other.* At first glance that may seem to be no different from what has already been discussed. Still in some ways "caring" is the combination of caring for and caring about. In other ways "caring" is more complicated.

First, *"caring" means that each of the two people is eager to do things that help the other.* Caring emphasizes the positive aspect of "caring for": action. Things are done by both people for the other. In the case studies, Nurse Adams cared for her patient, but he did nothing in return. That, perhaps, is to be expected in a hospital setting. In less structured situations, and when the relationship is closer, the caring for should be mutual. No one person in a relationship should attempt to be the only one who helps the other. No one person should demand that he or she always be the one helped. Helpfulness is part of caring, but the helpfulness should be reciprocal. In this way "caring" involves the very best of what I described earlier as "caring for."

Second, *"caring" means that people are genuinely and deeply concerned about one another.* The communing relationship is not created by one person caring about the other. Communion can only begin to develop when each person cares deeply about the other person. The wife who cares for her family but does not care about the individuals involved is not moving in the direction of communion. This does not mean, of course, that each person must begin to care about the other person simultaneously. Our culture is filled with stories of how one person won the "favor," the "hand," or the "love" of another person. Ryan's concern for Nell, the night nurse, seems to have begun as a result of her showing him she cared about him. So one person can obviously care about the other first. The point is that for caring to exist, eventually each person must become deeply and genuinely concerned about the other. In this sense "caring" is like what I called "caring about" in its most positive sense.

I defined caring as being "the helpful, genuinely felt, but mature concern of people for each other." So far, the discussion has involved "helpful" (as in caring for) and "genuinely felt" (as in caring about). What about "mature"? By this I mean that the caring relationship sometimes calls for more complicated responses between people.

Specifically, *"caring" means that you care about another person enough to treat him or her as a valued individual.* A person can absolutely be suffocated by the love and genuine concern expressed by another person. "Caring about," then, can be carried to an extreme. There is sometimes a very fine difference between "caring about" and overly protecting another person. Children, friends, and spouses can all be overprotected under a blanket of love and concern. Everyone needs space, time, and the opportunity to grow. The extreme expression of "caring about" can hinder that growth process. Anyone who cares deeply will be careful to let the other person be a responsible human being. Caring, then, calls for some maturity in controlling how much you "care about" another individual.

Similarly, "caring for" can be expressed in the extreme. Caring means you value the other person as a human being. This implies that people do not *do* everything for another. Good relationships are not established by one person completely taking care of the other person. That may work in hospitals and during times of extreme hardship of other types. But the relationship cannot develop positively by one person making the other appear to be—or feel—helpless. At times like these "caring for" needs to be balanced by "caring about." Hopefully, you will care enough about the other person to allow him or her to be a responsible person. Caring, then, means that some sophisticated decisions might have to be made: How much of my "caring for" is helpful? How much of it is detrimental to the person?

The caring relationship is based on the helpful, genuinely felt, and *mature* concern of two people for each other. In this way "caring" is more difficult than either "caring for" or "caring about." More decisions need to be made. Harder decisions need to be made: You have to decide what is a genuine help and what will hinder the other person's development. The problems are many, but the rewards are potentially great. The caring between two people is a key to the creation of the communing relationship.

CHAPTER SUMMARY

Caring is important in the interpersonal situation, and yet not all caring is equally constructive in the interpersonal situation: not all caring is alike.

"Caring for" another person means, or seems generally to mean, an almost mechanical response to the wants and needs of another. In focusing on role behavior and duty as key factors, "caring for" another person does not inevitably mean that there are feelings of warmth and closeness. In contrast, "caring about" another person means something about personal

feelings, but it may not include doing the things involved in "caring for."
You can "care for" other people without "caring about" them; you can
"care about" other people without "caring for" them. And, of course, you
can do both—or neither.

"Caring," in a more general and deeper sense, though, means that you
both care for and care about each other, but you do so responsibly. You
do not "care for" him or her so thoroughly that the person is not allowed
to grow and develop; you do not "care about" him or her so much that
the person is smothered in affection. "Caring" means that you approach
the other in a mature and thoughtful manner. You perceive the other to be
a full member of the relationship you are helping to build—one to another.

LEARNING BY APPLYING

1   Have you or your family ever volunteered to care for a pet while a relative
or neighbor was on vacation? That kind of situation can be used as an instance of when you may care for, but not care about something—in this
case, a pet. Let me give you an example. Our family volunteered to take
care of a neighbor's children's pet: a salamander. Spot—named for obvious
reasons—was to be fed an earthworm a day for about a week. About 7
inches long, this beast made a habit of nipping your finger as he took the
earthworm—he seemed unable to find earthworms if dropped in front of
him in the aquarium. This delightful nipping behavior aside, the neighbors
who returned home found a well-cared for, if not well-cared about, pet.
Have you had similar experiences?

2   Nursing homes, retirement homes, and the like provide the country with a
valuable service when there is no other way for an elderly person to receive
adequate care and attention. But one of the major problems faced by such
homes is that the families of people in these facilities often feel "guilty";
"After all," they are said to reason, "shouldn't we really have kept this person at home with us?" Do you think part of this reported guilt is due to
confusion between "caring for" and "caring about"? Explain your reaction.

3   "Caring" combines the best, most positive aspects of "caring for" and "caring about." More specifically, caring means a valuing of the individuals, so
that you do not "care for" them until they are helpless by themselves or
"care about" them until they are smothered with love. Can you think of
times that you have cared about a person too much? Sometimes parents attempt to keep secret the death of a grandparent or someone; are there ways
in which that may be too protective? Can you think of times when you have
cared for another person so that they became too used to your help? At
times a husband or wife is helpful all the time—about everything; are there
disadvantages for both people in this? See if you can think of other examples.

LEARNING
BY DISCUSSING

1 Explain any differences you see between and among: caring for, caring about, and caring.
2 How is it that caring implies the best of the other two ideas, but does not "push" either idea too far?
3 How can an attitude of caring help you build better interpersonal relationships?

LEARNING
BY READING FURTHER

Goffman, Erving, *Interaction Ritual.* New York: Doubleday-Anchor, 1967.
Mayeroff, Milton, *On Caring.* New York: Harper & Row, 1971.
Rapoport, Anatol, *Strategy and Conscience.* New York: Harper & Row, 1964.
Rogers, Carl, *On Becoming a Person.* Boston: Houghton-Mifflin, 1961.

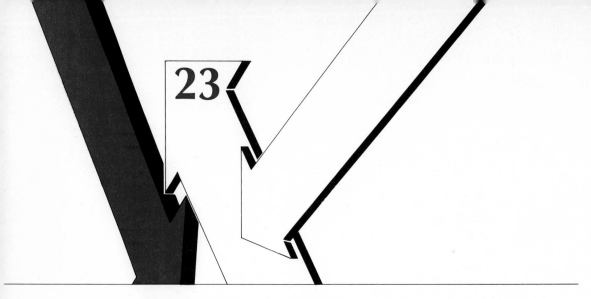

LOVING ABOUT, LOVING SOMEONE, AND LOVING

Eve	. . . and then he said, "I have something to tell you." I knew what he was going to say. . . . He said, "Eve, I want to marry you." Just like that—it was over! A marriage proposal. I knew what he was going to say, and I still couldn't believe it.
Gina	Oh, wow! You said that you had something exciting to tell me, but I didn't figure on this. . . . You said, "Yes," didn't you?
Eve	Well, . . . I didn't know what to say. He was the first person to ever propose to me. . . . I've seen all the movies where the girl just throws her arms around the guy and says, "Oh, yes, yes, yes."
Gina	And you did that, right?
Eve	Well, no—not exactly.
Gina	You didn't say "no," did you?
Eve	Well, no—not exactly.
Gina	Well, what exactly *did* you say.
Eve	I said I didn't know what to say.
Gina	Quick thinking. . . . Eve, do you know what a hunk Tim is? How could you say something dumb like that?
Eve	It's hard to explain.
Gina	I don't doubt it.
Eve	I told him I needed time to think—that marriage was a big step. . . .
Gina	You've been watching too many "B" grade movies. What were you trying to do—just make him worry a little bit?
Eve	I wouldn't do that.
Gina	You mean you don't know if you *love* him?
Eve	I didn't say that.
Gina	You haven't said much of anything. What are you going to tell him?
Eve	I don't know.
Gina	You're just full of information. . . . Do you *love* him?
Eve	I think he is the nearest thing to a perfect man that I'll ever find. . . .
Gina	Well, then . . .

275

Eve	He's handsome, and kind, . . . he's charming and intelligent. He dresses so . . . he always looks so sexy. . . . He is ready to graduate and already has a good job waiting for him. He's fun to be with. . . .
Gina	So where's the problem?
Eve	I love his smiles—the way he laughs. . . .
Gina	I ask again: Where's the problem, then? You have just created a catalog of all his virtues—you seem to love everything about him.
Eve	You're right. I love everything about him. But, Gina, I don't think I love *him*.

Loving about

"Love" seems to be a preoccupation with much of the world's population. People need love, want love, indulge in love, mourn the loss of love, seek love, win love, stumble into love, fall into love, and fall out of love. Love is the subject of conversation, much behavior, and every type of communication known to the human race. And still humans seem to understand so little about it. It presents a mystery to us even at a time when we can send people to the moon, talk around the world by telephone, and transplant bodily organs. Love can never be directly seen, touched, tasted, heard, or smelled. We have no good way of mechanically detecting its presence. Nor can we measure it in any sort of valid and reliable way. Yet love seems to be able to start and end almost any human situation.

I will not pretend to provide any ultimate definition of love. In fact, I will not define it at all. I will simply make the assumption that love—whatever it is—is an important factor in interpersonal relationships. What was illustrated in the opening case study was a special kind of love. The point of the illustration can be summed up into a single phrase: "Yes, I do love so many things about him." But what does this mean?

First, *"loving about" means that the love focuses on qualities or characteristics.* A very strong positive feeling—or "love"—is felt toward the factors that make up the person. When people say "Tell me about her," they probably are not asking for a life history but more likely want a description of some sort. When Eve was listing what she loved about Tim, she included descriptive words that had to do with appearance, attitudes, and behaviors. Any of them can help answer the question, "What is he like?" Any of them can become a focus for very strong positive feelings. So factors in any of these categories can be what someone "loves about" someone else.

Second, *"loving about" does not necessarily mean a general love of the person.* I may dislike a particular politician in general, but I may "love the way" he answers press questions. At the same time that I dislike him, there is one thing I may say I love about him—and mean it seriously. Hitler is a person who generally is not much admired, and yet there may be people who love his oratorical ability. This last, of course, is an extreme case. The point, however, is important: In the case study Eve *loved* many things *about* the young man. That did not mean that she either loved or did not

. . . "loving about" means that the love focuses on qualities or characteristics. [Smolan/Contact, DeWys]

love him. "Loving about" may mean nothing about general feelings toward the person.

In contrast, it is possible, obviously, to actually love someone. That is the topic of the next discussion.

Loving someone   *"Loving someone,"* as I shall use the phrase, has to do with *having strong, positive feelings for the person him- or herself.* This, I believe, differs from "loving about someone" in three important ways.

First, *"loving someone" is possible regardless of whether a person "loves (things) about" the other.* There are movie cliché situations where one person loves another, "in spite of" personal characteristics. Usually a woman (for some reason) thinks her "man" is sneaky, two-timing, jealous, dishonest, dirty, and physically repulsive — and yet she loves him. On the basis of qualities and characteristics the man does not deserve the love of the woman. But there she stands, loving him. "I'm not good enough for you, baby," he probably will say. We, in the audience, may agree. Alas, she says, "I don't care. I want you; I need you; I love you." Drama tends to exaggerate reality at times, and this is perhaps one of those times. It is the case, however, that "loving about" is not a requirement for "loving someone." Love can seem to exist and characteristics can be ignored.

In place of a focus on characteristics *"loving someone,"* second, *emphasizes the relationship.* In the case study Eve spent no time at all telling about the wonders of the relationship between her and Tim. The emphasis was on him and his qualities. Loving someone, however, seems to be much more focused on the couple and their relationship. For this reason, the specific qualities of either individual may not be so important. "We are so close," someone might explain. "We do things so well together," another person might suggest. "We are so well matched," is another expression of the same idea. "Loving about" may be irrelevant to the relationship. And, to reverse it, the relationship might be irrelevant to "loving about." But when someone loves another, one of the characteristics is a strong positive feeling for the joint relationship.

But this feeling for the relationship is not enough without a final characteristic. *"Loving someone" implies a concern for self-feelings.* Here the focus is not on either personal qualities of the other or on the relationship. The focus is on how one person makes the other feel. "I am so confident . . . and warm." "I feel like I'm the most important person in the world." "She makes me know how good companionship can be." "He makes me feel loved, and I love that." Throughout these examples the person's own feelings are emphasized. The point is not how the other person seems or how the people are together. The point is the degree to which someone is made to feel positive and good by a relationship.

These characteristics may all seem a bit abstract to you now. Yet the differences between "loving someone" as just described and "loving about" someone are real. Let's assume that Eve decided to put off a decision until later. During that time she has gone beyond loving the things about her young man. Again, she is talking to Gina.

Eve   Gina, guess what?

Gina   I'm afraid to.

Eve   Go on, guess.

Gina   Well, ...

Eve   I'm going to marry Tim.

Gina   What? Oh, Eve, I'm so happy for you.

Eve   Thank you. . . . You're the first to know, except for Tim and me, of course.

Gina   I'm so happy for you. . . . Wait a minute. I thought you weren't sure. . . . I thought you didn't love him. . . .

Eve   Oh, Gina, these last two months have been perfect. I really got to know him. When we were dating earlier, well, it was different. . . . After he proposed, we both looked at the relationship differently. We talked and talked. We used to be just romantic, . . . you know. . . .

Gina   I've had a little experience. . . .

Eve   Well, I mean I feel so safe now with him. I trust him. I feel so warm whenever we're close. You know, not just dating—it's a relationship that can build and build. I always liked him—I loved him for all the good qualities he has. But now I love him. I respect him. And he respects me. I am not just another girl. I am someone special to him. I even feel special. . . .

Loving someone, obviously, can be a positive human experience. Eve already loved the things about Tim. Now, however, her feelings were deeper than the level of qualities and characteristics. She loved *him*, their relationship, and herself.

What I have tried to describe in these first two sections are the ideas of "loving about" and "loving someone." "Loving someone," it seems to me, involves a deeper and more substantial set of positive feelings. Yet not everyone who is "in love with" someone loves people generally. Not every lover is a "loving person." The general concept of loving is the next idea for discussion.

Loving   So far, the chapter has focused on the concepts of "loving about" and "loving someone"—both of which deal specifically with feelings toward a single other person or a single person's characteristics. Yet love is a feeling that can involve more than one person's feelings for another individual. "Loving" is a term I shall use for a somewhat different sort of human emotion. "Loving" is *having strong, positive feelings for people and the world generally*. In this sense "loving" is broader and more encompassing than the other feelings discussed. Have "faith, hope, and love . . . but the greatest of these is love" is a phrase that implies the idea. Loving goes beyond a con-

... a generally "loving" attitude provides the necessary base for a communing relationship. [Gardiner, Stock, Boston]

cern for individual human qualities, or individual humans. It is possible to "love (things) about" someone and to actually "love someone" without being a "loving" person. Since all this may seem hopelessly abstract to you, let me explain both why "loving" is important and where I think "loving" begins.

First, it seems to me that *a generally "loving" attitude provides the necessary base for a communing relationship.* The communing relationship is an ongoing, continually developing state of affairs between two people. Yet the characteristics you "loved about" another person may seem less charming, interesting, and lovable through the years. In the same way, people do not seem always to "love someone" until death separates them. Both "loving about" and "loving someone" seem all too fleeting. One reason for this (and I suspect there are many opinions) is that these versions of "love" may be too specific. They focus on one characteristic (or a few) or on one person. It may (theoretically) be possible for someone to love another, while he or she hates — or is indifferent to — the rest of the world. But the history of humankind indicates this does not tend to occur: Dictators who are basically cruel to their subjects are reported to be cruel generally. There is a poster-type phrase that reads, "I love humankind; it's people I can't stand." I'm not sure that is possible, but I think the reverse of that is even less likely to be true: "I love people; it's humankind I can't stand." No, I shall argue that a loving attitude toward things and people generally is an important key to the development — and the sustaining — of interpersonal relationships. Loving, in general, seems to be important in loving (someone) specifically.

But if this "loving" is so important, it is also reasonable to ask, "Where does this love come from?" or "How do I become a loving person?" This is the second point I wish to make about loving: *"Loving," I think, is a reflection of your faith and belief in ultimate, substantial things.* By "ultimate" I mean something that is the absolute highest; by "substantial" I mean something that is strong and enduring. For you, this ultimate, substantial thing may be God (in some form); for others, it might be the love of nature or a basic belief in the worth of humankind. Whatever is at the base of your deepest, most reverent feelings can be the source of the love you reflect. It is difficult for me to believe that anyone can simply choose to be a loving person. That feeling of general loving, it seems to me, must have some more fundamental source. That source, whatever it is for you, can be the *intra*personal foundation for the *inter*personal communion you are trying to develop. Ideally, your source and the source of the other person can be compatible. As such, that source can be a common ingredient in the lives of both you and the other person. That source, in short, can play an important role in the building toward interpersonal communion.

"Loving (things) about" someone and "loving someone" can be powerful forces between two people. And yet, by themselves, they probably are incapable of being the base of a communing relationship. Interpersonal communion seems built most effectively by two generally "loving" individuals.

CHAPTER SUMMARY

Love. It is an indispensable part of the communing relationship and yet its influence is fairly complicated.

It is possible, for example, to "love (something) about" another person without actually loving the person. You can love some things (qualities or characteristics) about people whom, in fact, you hate in general. On the other hand, it is possible to "love someone" but to hate many things "about" him or her: temper, appearance, biases, and so on. The chapter discussed each of these instances of loving.

Yet, of course, there is a more general sort of love that has to do with an outlook on life and other people in general. This sort of "nondirected" love was explained as the basis for a communing relationship; it was explained as being a reflection of faith and belief in ultimate things. Somehow it makes more sense to think of communing relationships being developed in a context of a generally favorable, loving view of the rest of the world. It makes sense to think of your specific love for a specific other person based on something greater even than the relationship.

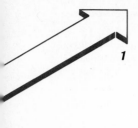

LEARNING
BY APPLYING

1   There are different ways of saying that we "love (something) about" some-
    one, but we do not actually "love" that someone. Common variations are:

    "Well, I don't love him but I do . . .
        a.   love the way he dances
        b.   respect and admire him
        c.   envy his manner with people
        d.   think he is very good at what he does
        e.   wish I had his ability to play piano"

    Can you think of other phrases that make the same sort of distinction?

2   As in exercise 1, there are different ways of saying that we "love someone,"
    but we do not "love (something) about" that someone. Common examples
    include:

    "Well, of course, I love her, but . . .
        a.   I hate it when she flirts
        b.   I dread for her to start drinking
        c.   I wish she wasn't so—you know— . . .
        d.   she never seems to be listening
        e.   she's so competitive"

    Can you add other examples?

3   I have argued that a truly loving attitude comes from a basic, ultimate
    source. If that sounds abstract to you, think of people such as Albert Sweit-
    zer, Gandhi—even Walt Disney. If these mean nothing to you, think about
    the person you consider the most "loving" individual you know. Is there not
    some deep, basic source of his or her expressed love?

4   The most perfect interpersonal situation, I assume, would be one in which
    you and another person loved one another, loved most things about the
    other, and were generally loving people. Do you have such a relationship?
    Are you building toward such a relationship? Such a relationship is ap-
    proaching communion.

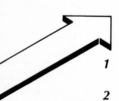

LEARNING
BY DISCUSSING

1   Explain the differences you see between and among: loving something
    about, loving someone, and loving.

2   Discuss your reactions to the idea that "loving" depends on some per-
    sonally important source.

3   How does the chapter enable you to "love something about," "love some-
    one," and "love" in ways that can help your relationships?

LEARNING
BY READING FURTHER

Berschied, Ellen and Walster, Elaine, *Interpersonal Attraction*. Reading, MA: Addison-Wesley, 1969.

Goodman, Paul, *Growing Up Absurd*. New York: Vantage, 1960.

Mayeroff, Milton, *On Caring*. New York: Harper & Row, 1971.

Morris, Desmond, *Intimate Behavior*. New York: Random House, 1971.

Murray, Davis, *Intimate Relations*. New York: Free Press, 1973.

SEXUAL INTIMACY, INTERPERSONAL INTIMACY, AND COMMUNION

STUDY OF THIS CHAPTER WILL ENABLE YOU TO

- *understand the nature of sexual intimacy*
- *understand the characteristics of sexual intimacy*
- *understand the nature of interpersonal intimacy*
- *understand the characteristics of interpersonal intimacy*
- *understand the nature of communion—in the context of intimacy*
- *understand the characteristics of communion—in the context of intimacy*
- *permit sexual intimacy, interpersonal intimacy, and communion to be handled knowledgeably in the interpersonal situation*

From a 1951 edition of *Webster's New World Dictionary:* "intimacy . . . 1. the state or fact of being intimate; intimate association; familiarity; 2. an intimate act; especially, illicit sexual intercourse; a euphemism."[1]

From the 1960s philosophy of a famous "man's magazine:"[2]

Between consenting adults, there is no such thing as illicit activities. Certainly, there are 'illegal' activities – based entirely upon repressive, out-dated, and personally-damaging laws. Laws which attempt to govern the private conduct between people are doomed to failure. Moreover, the attempt to make certain activity between consenting adults illegal prompts only hostility toward the law and personal guilt. In the mid-twentieth century, personal freedom and expression – in whatever form – are indispensable.

From the 1968 conversation between – what we would now sarcastically call – two "macho" young men:

Tom	*(Waking up)* How did it go last night?
Nels	Huh? Oh, man, don't wake me up like that. . . . I'm moving slow this morning.
Tom	How did it go last night – your date with Becky?
Nels	*(Getting more awake)* I don't want to think about it.
Tom	Struck out, huh?
Nels	Let's just say she has a 1968 body – and an 1890 mind.
Tom	That bad?
Nels	Worse. We were over at the fraternity house – lights were off, except the one 15-watt bulb. You know. We were on the couch. . . .
Tom	Sounds good so far. . . .

[1] *Webster's New World Dictionary* (Cleveland: World, 1951).
[2] Readers may decide that this is from a *particular* men's magazine. The description itself, though, is entirely my creation.

285

Nels	That's as far as it went. . . . I heard the word stop so often, I thought she was a traffic cop.
Tom	She looks nice enough . . . friendly and all that. . . .
Nels	Yeah, but under that sensual outer wrapping, there beats a heart of pure—and I mean *pure*—ice. I've dated fish before that were warmer. . . .
Tom	*(Suddenly finding it funny)* Do you date cold fish often?
Nels	On this campus, who has a choice?
Tom	Back to Diane tonight, then?
Nels	You know it. . . . Diane is so . . . open and honest . . . free as a bird . . . so . . .
Tom	Willing?
Nels	I wouldn't put it that way. . . .
Tom	How 'bout "eager"?
Nels	Yeah . . . that's closer.
Tom	I know what you mean. . . .
Nels	What do you mean? . . .
Tom	Hey, look, Nels. This is the twentieth century. I dated Diane for a while. . . . We, uh . . . always had a "good time."
Nels	Oh, . . . I didn't know that. . . . Did you . . . ? I mean . . .
Tom	Look, Nels, this is the twentieth century. . . .

From a 1970s edition of a popular "today's woman magazine:"[3]

The time has come when women need to be recognized as full human beings . . . It must be realized that as human beings, they have all the rights enjoyed by men. One of these rights involves the freedom to be as sexually self-expressive as men are. Old clichés, old moralities, and old social-conditioning have no place in the modern society. The modern woman is not an animal to be tracked down and captured by some supposedly-superior man. The modern woman need not wait to be captured in any sense. Intimacy is a normal female need. Intimacy is the right of the modern woman.

From the recent conversation between two "modern women":

Laura	Good morning.
Sheila	What's good about it?
Laura	Good point.
Sheila	Where did you go last night? You came in awfully late. . . .
Laura	I was out getting a little refreshment. . . . I met this really great guy. . . . We went to his apartment. . . .
Sheila	What about Joe?
Laura	That's just the point. I happen to know that Joe was out with someone else last night. . . . That's why *I* decided to go out.

[3] Again, this illustration is my creation, and does not necessarily refer to any particular publication.

Sheila	What will happen if Joe finds out?
Laura	What do you mean?
Sheila	I mean, won't he be jealous . . . or mad . . . or something?
Laura	Sheila, Joe and I are a mature couple. We like one another . . . and we love making love together. . . . But let's face it. We are still human—and we go our own ways.
Sheila	Oh! . . . This other guy. . . . What was his name?
Laura	I don't remember. . . . Roy, or Ralph . . . something like that. . . .
Sheila	Well, you didn't . . . I mean, when you got to his apartment, did you. . . ?
Laura	Did we have sex? . . . What did you think we did till three o'clock—play checkers?
Sheila	Oh . . .
Laura	You sound like my mother. . . . Sheila, wake up. This is the twentieth century. I have a right to be intimate with anyone I care to. . . . Joe knows that, and he understands. . . .
Sheila	Oh! . . . I see. . . .

Sexual intimacy   The comments and cases here illustrate something of a change in attitudes toward human "sexual intimacy." Clearly, not everyone would view the change from intimacy as "illicit sex" to a "right" as progress. Even more clearly, not everyone shares the attitudes expressed by all—or maybe any—of the characters in the cases. My goal is not to attack or defend any of the attitudes or behavior illustrated. My goal, simply, is to discuss the concept of sexual intimacy and its relationship to human communion.

Regardless of whether it is viewed positively or negatively, *"sexual intimacy" is close association that involves some form of sexual activity.* This means that sexual intimacy is generally characterized by a number of common factors. To begin with, *sexual contact, obviously, is required.* This might mean anything from "necking" to "petting" to "heavy petting" to intercourse—as I understand the use of those words. Sexual contact, then, might mean "necking": hugs and kisses. It may also mean "petting" which seems to mean contact with generally unexposed parts of the body such as breasts and genital areas. It may mean "heavy petting," which is generally said to mean more intense caressing, fondling, or massage—perhaps to sexual climax. Most often, however, sexual contact probably means intercourse itself. With sexual intimacy, sexual contact is a characteristic.

Second, *sexual intimacy actually may mean almost no physical contact except intercourse.* The stereotype of the prostitute is a person who may engage in intercourse without any less intense physical activity. Kissing, hugging, and stroking are not major parts of the task. In less extreme cases the same thing can be true. All of the popular books available on sexual techniques seem to indicate that most people do not handle the "preliminaries" of sexual intercourse well. In the rush to go beyond the necking and petting stages, these stages are often omitted altogether. In that sense sexual intimacy may mean very little nongenital physical contact.

Third, *sexual intimacy need not be enjoyable in any but a physical sense*. Prostitutes, again, are the traditional examples of people who simply "go through" the motions. Liking or loving the other person is not a requirement for sexual contact. In less commercial situations the same thing seems accurate. The relieving of sexual impulses is usually considered a natural human need—at a biological level. Biological needs can be attended to without there being any particular emotional enjoyment. Partly for this reason, fourth, *sexual intimacy need not involve anything except physical satisfaction.* Sexual intimacy may provide an outlet, an answer to physical needs. But it may not involve "satisfaction" in any other sense. The need for warmth, for affection, or for love may go unmet by even the most strenuous sexual activity. In some cases the sexual fulfillment may be considered enough satisfaction. In extreme cases, however, the purely physical satisfaction may lead either to an overpowering sexual drive—or to no desire at all.

Finally, *sexual intimacy may not even involve truly intimate behavior in some senses.* This may sound like a contradiction, but the point is im-

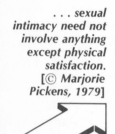

. . . sexual intimacy need not involve anything except physical satisfaction. [© Marjorie Pickens, 1979]

portant. Let's assume that intimacy means a kind of closely shared, closely guarded set of behaviors. There are other ways of viewing intimacy, but if this view is considered, an interesting thing happens. Very active sexual contact with several or many people may actually destroy the possibility of sexual intimacy in this sense. Sexual contact becomes a kind of community —not interpersonal—activity. The sex act no longer is a private, interpersonal phenomenon. It becomes a matter of public, not intimate, behavior. In the case study the relationship between Joe and Laura was open and free from rules. On the other hand, it was also a relationship that was in some ways shared by a variety of other people. Their belief in sexual freedom and the right to intimacy, ironically, may have destroyed the possibility of private sexual intimacy.

Not all "intimacy," of course, is sexual in nature. Currently, "intimacy" is not seen as being illicit sex. In fact, it may not involve sex at all.

Interpersonal intimacy

"Interpersonal intimacy" involves close, deep, interpersonal relationships. In a number of important ways interpersonal and sexual intimacy are very different.

First, *interpersonal intimacy does not necessarily involve sexual activity.* Such intimacy can exist regardless of age, sex—or sexual preference. The relationship, for example, between two people of the same sex can be as *interpersonally* intimate as a relationship between a husband and wife. The closeness that each feels for the other may simply be irrelevant to any sort of sexual concern. Relatedly and second, *interpersonal intimacy may involve* either *much or little physical, but nonsexual, contact.* Touching and stroking may be completely nonsexual, but still important to the relationship. Handshakes, friendly hugs, and pats on the shoulder may be an important expression of feeling between two people—again, regardless of any sexual factors. In contrast, though, it is possible—but perhaps less likely—that an interpersonally intimate relationship is completely unphysical. Some people are what we called earlier "touchers" and enjoy touching and being touched physically. Others are simply uncomfortable with touching, hugging, and stroking. Besides these personal differences, culture and conditioning are factors. In the American culture nonsexual but physical contact is less popular than in other cultures. Again, in American culture the "proper" physical contact is "taught" by the influence of subculture, social position, national region, and family tradition. In sum, interpersonal intimacy may or may not involve physical (nonsexual) contact as an important factor.

Third, *interpersonal intimacy is more than* physically *enjoyable and satisfying.* Sexual intimacy is often physically enjoyable and satisfying, but need be nothing more. Interpersonal intimacy can be emotionally, intellectually—even spiritually—enjoyable. The relationship is fun, pleasurable, comforting, love-inspiring—all of the things that sexual intimacy need

289

not be. Emotional stability, warmth, "completion," and (not necessarily physical) gratification can be the rewards of interpersonal intimacy. Interpersonal intimacy, then, involves and satisfies a wider range of levels in human existence.

Finally, *interpersonal intimacy is—by nature—more exclusive than sexual intimacy.* History tells us of people of the past who seemed to have insatiable sexual appetites: The more partners, the better. Some of those exploits may be somewhat exaggerated—either by others or the participants themselves. Still, with humans being one of the rare animals always potentially available for sexual activity, the potential for sexual intimacy is not very limited. In contrast, interpersonal intimacy seems necessarily to involve fewer potential "partners." The truly close human relationship is not something that can be formed indiscriminately by every pair of people. So we may speak of associates, acquaintances, friends—and certain other "special" people. These special people probably will be few in number. The number may not include even all those within the immediate family. In fact, there is no reason to predict that any two members of a family will have that very "special relationship." The husband–wife, parent–child, and sibling relationships do not automatically become intimate. True interpersonal intimacy probably will be experienced in relation to some small number of people—or sadly, in relation to no one at all.

Clearly, there is no reason for sexual intimacy and interpersonal intimacy to be in conflict. It is entirely possible for two people to enjoy both sorts of close, human contact. On the other hand, it is possible for sexual intimacy to exist without interpersonal intimacy. And finally, it is possible for interpersonal intimacy to exist without sexual intimacy. Consider the following situation:

You know what?
What?
I wanted to say "good night" before I went to bed. . . . I hope you don't mind. . . . I
      know you're busy. . . .
Come over here. . . . You know, you get bigger every day.
I know. . . . What are you doing?
Writing. . . .
Oh . . . about what?
About people like us. . . .
Me?
You *and* me, and all kinds of people like us. . . . What do you think about that?
I think it's silly.
Ah, come on. . . . Hey, you need to get to bed. . . .
I know. . . . Oops, I forgot kisses. . . . I don't want to kiss your mustache—it tickles.
I know. . . . Good night; God bless.

Interpersonal intimacy is a great and valued human condition. Yet it

need not have anything at all to do with sexual intimacy. Those feelings of closeness, of caring, of love – they are the elements of interpersonal intimacy.

Communion

In this final section of the book, I want to discuss most directly the concept that I hope you have found forms the basis of the text: communion. Communion is a special kind of intimacy that seems much deeper than sexual intimacy – and even more special than interpersonal intimacy. *Communion is the almost complete melting of two people into two strong members of a single strong relationship.* Let me explain in more detail.

First, *communing relationships are the most exclusive of relationships.* Sexual intimacy may involve dozens or – if we can believe the stories – hundreds of partners. Even interpersonal intimacy can be experienced with a small number of other people. Communion, though, seems even more restrictive. No one I know – or have ever heard of – experiences more than one communing relationship at any one time. More common probably is the situation where one person experiences no relationship that approaches the communing level. That is not to say that the person is not interested. It is to say that communion is such a unique situation that some people miss the opportunity altogether. The wrong marital partner is chosen, a friend moves away when the relationship is finally becoming truly close, or children become independent – just at the time you feel communion is a possibility. For a variety of reasons, the communing relationship is

291

difficult to achieve. Even when people take seriously the ways in which communication can build toward communion, the effort may fail. Communion is simply the rarest and most exclusive kind of relationship.

Second, *in communion, the emotional, intellectual, and spiritual factors are symbolic.* The admiration and deep feelings you have for the other are not only important in themselves, but also as symbols of the strong relationship. So it is not that you have communion, and, thus, you feel very good about the relationship. The point is rather that you have the feelings and thoughts which indicate or symbolize how *very* strong the relationship is.

Third, *in the same way, communion means that any sexual intimacy is symbolic.* Sexual activity is not good simply because you feel the communion. On the other hand, communion is not good because the sex has never been better. Sex is important for its own sake—but that is sexual intimacy. Here sex is important as an expression of the depth of feeling between two people. That does not necessarily mean that sex should always be a solemn, serious act. Indeed, most people agree that sexual activity can be enjoyable —and that there is room for playfulness. Still sexual activity is not "just a part" of the communion. It can symbolize the oneness, the completion of the people involved in communion. There can be sex without communion. There can be communion without sex. But when sexual activity is a part of the communion, it will be emotionally, spiritually, and physically fulfilling. It will be a symbol of the utter communion between two devoted people.

Communion, then, is exclusive. Its emotional, spiritual, and physical satisfactions will be at least in part symbolic of the communion itself. Then, too, as discussed earlier, communion is a very high level of human relationship. Whether that stage will be completely reached is impossible to predict. At worst, human communion is a goal to be approached and neared. It does not occur magically between two people who simply "fall into" the relationship. Communion will be the product of sensitivity and caring. The possibilities of developing a communing relationship are strengthened by putting into practice an understanding of interpersonal communication—communication one to another.

CHAPTER SUMMARY

Interpersonal communication, intimacy, and sex are three terms that form the core of this final chapter. They are all important in one way or another, but they are hardly interchangeable.

Sexual intimacy was described as a close association involving some form of sexual contact. It involves, by definition, sexual behavior but may include little except intercourse—which may not be enjoyable in any except a physical sense. For some people, even that satisfaction is missing.

In contrast, interpersonal intimacy has to do with relationships and does not necessarily involve sexual factors at all. In fact, there may be no physical (even nonsexual) activity. Yet such interpersonal intimacy can be more than physically enjoyable and satisfying. Finally, interpersonal intimacy is exclusive—more exclusive than sexual intimacy. The individuals with whom we can be intimate interpersonally are generally limited.

But "communion" as discussed in the chapter is an almost complete melting of two people into two strong members of a single strong relationship. Communion is the most exclusive of relationships. In communion, the emotional, intellectual, and spiritual factors are symbolic of the quality of the relationship. Any sexual activity, though perhaps important in its own right, is even more important for its symbolic value.

Communion, then, is the highest form of human relationship. It occurs rarely in the life of one person, but can serve as both a goal in its own way and a guideline for all sorts of other, less intimate human relationships. This book is subtitled "A Guidebook for Interpersonal Communication." It has been written to help you use communication as a way of helping you build better relationships . . . "one to another."

LEARNING
BY APPLYING

1   This is an optional exercise, of course! *Buy (or borrow) a copy of a "men's magazine"—one even more questionable than the "established ones." Read a story included for some other reason than the intellectual challenge of the reader . . . if you know what I mean. Such a story—I suspect—will illustrate what I mean by sexual intimacy without any attendant interpersonal intimacy.*

2   *If you have the opportunity to see rerun, syndicated situation comedies from the 1950s, you will have a rare chance to see marital situations with interpersonal intimacy without sexual intimacy. The major husband–wife couple probably slept in separate beds, never kissed except on the cheek, and never ever discussed "S-x." Now, compare such a television show to one in the late 1970s or early 1980s. Has the interpersonal intimacy–sexual intimacy balance changed—or have they both become more explicit? Discuss your thoughts.*

3   *Interpersonal intimacy does not mean that sexual intimacy has to occur. Fictional relationships between the Three Musketeers, the Magnificent Seven, and the Lone Ranger and Tonto seem to illustrate the point . . . and yet, closeness and companionship do not necessarily mean intimacy. Do you or don't you agree? Discuss your feelings.*

4   *Think of the relationship you know about in which "communion" seems to occur—you may or may not be a member of the relationship. Why do you think the relationship is at or near a communal level? What feelings do you*

have about it? What thoughts? What does this tell you about the beauty and wonder of the communing relationship?

LEARNING BY DISCUSSING

1 *Discuss the nature of sexual intimacy.*
2 *Discuss the nature of interpersonal intimacy. How does that differ from sexual intimacy?*
3 *How are communion and intimacy related in discussions of interpersonal relationships?*
4 *How can your knowledge of sexual intimacy, interpersonal intimacy, and intimacy help you in creating better, more desirable relationships?*

LEARNING BY READING FURTHER

Greer, Germaine, "Seduction is a Four-Letter Word." *Playboy Magazine,* January 1973.
Lederer, William and Jackson, Don, *Mirages of Marriage.* New York: Norton, 1968.
Masters, W. H. and Johnson, Virginia, *Human Sexual Response.* Boston: Little, Brown, 1966.
Morris, Desmond, *Intimate Behavior.* New York: Random House, 1971.
Murray, Davis, *Intimate Relations.* New York: Free Press, 1973.
Slater, Philip, *The Pursuit of Loneliness.* Boston: Beacon Press, 1970.

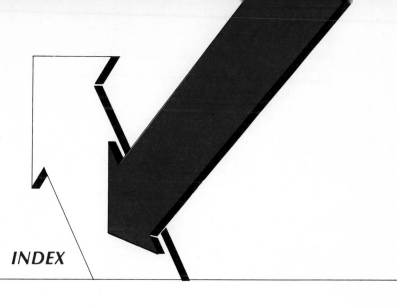

INDEX

295

299